QUICK
ESCAPES
from
Chicago

25 Weekend Trips from the Windy City

by

Bonnie Miller Rubin
and
Marcy Mason

A Voyager Book

The Globe Pequot Press

Old Saybrook, Connecticut

Photo credits: P. 1: courtesy Illinois State Library; p. 3: Steve Stout, courtesy Starved Rock Lodge & Conference Center; p. 9: courtesy Maxon Manor; p. 15: courtesy The Heartland Health and Fitness Retreat; p. 20: courtesy Springfield Convention & Visitors Bureau; p. 28: Galena/Jo Daviess county Convention & Visitors Bureau; p. 40: Ron Bailey, courtesy the *Chicago Tribune;* p. 51: courtesy Milwaukee Department of City Development; p. 53: courtesy Milwaukee Department of City Development; p. 65: courtesy Geneva Lake Area Chamber of Commerce; p. 85: courtesy of the Wisconsin Dells Visitor and Convention Bureau; p. 95: Gary Tuescher, Tuescher Photography, courtesy Platteville Chamber of Commerce; p. 102: EAA photo; p. 108: courtesy the Kohler Company/The American Club; p. 115: Erol Reyal; p. 123: courtesy The Indianapolis Project; p. 125: courtesy LaPorte County Convention & Visitors Bureau; p. 133: courtesy Public Relations and Information, Notre Dame; p. 139: courtesy Elkhart County Convention & Visitors Bureau; p. 145: Delores Wright, courtesy The Indianapolis Project; p. 153: courtesy Brown County convention & Visitors Bureau; p. 160: Balthazar Korab/Columbus Visitors Center; p. 167: courtesy Lakeshore Convention & Visitors Bureau. p. 169: courtesy Harbor Country Chamber of Commerce; p. 177: courtesy Lakeshore Convention & Visitors Bureau; p. 183: J.O.L. Finucan, courtesy Saugatuck/Douglas Convention & Visitors Bureau; p. 190: courtesy Holland Convention & Visitors Bureau; p. 199: courtesy Greenfield Village and Ford Museum.

Library of Congress Cataloging-in-Publication Data

Rubin, Bonnie Miller.
    Quick Escapes from Chicago : 25 weekend trips from the Windy City
    / by Bonnie Miller Rubin and Marcy Mason. — 1st ed.
        p.   cm.
    "A Voyager book."
    Includes index.
    ISBN 1—56440-025-5
    1. Chicago Region (Ill.)—Tours. I. Mason, Marcy. II. Title
F548.18.R83 1992
917.73'110443—dc20   92-1362
                                                    CIP

Manufactured in the United States of America
First Edition/Fourth Printing

To Wayne and Gale, my brother and sister,
with whom I once shared the back seat of a station wagon
and now share some pretty terrific memories

—Bonnie Miller Rubin

For all those who've ever wanted to travel
but couldn't afford to do so

—Marcy Mason

Wisconsin

Lake Michigan

Michigan

8

6

7

4

3

5

1

2

5

CHICAGO

2

1

4

3

2

1

6

4

3

2

1

5

1

2

3

3

Indiana

4

5

6

4

Illinois

Contents

Introduction .... **vii**

The Best of the Midwest ix

ILLINOIS ESCAPES **1**

    Map 2

    1. Starved Rock State Park 3

    2. Rock River Valley 9

    3. Gilman 15

    4. Springfield 20

    5. Galena 28

    6. Downtown Chicago 40

WISCONSIN ESCAPES **51**

    Map 52

    1. Milwaukee 53

    2. Lake Geneva 65

    3. Madison and Spring Green 73

    4. Wisconsin Dells 85

    5. Platteville and Mineral Point 95

    6. Oshkosh and Horicon Marsh 102

    7. Kohler 108

    8. Door County 115

INDIANA ESCAPES **123**

    Map 124

    1. Michigan City 125

    2. South Bend 133

    3. Elkhart and Crystal Valley 139

    4. Indianapolis 145

    5. Brown County 152

    6. Columbus 160

MICHIGAN ESCAPES **167**

    Map 168

    1. Southwest Michigan 169

    2. South Haven 178

    3. Saugatuck 183

    4. Holland and Grand Haven 190

    5. Detroit 199

INDEX **209**

About the Authors

BONNIE MILLER RUBIN is Home Editor of the *Chicago Tribune*. She has spent almost twenty years working for daily newspapers, including the *Minneapolis Star Tribune* and the *Gary Post Tribune*. She is the author of *Time Out,* a handbook on taking sabbaticals, which was based on her own year-long travels through Europe and the Middle East. Bonnie lives in the Chicago area with her husband and two children.

MARCY MASON is a Chicago-based freelance writer. She is a regular contributor to the *Chicago Tribune* and has written for numerous publications, including *Crain's Chicago Business* and *Commerce* magazine. Her subjects range from the arts, broadcasting, and food to travel, real estate, and finance. A former high school English teacher, Marcy has spent eight years in the advertising and public relations fields. Most recently she was promotions director at WLS-AM, a talk radio station in Chicago.

Introduction

Chicago has it all—from architecture to zoos. In between you'll find one world-class symphony, six professional sports teams, fifty-five museums, and more than a hundred theaters (no wonder *Newsweek* calls it "the hottest theater town in America").

But sometimes you've just got to get out of town. So pack up the car, crank up the radio, and hit the road. A weekend escape can do wonders to clear your head—especially if you're short on time, money, or both. *Quick Escapes from Chicago* provides details of twenty-five cities or areas, some as close as 75 miles to Chicago and one as far away as 300 miles, to be seen on two- to four-day getaway trips. If you're a spa lover, antique hunter, art enthusiast, fisherman, history buff, avid shopper, hiker . . . you name it, this book can point you in the right direction.

Each chapter is based on a different city or area to explore. The itinerary for each destination gives specifics on restaurants, lodgings, sights, and activities. Don't feel, however, that you must follow these itineraries verbatim. Just refer to them for some reliable suggestions about things to do and places to go. If you can't do it all in the time allotted, plan to return on another escape weekend.

At the end of each chapter, **There's More** suggests additional attractions and recreational activities. The **Special Events** section lists the area's noteworthy festivals and annual events. In case you want to try a different lodging or restaurant than we suggested, you'll find **Other Recommended Restaurants and Lodgings** at the end of each chapter. Finally, **For More Information** is your reference for names and addresses of chambers of commerce or tourism bureaus.

With many restaurant descriptions we've given price ranges, so you'll have an idea of what to expect. These are Inexpensive (under $8.00), Moderate ($8.00–$15.00), and Expensive ($15.00 and up). Other rates and fees are given as precisely as possible throughout the book, but they often change. When you plan a trip, we recommend you call ahead for rate confirmation, reservations, and other specific information such as handicapped accessibility or smoking policy.

Most of these itineraries can be relied upon year-round, but a few, because of the location of the destination, may seem to be more suited to warm-weather travel. Nevertheless, every itinerary includes indoor activities and attractions that will come in handy on rainy or cold days.

Our itineraries can be as helpful to you as parents as they will be to couples traveling alone, and in several cases we've offered two alternatives of lodgings or attractions.

If you are going to take our recommendations, you should know something about us and our preferences. I did all my traveling with a husband and two children, while Marcy traveled on her own or with friends. Those differences aside, we both like the same things: firm mattresses, soft towels, thick walls, and thin pancakes. Antiques are lovely, but bathrooms should be strictly modern. To say that bed and breakfasts have been overly romanticized is an understatement. Not every old house is necessarily an inn, any more than the people who own them are innkeepers. (My husband and I once stood in the hall until the conclusion of "All My Children" so the proprietor could check us in.) Charm is great, but it is no substitute for professionalism.

The best advice is to zero in on what you want. Sometimes it will be old-fashioned quilts, a screened porch, and sharing lively conversation with fellow travelers. Other times it will be a heated pool, wall-to-wall carpeting, and the blessed anonymity of a national chain.

Food should never be treated as mere fill, which, unfortunately, is what you'll find all too often. Pass up the safe franchise for a local gem—the kind of place that's been in the same family for generations. It doesn't have to be fancy; a bowl of homemade soup and crusty bread beats a microwaved duck á l'orange any day.

Of course, chefs change as do prices, and the place that was extraordinary a year ago may be merely ordinary now. What we have attempted to do here is to be both comprehensive and discriminating. Let us know if we've succeeded.

If you would like to make a correction or suggest a new find that should be considered for a future edition, please write us at Globe Pequot Press, P.O. Box 833, Old Saybrook, CT 06475. In the meantime, we hope you enjoy these twenty-five quick escapes from Chicago as much as we have.

Bonnie Miller Rubin

The prices and rates listed in this guidebook were confirmed at press time. We recommend, however, that you call establishments before traveling to obtain current information.

The Best of the Midwest

In a region as delightfully diverse as the Midwest, there's something for everyone. But here are a few favorites that still remain standouts, even after months of travel.

Regional dining delights:

A fish boil in Door County, Wisconsin
Any breakfast with blueberries at North Beach Inn in South Haven
A hearty German meal in Milwaukee
A hot fudge sundae at Beernsten's, Manitowoc, Wisconsin
A sinful scoop of ice cream at Sherman's Dairy, South Haven, or Babcock Hall at the University of Wisconsin, Madison
A slice of shoo-fly pie at Essenhaus Country Inn, Middlebury, Indiana

Attractions:

Henry Ford Museum and Greenfield Village, Dearborn, Michigan
Museum of Science and Industry, Chicago
House on the Rock, Spring Green, Wisconsin
Abraham Lincoln's home, Springfield, Illinois
Children's Museum, Indianapolis

Quirky attractions:

Motown Museum, Detroit
Circus World Museum, Baraboo, Wisconsin
The Musical Fountain, Grand Haven, Michigan

Hotels and resorts:

The American Club, Kohler, Wisconsin
The Pfister, Milwaukee, Wisconsin
The Four Seasons, Chicago
Eagle Ridge Inn & Resort, Galena

Natural wonders:

Cave of the Mounds, Blue Mounds, Wisconsin
The Dunes (either in Chesterton, Indiana, or Warren Dunes State Park, Bridgman, Michigan)
Migration of Canada geese, Horicon Marsh, Wisconsin
The Dells, Wisconsin Dells, Wisconsin

Illinois Escapes

Starved Rock State Park

The natural beauty of Starved Rock makes for exhilarating hiking.

Take a Hike

———————————— 1 NIGHT ————————————
Cycling · Winter sports · Hiking · Camping · Bird-watching · Fall foliage

If the idea of spending any time at all in a government-supported park lodge sounds like reliving Boy Scout camp, then it's probably been a while since you've been a guest of the state.

In 1984 Governor James Thompson pumped $100 million worth of renovations into Illinois' sixty-seven state parks. Seven of them—Starved Rock, Illinois Beach, White Pines Forest, Pere Marquette, Eagle Creek, Giant City, and Cave-in-Rock—are equipped with lodges.

Starved Rock, one of the state's most popular attractions, now includes a complex that could compete with some of the best luxury resorts from Lake Geneva to Upper Michigan, and at a fraction of the price. Swimming is no longer relegated to some slippery riverbank; the lodge's new wing, completed in 1989, offers an Olympic-sized pool, flanked by whirlpool, sauna, and kiddie pool. Thirty new rooms have been added, too, along with cable TV.

But the face-lift has not altered Starved Rock's rustic charm, which has been in place since the Civilian Conservation Corps built the lodge back in the 1930s. Douglas fir logs (some nearly three feet in diameter) and a 700-ton double fireplace still dominate the Great Room, where it seems downright quaint to see families playing board games. (It doesn't take kids too long, however, to discover the video games on the second floor.)

Another big factor in Starved Rock's favor is its proximity. Located on the Illinois River, the park is a mere 80 miles west of Chicago (just off I–80), in Utica. You can leave downtown at five on a Friday afternoon and easily make dinner at seven. Because it is so close, it also makes a very nice day-long excursion.

Day 1

Morning

Take I–80 west. Just as the suburbs turn to countryside, make a stop in Morris at the **Gebhard Woods State Park.** The thirty-acre park has four ponds for fishing, including one for kids' fishing only. Bass, bluegill, and sunfish are the catch of the day.

Gebhard Woods is part of the Illinois Michigan State Canal Trail. The I & M was dug in the 1840s to link Chicago to St. Louis, and it helped clinch the Windy City's reputation as a commercial center. Today a 15-mile section—from Morris to Channahon (near Joliet)—provides excellent recreational facilities for hikers, bikers, and cross-country skiers.

This scenic area is heavily forested with oak, maple, walnut, and ash. In fact, trivia experts may note that the largest tree in the state, a 120-foot-tall cottonwood, is located one mile west of Gebhard Woods. The area doesn't offer much in the way of food service, but there are fine picnic facilities, so plan on bringing your lunch. For more information contact the park at (815) 942–0796.

Afternoon

Get back on I–80 and continue west another 30 miles or so to **Starved Rock State Park.** Legend has it that during the 1760s a group of

Illinewek Indians, under attack by an Ottawa-Potawatami war party, sought refuge atop the rock. The Illini were surrounded and eventually starved—hence the name.

The infamous rock, a 125-pound sandstone butte, is still the park's main attraction, and you can explore it yourself. There are also trickling waterfalls, rock formations, and eighteen canyons formed during the glacial drift; the biggest rock formations are in St. Louis, French, and LaSalle canyons. There are more than 600 species of plants, making the park a veritable feast for everyone from photographers to bird-watchers. The well-marked trails offer easy accessibility for young children, but the rugged terrain will challenge even the most advanced hiker.

Depending on the season, you also can paddle a canoe, fish, cross-country ski, play a few sets of tennis (the lodge has one lighted court), or explore the scenery by horseback.

As you return to the lodge, be sure to notice the wood carvings that dot the landscape. The bald eagles, ducks, and black bear cubs are the work of Larry Jensen, one of the best chainsaw sculptors in the country.

Dinner: The Starved Rock lodge dining room is where you'll probably end up eating all your meals. And given the limited number of dining choices, it's a lot better than it has to be. The chef serves up honest fare—fried chicken, fish, steaks. The prime rib and red-jacketed potatoes are better than what you'd find at many city restaurants. And who would ever expect to see a dessert tray, complete with flourless chocolate torte and caramel pecan cheesecake, at a state park dining hall? Dinners are in the $8.00–$12.00 range, but there is a child's menu with little portions and prices to match. Insider's tip: Make your dining reservations as soon as you arrive.

Lodging: Since your tax dollars help defray operating expenses, room rates at the lodge are a bargain that even budget motels would find hard to match. Accommodations range from about $58 per night for a double in the main wing to $75 for a deluxe cabin with a fireplace and a king-sized bed. The most difficult part is booking a room, not affording it. It is not unusual to hear about waiting lists of a year or more. If you find yourself thwarted by the reservations desk, play hooky during the week, when the demand for rooms is much less. The lodge also deserves high marks for being totally handicapped-accessible (including the pool). For reservations, call (815) 667–4211.

Day 2

Morning

Breakfast: The lodge dining room offers the usual choice of pancakes, waffles, eggs. Prices range from $3.00 to $5.00.

The **Waterway Visitors' Center** (Starved Rock Lock & Dam, Dee Bennett Road and Route 178, Utica) presents an audiovisual display on early Midwestern river travel. A visit to the center is especially worthwhile if you are a transportation buff or it's a rainy day and you have kids in tow. The observation deck offers a great view of the locks along the 327-mile Illinois Waterway, which forms a link between the Great Lakes and the Mississippi River. Open 9 A.M.–8 P.M. from Memorial Day to Labor Day; 9 A.M.–5 P.M. from the day after Labor Day to mid-December and from March 1 until day before Memorial Day. Closed between mid-December and March 1. Call (815) 667–4054.

There's still another state park to hit. **Matthiessen,** southeast of Starved Rock, is smaller, but take a look at the upper dells, which include a staggered series of waterfalls that plunge into the Vermilion River. This park is made for winter activities. The terrain is challenging, and equipment (skates, skis, even snowshoes) can be rented at a nominal charge.

If your timing is good, return to Chicago via I–39. Travel north to Highway 52 and go east to Sandwich, about 60 miles west of the city. Take the Sugar Grove exit to Hinkley and then follow the signs to **Sandwich Antiques Market.** The market is open only five Sundays a season, from May to October, but it's worth a detour. It has a national reputation for top-quality furniture and collectibles and was recently listed in *Metropolitan Home* as one of the best in the country. Call (815) 786–6122. (Note: If you're making this a day trip from Chicago, take I–88 west to Sugar Grove exit to Hinkley.)

There's More

Reddick Mansion, 100 West Lafayette, Ottawa (northeast on I–80); (815) 433–0084. This ornate Italianate mansion, one of the most elaborate ever built in northern Illinois, was a stop on the Underground Railroad.

LaSalle County Historical Museum, Highway 178, LaSalle; (815) 667–4861. Artifacts and relics from the Prairie State.

Hoffman's Patterns of the Past, 513 South Main Street, Princeton (about 20 miles west of Starved Rock off I–80). This shop has achieved a national reputation for locating discontinued china patterns. In fact, they have many in stock. Call (815) 875–1944.

Special Events

Starved Rock State Park offers a number of theme weekends, which are very popular. For exact dates and reservations, call (815) 667–4906.

Mid-January. Winter Wilderness Weekend. Cross-country skiing with basic instruction. Ski rentals are available.
Early February (first weekend). Cross-Country Ski Weekend. Similar to above, but at Matthiessen State Park, which is 2 miles south of Starved Rock on Route 178.
Early May. Annual Wildflower Pilgrimage. An outstanding area for wildflowers. Guided hikes take place twice daily.
Mid-September. Turn-of-the-Century Celebration. Arts and crafts, stage shows, hot-air balloons.
Mid-October. Fall Colors Weekend. Guided hikes to view Mother Nature's grandest annual show.

Elsewhere:

September. Mendota Sweet Corn Festival. There is literally tons of the stuff. Festivities include a corn-shucking contest.
October. Utica Burgoo Bash. Burgoo is a stew of meat, fowl, and vegetables that simmers in large kettles for as long as eighteen hours. The name comes from the combination of seasonings that is known only to the burgoo-master. Such festivals are common in the South, but this one may be the closest to Chicago. Call (815) 667–4861.

Other Recommended Restaurants

Peru

Red Door Inn, 1701 Water Street; (815) 223–2500. This is a lovely restaurant, located in a restored 1850 river house in nearby Peru. Fine dining, with steak Diane the signature dish. Three miles south of I–80. Reservations recommended.

Utica

Duffy's, downtown Utica, across from the LaSalle County Historical Museum. An Irish pub on the prairie, where you can get a tasty burger. (815) 667–4324.
Kickapoo Club, Starved Rock Marina; (815) 433–0275. Dine alfresco on the deck, which overlooks the Illinois River. Steaks, chicken, fish. A popular spot for Sunday brunch.

LaSalle

Uptown Bar and Grill, 613 First Street, (815) 224–4545. Salads, sandwiches. Local folks recommend the sizzling fajitas. Choose a frosty brew from their large selection of domestic and imported beers.

For More Information

Heritage Corridor Convention and Visitors Bureau, 81 North Chicago Street, Suite 103, Joliet, IL 60431; (800) 535–5682.

Starved Rock Visitors Center, Box 116, Utica, IL 61673; (815) 667–4211.

Rock River Valley

The *Rose of the Rock River* paddleboat affords views of pristine scenery.

Country Roads Come Alive

1 NIGHT

Antiques · Historical sites · Canoeing · Fishing · Horseback riding ·
Fall foliage · Hiking · Camping · Golfing

It was rumored that after a visit to the Rock River Valley, John Denver wrote "Country Roads." Whether that's true or not, this little cradle of tall trees and limestone bluffs shrouded in an almost eerie quiet is a well-kept secret—rather remarkable, considering that it's barely 100 miles from Chicago.

It's also the home of three state parks—White Pines, Lowden, and Castle Rock—so you would think it would attract a steady stream of day-trippers. Not so. In addition, it has just enough quirky tourist attractions, such as the homes of John Deere and Ronald Reagan, to make it a more popular destination. To our good fortune, the masses have not made those same discoveries—yet.

If you're lucky enough to be traveling during the time that the leaves are turning, don't miss the ride on Highway 2 north from Dixon to Rockford. It follows the Rock River shoreline and is considered by many veteran leaf-peepers to be the most scenic route in the state.

Day 1

Morning

Take Highway 64 west into Oregon. An early start is recommended, as you'll want to make it into town by 11:00 A.M. for the *Rose of the Rock River* paddleboat ride, which departs from Maxson Manor Restaurant at 11:30. If you're late, though, don't worry. There are two more departures, one at 2:30 and one at 6:30; the latter includes dinner. This two-hour cruise is a visual feast, especially in the fall. Prices range from $9.00 to $27.00 (depending on whether or not meals are included). Call 1–800–468–4222.

Lunch: Lunch is served on board the *Rose of the Rock River.* The scrumptious orange rolls are almost as famous as the scenery.

Afternoon

Head over to **White Pines Forest State Park** (6712 West Pines Road, Mt. Morris; 815–946–3717. The official address is Mt. Morris, but it's 8 miles west of Oregon.) The park offers unlimited recreation and is significant for being the southernmost stand of virgin white pine in the Midwest, which means something to botanists, if not tourists.

Explorers will find an area rich in Indian history, as well as an abundance of natural resources spread over 385 acres. The park has seven well-marked hiking trails running through it. The Chicago-Iowa trail, which borders the south side of the park, once served as the main east-west road through Illinois. White Pines is the most popular of the area's three parks primarily because it offers the most amenities, including a lodge, cabins, a gift shop, and a restaurant (see "Other recommended restaurants and lodging" at the end of this chapter).

Castle Rock (Route 2, Oregon; 815–732–7329) is the largest of the three state parks, with 2,000-plus acres, and attracts more die-hard nature lovers. Rockhounds take note: This is one of the few places where you can see St. Peter sandstone, which underlies nearly all of Illinois, at the surface. For a panoramic view of the river, climb the wooden stairs to the top of Castle Rock.

Lowden State Park encompasses 207 peaceful acres just across the river from Oregon. It is situated on a bluff. Sharing that vantage point is "Black Hawk," a stern, 48-foot statue that stands guard over the Rock River Valley. The chief is the most famous work by Lorado Taft who, along with a few fellow artists, set up an artists' colony here during the 1920s called Eagles Nest. To reach the park, go north on River Road from Route 64 to Route 2 (815–732–6828). Regardless of where you choose to do your hiking, be sure you end up in front of White Pines Inn just in time for dinner.

Dinner: Like most state-run properties, the menu at the **White Pines Inn** is a terrific value. Entrees lean heavily toward baked chicken, fresh fish, and barbecued ribs—fare that fits nicely with the knotty pine decor. After dinner take your coffee out onto the porch and settle into a wicker rocker or browse the gift shop, stocked with equal parts of Illinois crafts and tacky souvenirs. For reservations call (815) 946–3817.

After dinner return to the sixties at **Washington Street Mercantile and Coffee House,** 221 Washington Street, which features folk singers. There are two shows nightly, at seven and nine. Admission is $5.00; call (815) 732–6568.

Lodging: **Pinehill Bed & Breakfast,** 400 Mix Street, Oregon; (815) 732–2061. Innkeeper Sharon Burdick is very proud of her 1874 Italianate villa, with its five charming rooms, all with private bath and three with original working marble fireplaces. The rooms have whimsical names, such as the Somerset Maugham (Maugham often visited Pinehill during the 1930s). A truly kid-friendly inn, activities include Easter egg hunts, story telling, and ice cream socials. Christmas teas are daily rituals during the holiday season. Rates: $75 to $150.

Day 2

Morning

Breakfast: A full breakfast at Pinehill may include eggs and homemade blueberry or banana–chocolate chip muffins, cinnamon sticky buns, crumpets, and such hot entrees as granola pancakes with real maple syrup or cheese blintz souffle.

Drive down Highway 2 to **John Deere Home,** Grand Detour (5 miles north of Dixon). Grand Detour is to agriculture what Detroit is to transportation. This prairie hamlet is where a blacksmith named Deere built a plow that would forever change the way people farmed. Much of the original shop was destroyed by fire, but it has been carefully restored, right down to the white picket fence. Admission charge. Call (815) 652–4551.

You can swing back onto Highway 2 and head up to DeKalb, home of Northern Illinois University, the second largest school in the state. If you would like a tour, call the Administration Office (815–753–0466).

Lunch: Crystal Pistol, 1312 West Lincoln Highway, DeKalb; (815) 758–1000. Steaks and seafood in a New Orleans decor. The sixteen-ounce sirloin is a local favorite. Closed Monday. Moderate.

Afternoon

If your time is short, limit your touring to two architecturally important sites in DeKalb. The first is **Ellwood House Museum,** 509 North First Street. Colonel Isaac Ellwood, who made his money in barbed wire (it was invented here, an ironic touch in such rural surroundings), built a grand Victorian mansion and furnished it in an equally grand manner. It's open from April to early December every day except Monday. Admission: adults, $2.50; children, free. Call (815) 756–4609.

Your other stop should be the **Egyptian Theater,** 135 North Second Street (near Lincoln Highway). The terra-cotta exterior and Egyptian-revival style (circa 1929) recalls a time when vaudeville was king, despite the fact that touring companies still play here. For a schedule, call (815) 758–1215.

There's More

Antiques. Conover Square, corner of Third and Franklin, Oregon; (815) 732–2134. Renovated piano factory, mostly of crafts and antique shops.

Merlin's Florist and Greenhouse, 300 Mix Street, Oregon; (815) 732–7081. Collectibles and furniture are sold amid the blooms.

White Pines Ranch, 3581 Pines Road, Oregon; (815) 732–7923. This ranch (one of two working ranches in the state) offers horseback riding and an outdoor education program for kids that teaches everything from reading headstones to searching for fossils. By reservation only.

Silver Ridge Golf Course, Highway 2 (1½ miles north of Oregon); (815) 734–4440. This is a serenely beautiful course, high up on the ridge, overlooking the Rock River.

White Pines Deer Park, 1900 South Harmony Road, Oregon; (815) 732–2088. Feed the deer, peacocks, and even llamas. For 50 cents you get a cone of food. Another photo opportunity with the kids.

Sinnissippi Forest, 3122 South Lowden Road, Oregon; (815) 732–6240. If the season's right, this is the perfect spot to cut down your own Christmas tree. Here the job is done so well that the experience is turned into a Currier & Ives print. A horse-drawn wagon takes you into the 290-acre tree farm. After you've cut down your tree, sip a cup of cocoa while you warm your toes by the fire. (For Scrooges, there are also precut trees.)

Special Events

June. Canoe Rally. Pleasure canoeing and breakfast. Rock River near Maxson Manor.
July. Ogle County Airport Open House. Antique planes and rides.
July. Petunia Festival, Dixon. Dutch Reagan's hometown pulls out the stops with more than 7 miles of petunias.
October. Autumn on Parade, Oregon. One of Northern Illinois' oldest and largest festivals. Food, crafts, and games on the main square.
November. Christmas Walk. Decorated homes, crafts, etc. Downtown Oregon. Starts at Ogle County Historic Courthouse with the lighting of the tree.

Other Recommended Restaurants and Lodgings

Dixon

Best Western Brandywine Lodge, 443 Highway 2; (815) 284–1890. A full-service motel with pool and all other amenities. Four rooms have whirlpools. Rates: $45–$100 per night.

Detig's Bed and Breakfast, 3708 West Illinois; (815) 652–4750. Despite the Dixon mailing address, this New England–style inn is located across from the John Deere Museum. The fact that it is also a custom-lamp shop just adds to its character. The three cozy bedrooms are furnished in antiques. Rates: $45 per night.

Grand Detour

Colonial Inn, 8230 South Green Street; (815) 652–4422. An 1850 red-brick Italianate house of twelve rooms (four with private bath), with lots of period furniture, such as iron-rail and brass beds. The continental breakfast includes fresh fruits and croissants.

Mt. Morris

White Pines Inn, 6712 White Pine Road; (815) 946–3817. Like Starved Rock, this state park lodge has undergone extensive renovation and is a steal. The lodge has 25 cabins, each accommodating four people. The Sweetheart Cabin has a canopied waterbed. Open year-round, although the restaurant closes in January and February. Rates: $54 per night.

Kable House, Sunset Hill; (815) 734–7297. This B&B is located right in the middle of a nine-hole golf course. That's right, you walk out and you're on the fairway. Six rooms. Breakfast is not served. Rates: $45–$75.

Oregon

LynDel Mansion, 400 North Third Street; (815) 732–7313. An air of romance permeates this 1877 Victorian home, which features two parlor rooms with marble fireplaces. All four guest rooms are furnished with antiques. Rates: $55–$75.

Maxson Manor, Highway 2 (1½ miles north of Highway 64); (815) 732–6761. This is beef country and the prime rib is a specialty, although the lobster and seafood entrees were mentioned by several fellow travelers. Lunch ($4.00–$6.00) and dinner ($10.00–$12.00).

Blackhawk Steak Pit, Highway 2; (815) 732–2500. Just as it sounds. A place to indulge in prime Midwestern beef, which is charbroiled before your eyes. Moderate.

Polo

Barber House Bed and Breakfast, 410 West Mason; (815) 946–2607. Built in 1891 by prominent Polo banker Henry Barber, this Georgian Revival home in the town just west of Oregon is listed on the National Register of Historic Places. Five bedrooms are furnished with period antiques. Rates, which include a full country breakfast, range from $50 to $75 per night.

For More Information

Northern Illinois Tourism Council, 1740 Bell School Road, Cherry Valley, IL 61016. (815) 964–6482.

Gilman

Get the kinks out during morning stretch at The Heartland.

The Ultimate Midwestern Spa

_____ 2 NIGHTS _____

Health · Fitness · Self-indulgence

At the first sign of a few extra pounds, Cher retreats to the Golden Door in California. When too many late nights take their toll on Frank Sinatra, he flies off to Switzerland for an injection of sheep's cells. But for many Midwesterners, luxury is in Gilman, Illinois, just south of Kankakee.

The Heartland may be just an hour and a half from Chicago, but it could just as easily be a world away. This seven-year-old spa, situated on thirty-one acres of lush central Illinois countryside offers equal parts of clean living and indulgence.

The Heartland operates a complimentary shuttle from Water Tower Place downtown. But making the short drive is a pleasant option, not only because it clears your head as you get out into the country, but also because it lets you explore some interesting stops along the way.

Day 1

Afternoon

The Heartland's weekend starts with dinner on Friday. If you are an antique buff, however, take I–94 to Highway 1 and stop in **Crete.** This far-southern suburb doesn't get half the attention of other Chicago area antique "meccas" such as Long Grove, St. Charles, or Geneva; therefore, it has twice the bargains.

Start at **Marketplace Antiques** (550 West Exchange; 708–672–5556). It has about a dozen dealers and is filled to the rafters with china and glass primitives, quilts, furniture, and jewelry.

From there, head to **Surrey Antiques & Collectibles** (280 West Exchange; 708–672–4818). Talk about a specialty—the shop only handles items related to drinking. You can find everything from old beer signs to Coke vending machines from the 1950s.

Next is the cluster of shops on Main Street. If you have time for only one, make it the **Crete Antique Mart** (1292 Main Street; 708–924–5489), which has fifty dealers.

Continue on Highway 1 to the Heartland in Gilman. (If you're going straight to Gilman and bypassing Crete, I–57 is the most direct route.)

The Heartland is a beautiful, country estate with every conceivable amenity and an attentive, knowledgeable staff. There is just the right combination of health without hysteria, luxury without snobbery, and gain without pain.

The weekend we were there, a quick look around at the other twenty-seven guests confirmed that this was a place for real people, and there were few washboard-flat abdomens among us. One woman came to celebrate a 75th birthday; another was there to hide out from a 50th. Some guests came with their spouses, others with their mothers, and quite a few came alone. One woman was a waitress who decided that she needed to break the milkshake-a-day habit she had acquired on the job. Another, an accountant, was trying to wean herself off a nasty candy bar habit, a result of too much stress during tax season.

Stress is considered as much a no-no as a hot fudge sundae. Consequently, everything is designed to achieve maximum mellowness. The rooms are comfortably appointed, and there are no phones or TVs to break the mood.

Perplexed about what to wear? Everything is provided, from sweat suits to bathrobes to cozy socks. As for laundry, you just drop your clothes on your doormat and the "laundry fairies" whisk them away and replace them with a new stack. (Alas, one woman took her door-mat with her, only to find that the magic does not work at home.)

And because there's no tipping, there's no need for money—at least until you check out. A two-day stay, which includes everything, even a facial and a massage, costs $500. (Week-long stays are also available, for people who are lucky enough to have that unbeatable combination of time and money.)

The moderate tone is set right on the first page of the spa's manual, which each guest gets to take home: "Try as much or as little as is comfortable for you. This is your time to concentrate on yourself and nothing else."

Dinner: Pasta with a basil-tomato sauce is so delicious you don't even miss the fat. There's always plenty of fresh fruit to get you back on the straight and narrow.

Day 2

Morning

A typical morning at the Heartland starts with stretching exercises and a brisk, 2-mile walk through pastoral farmland. If you'd rather sleep in, however, no one will come pounding on your door.

After breakfast (hearty muffins or ricotta pancakes with fresh fruit), you can participate in a scheduled activity, such as Bodyworks (a conditioning class for exercise dropouts), weight training, water exercises, or advanced aerobics.

Lunch is a high point of the day. It can be a slice of vegetarian quiche or a beautifully presented salad. It is surprisingly satisfying.

Afternoon

Lunch may be followed by more activity, maybe on such high-tech equipment as Stairmaster or Nordictrack. Or perhaps you'd like to schedule a yoga class or head for the sauna and whirlpool. You can turn the self-indulgence up a notch with a full-body massage, a manicure, or a soothing facial.

After a dinner of grilled fish and a salad, an evening walk feels just right. The brave may want to try an obstacle course that starts with meeting simple challenges and works up to scaling a 40-foot-tall telephone pole. In the summer you can play a few sets of tennis or take a paddleboat out on shimmering Kam Lake; in the winter guests don cross-country skis and ice skates.

A series of educational programs, called "The Heartland Institute," takes place every night in a cozy den complete with stone fireplace and overstuffed furniture. Topics range from "how to read food labels" to "stress management." You can skip class and retire to your room with a steamy novel if you want to; class—and guilt—are not required.

Day 3

After saying good-bye, get back to I–57 (the Heartland will give you directions) and head north. At Kankakee, you can keep up the healthy life-style with an easy canoe trip on the **Kankakee River,** considered by many to be the best canoeing river in the state. Reed's Canoe trips will outfit you completely, from the boat itself to the life jackets. After your two-hour trip, buses are waiting at your destination to take you back to your car. There are longer options as well; some last as long as two days. April to October (815–932–2663).

Lunch: Take a short jog east on Highway 17, before hitting Highway 1 for the drive home. Stop at **Dionne's** in Momence, at the intersection of highways 17 and 1 (815–472–6081). You may have learned a lot about nutrition over the last two days, but who can resist French onion soup with a thick blanket of cheese? It goes especially well with a crisp salad and a basket of crusty bread. If you go for the chocolate mousse, no one will ever tell.

What tulips are to Holland, gladioluses are to **Momence.** There are several major growers here that produce about sixty varieties of blossoms, which are shipped all over the country. An annual three-day festival, held usually the second weekend of August—when some 500 acres of flowers are in bloom—is alone worthy of a day trip.

There's More

Kankakee County Historical Society Museum, Eighth Avenue at Water Street; (815) 932–5279. The French and Indian heritage of the Kankakee River Valley is on display here, as are housewares, furniture, and Civil War memorabilia.

Fishing, hiking, snowmobiling (3 miles of designated trails). Kankakee River State Park, 8 miles northwest of Kankakee on Highway 102 (815–933–1383).

Special Events

Mid-July. Kankakee Fishing Derby. Anglers from all over the Midwest compete for cash prizes. Held throughout the county on the Kankakee River.

August. Kankakee County Fair and Rodeo Exposition. Carnival, entertainment, food.

Other Recommended Restaurants and Lodgings

Grant Park

Bennett-Curtis House, 302 West Taylor; (815) 465–6025. Senator Edward C. Curtis built this stately Victorian home in 1900. Senator George Bennett bought it in 1919. Today you can stay in it or have a gourmet dinner (fixed price $43). The specialty is Beef Wellington, and all pastries are baked in the kitchen. Open for lunch at noon, Monday–Saturday. Open for dinner weekends only except in December when open daily. Open for Sunday brunch. Reservations required.

For More Information

The Heartland, 20 East Jackson Boulevard, Chicago, IL 60604. (800) 545–HTLD or (312) 427–6465.

Kankakee Convention and Visitors Association, 4 Dearborn Square, 2nd floor, Kankakee, IL 60901. (815) 935–7390.

Springfield

Lincoln's Springfield residence today—much as it was in Abe's time

Land of Lincoln

_____ 2 NIGHTS _____

Sightseeing • Architecture • Historic sites

It's amazing to consider the number of adults who have been to Paris, London, and Rome but somehow have never made it to Springfield.

Lacking both the proximity and cachet of, say, a Lake Geneva, Springfield is easy to overlook. And while it's true that there are no beautiful beaches or sunset cruises to seduce you, the sheer dignity of Abraham Lincoln's life will provide more than enough sightseeing fodder for one weekend.

A trip to Springfield, however, is not just a glorified history lesson. You'll find several surprises strictly of the hedonistic variety. For example, the Ramada Renaissance hotel is one of the best in the Midwest. Not only does it have every creature comfort one would expect from Michigan Avenue accommodations, but it is also an incredible bargain. On weekends—when lobbyists on fat expense accounts have left town—rooms go for nearly half the weekday rate. (More on lodging later.) With virtually all the historic and government buildings free of charge, Springfield can be a lot cheaper than a getaway closer to home.

You'll also find that, despite the many attractions that capitalize on the popularity of its most famous citizen, the town still retains an unpolished quaintness. While you will see Mr. Lincoln's Campgrounds, Abe's Antiques, and even the Abe Lincoln Barber College, the landmarks, at least, are remarkably scrubbed of crass commercialism. Virtually all are free and disarmingly accessible. No lines, no barrage of billboards, no one hawking T-shirts. Just the Lincoln legacy—even kids raised on Nintendo come away impressed.

A few postscripts: While there are more than twenty attractions, many would be of interest only to the most passionate history buff. The top draws—Lincoln's home, Lincoln's tomb, the State capitol, the Illinois State Museum, the Dana-Thomas House—can be accomplished in a weekend. While the Governor's Mansion is undoubtedly worth a stop, hours are limited to Tuesdays and Thursdays.

Day 1

Take I–55 south to Springfield, about a 200-mile trip. You might want to put in a few hours of driving before stopping for breakfast in the Bloomington/Normal area, about 75 miles north of your final destination. (The usual selection of Bob Evans, Denny's, etc. can be found right off the highway.)

The break will also allow you to visit the **David Davis Mansion State Historic Site** (1000 East Monroe Street, Bloomington, 309–828–1084), a large, exquisite Victorian home built in 1872 for Judge David Davis and his wife. The home of this wealthy landowner and crony of Abraham Lincoln has been faithfully restored and contains a great many period furnishings. Fans of Victoriana will find it especially worth a stop at Christmas, when it is decked out for the holiday season. Admission: free.

Back on 55, Springfield is a little more than an hour away. Not only will you find the Lincoln sites close together, but the block of Eighth Street between Capitol Avenue and Jackson Street is closed to auto traffic, so travelers can immerse themselves in nineteenth-century history without any twentieth-century intrusions. The gaslights and wooden sidewalks add to the ambience, as well.

Stop first at the **Lincoln Home Visitors Center** to pick up tickets for the tour of Lincoln's home, just a block away. Tickets are free but are dispensed on a first-come, first-served basis. It's worth a stop to check availability when you come into town. If tickets are sold out, make this the first stop of the day tomorrow. Tickets are stamped with the time of your tour; this way you can visit other stops and return in time for the tour. The visitors center is also a good place to get oriented. You'll find special exhibits and an excellent bookstore, with a wealth of material on the Lincoln years and the Civil War. The Lincoln Home Visitors Center is located at 426 South Seventh Street. Hours are 8:30 A.M.–5:00 P.M. (217) 789–2357. Free.

When you tour Abraham Lincoln's home, where the family lived for the seventeen years before Lincoln was elected president, you'll actually feel good about your tax dollars at work. Beautifully restored and impeccably maintained, the home sits squarely in the middle of a four–square-block area. Tours, conducted by knowledgeable park rangers, are about twenty minutes in length—short enough to hold the interest of even a five-year-old, but still substantial enough to satisfy adults. The home—the only one Lincoln ever owned—is furnished (mostly with reproductions) as it appeared in 1860. The Lincoln Home National Historic Site, Eighth and Jackson streets, is open daily 8:30 A.M.–5:00 P.M. Call (217) 492–4150. Free.

When you leave Lincoln's home, head north on Ninth Street to Monroe. Turn right and you'll find the **Lincoln Depot,** where president-elect Lincoln said good-bye to Springfield and boarded a train for Washington, D.C. The depot contains restored waiting rooms and a multimedia presentation. Open daily, 10 A.M.–4 P.M. Call (217) 544–8695. Free.

Head west on Monroe a couple blocks and stop at the **First Presbyterian Church** (Seventh and Capitol streets; 217–782–4836) to view the Lincoln Family pew. Another block to the northwest, at Sixth and Adams, is the Lincoln Herndon Law Offices. Lincoln practiced law here for ten years. It is the only surviving structure in which he maintained working law offices. Open daily, 9 A.M.–5 P.M. Free.

That's a lot for one day. Time to break for dinner.

Dinner: **Alexander's Steak House,** 620 Bruns Lane; (217) 793–0440. Carnivores will think they've died and gone to heaven at Alexander's, where T-bones weigh in at twenty-five ounces. The gimmick of picking out your steak and cooking it over a charcoal grill adds to the fun. Moderate.

Lodging: **The Ramada Renaissance,** 701 East Adams Street; (217)

544–8800. This is the only AAA four-diamond hotel in the state (outside Chicago). The furnishings are lovely, the service impeccable, and the food exceptional, which is not quite typical of central Illinois. Use of the clean, comfortable health club is included in your room rate (during the week it's often used by legislators). You'll find small, unexpected touches everywhere, from complimentary newspapers to a jigsaw puzzle-in-progress in the lobby, just waiting for you to sit down and add a piece. Weekend rates are $65 per night.

Day 2

Morning

Breakfast: Ramada Renaissance Hotel.

If you didn't see the Lincoln home, go to the visitors center as early as possible and get your tickets. If you've already seen it, then pick up the Lincoln trail where we left off.

Go 2 blocks north and 1 block west from the the First Presbyterian Church to the **Old State Capitol.** This is where Lincoln served as a state representative and made his famous "House Divided" speech. It is completely furnished and restored to duplicate his legislative years. There is also a tour, called "Mr. Lincoln's World," provided by costumed interpreters. The Old State Capitol, located at the Downtown Mall, between Adams, Washington, Fifth, and Sixth streets, is open daily, 9 A.M.–5 P.M. Call (217) 782–4836. Free.

If you want to view modern-day government in action, the **new state capitol** houses the Illinois state legislature and constitutional offices. The capitol complex includes the Centennial Building, which houses the Hall of Flags, and the state archives. Built in 1868, the capitol offers free guide service. The Illinois State Capitol Building, Second Street and Capitol Avenue, is open to visitors. Monday through Friday, 8:00 A.M.–4:00 P.M.; Saturday and Sunday, 9:00 A.M.–3:30 P.M. Call (217) 782–2099. Free.

Just next to the capitol, is the Illinois State Museum (Spring and Edwards streets; 217–782–7386). For kids with access to the Field Museum, this will seem a bit tame. The emphasis is on the state's history, geology, and anthropology. Art galleries feature photography and fine and decorative arts, but easily the most popular displays are the Carson miniatures and a mastodon skeleton. There is also a special hands-on discovery room for kids. The museum is open Monday through Saturday, 8:30 A.M.–5:00 P.M.; Sunday, noon–5 P.M. Free.

Lunch: **Maldaner's,** 222 South Sixth Street; (217) 522–4313. A Springfield establishment, where as much state business is conducted as on the capitol floor. The historically appointed 1896 building serves hearty American fare, while downstairs features a lighter menu of salads, soups, and sandwiches (the horseshoe sandwich is the specialty of the house).

Afternoon

If you feel as if you've burned out on government and need to shift gears, about 3 blocks away, at 301 East Lawrence Avenue, is the **Dana-Thomas House.** After a three-year restoration project, the Dana-Thomas House reopened in 1990 to rave reviews. Designed and built by Frank Lloyd Wright in 1910, the house and its contents have been brought back to a time when Springfield socialite Susan Lawrence Dana entertained dignitaries there with great flourish.

This is the Wright mother lode, containing the largest collection of original Wright-designed oak furniture and art glass (about 450 windows, skylights, light fixtures, lamps, and door panels). Fully narrated tours last about one hour and are preceded by a slide show. Visitors should also take note of the Sumac Book Shop, which offers architectural books, gifts, and home furnishings of a superb quality. The house is open daily, 9 A.M.–5 P.M., and admission is free. (217) 782–6776.

Lodging: Return to the Ramada Renaissance for some swimming and a soak in the whirlpool before dinner.

Dinner: **Floreale/Lindsay's,** Ramada Renaissance Hotel. Floreale is one of Springfield's most upscale restaurants—with prices to match ($15 to $20 per entree). The emphasis is on Northern Italian cuisine, and the service is top-notch—lots of tableside showmanship, for example. Floreale also offers an extensive wine list. Note that there is a dress code. If you're on a budget, opt for an early (before 6:30) reservation, when prices are lower. Lindsay's, the hotel's less expensive dining alternative, is more casual. Such basics as chicken, steak, and fish range from $9.00 to $16.00. Call (217) 544–8800 for either restaurant.

Day 3

Morning

Breakfast: Ramada Renaissance.

Start your day with a visit to **Lincoln's Tomb,** about a ten-minute drive from downtown. This is the final resting place of Lincoln, his wife, and three of their four sons. (A fourth son, Robert Todd Lincoln, is buried at Arlington National Cemetery.) Inside the tomb are statuettes of Lincoln that celebrate various periods of his life. The popular bust of Lincoln that stands at the tomb's entrance has a "nose" that has been rubbed smooth by visitors for luck. Despite this one bit of folly, the tomb is as dignified a monument as you'll see, mercifully free of anything but solitude. Along with Lincoln's Home, this should be a priority for any Springfield visitor. While you're at the cemetery, take a moment to view the Vietnam Veterans Memorial, which pays tribute to all Illinois residents who served in the war.

The Lincoln Tomb State Historic Site is located at Oak Ridge Cemetery. Entrance is at 1500 North Monument Avenue or at North Walnut Street. The monument is open daily, 9 A.M.–5 P.M. The cemetery's hours are seasonal. From May to October it is open 8 A.M.–8 P.M.; from November to April it is open daily, 8 A.M.–5 P.M. (217) 782–2717. Free.

There are a number of other attractions in Springfield, which are listed below. In order to fit everything into a weekend, however, start making your way back home, so you can hit **Lincoln's New Salem State Historic Site,** which is about 20 miles northwest of Springfield on Highway 97 near Petersburg.

Lincoln lived and worked in New Salem for six pivotal years of his life. He arrived at this tiny hamlet in 1831 as an awkward youngster and left in 1837 as an adult poised for a career in law and politics. In between, he worked as a store clerk, postmaster, surveyor, and steamboat pilot.

Ironically, the years Lincoln spent here almost entirely encompass the town's brief history. Shortly after Lincoln left, the county seat was moved to nearby Petersburg, and New Salem blew off the map like a tumbleweed. Today the restoration is virtually all that is here, but that is more than enough to warrant a detour.

Dozens of buildings—from the tavern to the church—have been reconstructed and furnished to take you back to the 1830s. The only original building is the Henry Onstatot Cooper Shop; this is the place where Lincoln pored over his law books. Children will enjoy the horse-drawn carriage that trots through the village. (While there is a small snack shop, either eat in Springfield or pack a picnic.)

Summer hours for New Salem are 9 A.M.–5 P.M.; winter hours are 8 A.M.–4 P.M. Call (217) 632–7953 for admission fees and other information. New Salem offers two additional seasonal attractions. During the summer months you can board *The Talisman,* a replica of the steamboat that paddled along the Sangamon River in Lincoln's day. The boat leaves hourly, between 10 A.M.–5 P.M. For information call (217) 632–7681.

Also, from mid-June through late August a dramatic production chronicling the life of Lincoln is performed in the outdoor amphitheater. For information and reservations call (217) 632–7754.

If you are a Lincoln scholar (or would like to be) and don't have to head back home yet, you can take the Lincoln Heritage Trail, which wends through the central Illinois cities of Decatur, Mattoon, Charleston, and Vandalia. You can obtain a complete map of this trail from the Springfield Convention and Visitors Bureau (address below).

There's More

Governor's Mansion, Fifth and Jackson streets; (217) 782–2525. Home to Illinois' first family, this is the third oldest continually occupied governor's mansion in the country. Of the fourteen rooms open to the public, the State Dining Room, Lincoln Bedroom, and Library are especially worth noting. So are the antiques, which grew impressively during the years Jim Thompson was governor, thanks to Big Jim's passion for collecting. While this is a splendid stop, note that it's only open to midweek visitors. Open Tuesday through Thursday, 9:30 A.M.–10:45 A.M. and 2:00–3:15 P.M. Free.

Vachel Lindsay Home, 603 South Fifth Street; (217) 528–9254. This home gets overshadowed by the magnificence of Dana-Thomas, but if you love house tours, you'll enjoy viewing the original fixtures, furnishings, artwork, and writings of this poet, known as the "Prairie Troubadour." This is another site open only during the week. Open March–October, Tuesday–Thursday, noon–3:30 P.M.; rest of the year, by appointment. Free.

Lincoln Memorial Garden & Nature Center, 2301 East Lake Drive; (217) 529–1111. Lush gardens designed by Jens Jensen, America's leading landscape architect in the early twentieth century. Five miles of trails, blanketed with wildflowers, which give their peak performance in late April and May. In winter try the cross-country skiing. The nature center will be of interest to the little ones. Open Tuesday–Saturday, 10 A.M.–4 P.M.; Sunday, 1–4 P.M. Free.

Washington Park Botanical Gardens, Springfield; (217) 787–2540. For serious gardeners, Washington Park features a domed conservatory, formal rose garden, and seasonal floral shows. Open Monday–Friday, noon–4 P.M.; Saturday–Sunday, noon–5 P.M. Free.

Henson Robinson Zoo, 1100 East Lake Drive; (217–529–2097). This 14-acre zoo, which includes a nifty reptile house and nocturnal animal building, is a good place to remember when the kids have endured just about all the educational stuff they can stand. Open April–September, 10 A.M.–5 P.M.

Candy tour. Nestle-Beich Candy Factory, 2501 Beich Road, Bloomington; (309) 829–1031. Tour the factory that produces Bit O'Honeys and Laffy Taffys. The highlight is the free samples.

Antiques. Springfield Antique Mall, 3031 Reilly Drive; (217) 522–3031. Sixty dealers, with an impressive selection of estate jewelry.

Vinegar Hill, First and Cook streets. This quaint mall, 1 block south of the Capitol, has several antique shops.

Golf. Springfield Park District operates three public courses. Reservations accepted but not required. Call (217) 544–1751.

Knight's Action Park, Bypass 36 and Chatham Road; (217) 546–8881. Includes eighteen-hole miniature golf courses, driving range, batting cages, gameroom, and waterslide.

Special Events

Mid-February to early March. Maple Syrup Time, Lincoln Memorial Gardens & Nature Center. Get some pancakes ready as you watch the process from sap to syrup. Weekends only.

Mid-August. Illinois State Fair (Sixth to Ninth streets and Sangamon Avenue). A good excuse to pig out on corn dogs and cotton candy. (During the fair hotel accommodations can be tough and all special weekend rates are off, so plan accordingly.) For fair information write Box 576, Springfield, IL 62705.

Other Recommended Restaurants and Lodgings

Springfield

Baur's, 620 South First Street; (217) 789–4311. Another menu heavy on Midwestern beef. Also known for its mesquite cooking and one of Springfield's best Sunday brunches.

Hampton Inn of Springfield, 3185 South Dirksen Parkway; (217) 529–1100. Heated indoor pool, whirlpool. Rates: $50–$55 per night.

Hilton, 700 East Adams Street; (217) 789–1530. Recently renovated, the Hilton offers indoor pool, sauna, and all the other extras you'd expect from this upscale chain. Weekend rates. Like the Ramada, the Hilton is walking distance from all the major sights. Rates: $65–$175 per night.

Holiday Inn East Conference Center, 3100 South Dirksen Parkway; (217) 529–7171. Two heated pools, sauna, whirlpool, putting green, playground. Rates: $60–$150 per night.

For More Information

Springfield Convention and Visitors Bureau, 642 East Adams Street, Springfield, IL 62701. (217) 789–2360.

Galena

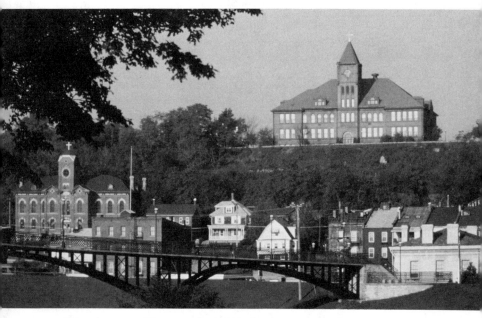

Galena is a town still very much rooted in the nineteenth century.

A Trip Back In Time

_____ 2 NIGHTS _____

Antiques · Architecture · Historical sites · Museums · House tours ·
Golfing · Horseback riding · Shopping · Downhill skiing ·
Cross-country skiing · Riverboat gambling · Hiking · Camping

When you tire of all the high-tech gadgetry and helter-skelter of this
century, pack a bag for Galena and take a trip back in time. Cradled
in the rolling countryside and wooded hills of Illinois' great northwest
lies a land of quintessential quaintness. A real-life nineteenth-century
Brigadoon, Galena is a haven for the historic minded, with 85 percent
of its community listed on the National Register of Historic Places.

During the mid-1800s the town was the largest Mississippi River
port north of St. Louis and a thriving capital of commerce. This was

the site of America's first mining rush, an 1820s boom town in search of lead (or "galena," the ore's name in Latin). As Galena's star rose, her wealth was transformed into elegant mansions and other architecturally distinct buildings. Today virtually every street boasts fine period examples (many beautifully preserved), ranging from Federal, Greek Revival, and Italianate styles to Queen Anne, Second Empire, and Gothic Revival (to name a few).

Galena was also the hometown of President Ulysses S. Grant. Oddly enough, it was about the time Grant and his family arrived here (shortly before the Civil War broke out) that the seeds of Galena's demise were sown. Among the contributing factors was the decision to relocate the Illinois Central Railroad terminal in neighboring Dubuque.

Ironically, it was the town's slumber that renewed its prominence. After Chicago and Springfield, Galena, populated with fewer than 4,000, is considered the third most popular destination in Illinois.

Keep in mind that reservations are a must in Galena; be sure to contact restaurants and bed and breakfasts well in advance. Parking can be troublesome, too, so plan on doing a lot of walking, and bring a comfortable pair of shoes. Casual attire is appropriate; don't worry about dressing up. And although there is much to be enjoyed by the young and old alike, Galena is primarily a getaway for adults with a hankering to experience a little history.

Day 1

Morning

The drive to Galena, roughly 3¼ hours, is picturesque, especially as you approach Jo Daviess (pronounced Davis) County in the state's far northwest corner, where Galena is situated. Lovely farm vistas stretch for miles, and the panorama, particularly in autumn, is invigorating.

Head west out of Chicago on I–90. About an hour outside of the city, stop in Rockford to see the **Time Museum** in the Clock Tower Resort (7801 East State Street, at the junction of I–90 and U.S. Highway 20; 815–398–6000). This exquisite little museum is a fitting start for your journey to the "land that time forgot." Since the museum doesn't open until 10 A.M., take a quick detour to the Clock Tower coffee shop for breakfast. The menu is complete with all the early morning regulars: eggs, sausage, biscuits, pancakes, waffles, and the like. Then, on to the museum.

Housing an extensive collection of timekeeping devices from around the world, the Time Museum will delight you with clocks and watches of all kinds. An atomic clock so precise that it registers time in atoms and a waterfall clock run by circulating water are two of the favored treasures. You'll also find an elaborate display of decorative and novelty clocks such as the ornate Singing Bird clock made by Ingold in Paris in 1834 or the "Mudge Green," an English marine timekeeper made by Thomas Mudge in 1777. Allow at least an hour to marvel. Admission: adults, $3.00; seniors and students, $2.00; children under 18, $1.00. Open 10 A.M.–5 P.M., Tuesday–Sunday.

Back on the road again, head west on U.S. Highway 20, enjoying the countryside's winding twists and turns.

Lunch: As you enter town (off of U.S. Highway 20) heading north on Main Street, you'll find **Grant's Place** (515 South Main Street; 815–777–3331). This adorable pub is just upstairs from the Galena Cellars Winery (both are housed in a restored 1840s granary). Hamburgers and big sandwiches are specialties of the house, as are the servers, the real novelty here. The costumed crew are dressed as Civil War soldiers complete with Union blues and forage caps.

Note: If you opt to tour the winery, plan on spending forty-five minutes at **Galena Cellars.** You'll learn via video how the family-run winery presses, ferments, and ages its wines. Tasting is also part of the tour, but you'll have to savor your sample. The guides teach you how to extract three different tastes from a single serving. The $1.00 tours begin daily at 1:30 P.M.

Afternoon

Exploring Galena is hardly an activity you'll accomplish in a single afternoon. And while there are several touring services that will take you to the historic sites by trolley, van, bus, or even a 1929 Buick, you may want to rely on your own resources and set off on your own.

Begin your introduction to the town at the **Galena/Jo Daviess County Historical Society and Museum** (211 South Bench Street; 815–777–9129). Along with the lead mining, steamboating, and Civil War exhibits housed in this nineteenth-century mansion is a concise slide presentation that will give you a fairly good overview of Galena's history. The museum also offers two thirty-minute, self-guided walking tours. Open daily, 9:00 A.M. to 4:30 P.M.; closed on major holidays. Admission: adults, $2.50; students 10–18, $1.50; children under 10, free.

Next walk across the Galena River (over the foot bridge) to the **Galena/Jo Daviess County Visitor Information Center,** a train depot built in 1857 (101 Bouthillier Street; 800–747–9377). This is the same station Colonel U. S. Grant first departed from on his way to war. Today you can sit on one of the long wooden benches and watch the freight trains go by. You'll also be able to stock up on maps, brochures, and plenty of pamphlets. Admission is free.

At this point, check out the **Ulysses S. Grant Home,** which is just a short walk up the street. The house is located on a hill at 500 Bouthillier Street (815–777–3310 or 815–777–0248). Certainly not the largest or grandest home in Galena, this two-story Italianate brick house was a gift presented to Grant upon his heroic return from the Civil War in 1865. Although Grant actually spent little time in the home (he was elected to the presidency in 1868 and only briefly returned to Galena in 1879), it contains many of the family's possessions, including Grant's White House china and silver. Additionally, most of the home's original furnishings are still intact. Open daily, 9 A.M. to 5 P.M.; closed major holidays. Admission is free.

Retrace your steps down Bouthillier Street, turn south on Park Avenue, and venture into **Grant Park** for a leisurely stroll. Straddled alongside the Galena River, the park provides an excellent vantage point to view the town. The park's highlights are a statue of its namesake, a Civil War monument, and a charming gazebo where you'll be tempted to linger.

Next travel back over the bridge and into town. Stop at the **Old General Store Museum,** a replica of a nineteenth-century general store with authentic artifacts, but nothing for sale (223 South Main Street; 815–777–9129). Tours take thirty minutes and admission is only $1.00. Hours are from 10 A.M. to 4 P.M. daily, June–October; weekends, November–December.

Try to visit the **Old Market House State Historic Site** (423 North Commerce Street; 815–777–2570 or 815–777–3310). Built in 1845, this is one of the oldest remaining market houses in the Midwest. During Galena's most prosperous years, it was the hub of the town's community life. Fully restored, the building currently holds an exhibit on Midwestern architecture. You'll find a short audiovisual show here as well. Open daily, 9 A.M. to 5 P.M.; closed major holidays. Admission is free. Allow a minimum of thirty minutes.

Finally, head on over to the **Old Stockade Refuge,** situated only a few steps away on Galena's only remaining cobblestone street (208 Perry Street; 815–777–1646). Built of rough-hewn logs, the refuge was used by pioneers during the Blackhawk War of 1832. Today an Indian museum can be found on the premises. Arrowheads, tomahawks, beadwork, wampum, pottery, and a birchbark canoe are among its contents. Don't forget to take a peek in the "basement" where you'll find a room carved out of solid rock. Open daily, 9:30 A.M.–4:30 P.M., May–August; 10 A.M.–4 P.M., September and October; and on weekends in April, 10 A.M.–4 P.M.; closed November through March. Admission: adults, $2.00; children ages 13–16, $1.00; children ages 5–12, 75 cents.

Dinner: One of the local favorites is the **Kingston Inn** (300 North Main Street; 815–777–0451). Accompanied by an excellent pianist, the waitstaff takes turns bursting into song. Food specialties are varied including Spanish, Mediterranean, Northern Italian, French, and regional American dishes. Seating in the dining room is limited, so be sure to make a reservation. Dinners range from $8.00 to $20.00.

Lodging: The **DeSoto House Hotel** (230 South Main Street; 800–343–6562) is a Galena landmark. Recently renovated (at a cost of $8 million), the DeSoto was considered the largest hotel west of New York when it opened in the mid-1850s. Such notables as Abraham Lincoln (who once spoke from its balcony), Mark Twain, Susan B. Anthony, and Lorado Taft were all guests here. The hotel features an elegant Victorian lobby and rooms are decorated to reflect the period. Furthermore, its location is convenient, right in the heart of Galena's historic district. Parking (which is at a premium in downtown Galena) is also included. Rates: $69 (single) to $150 (two-room suite), depending on season.

Day 2

Morning

Breakfast: The **DeSoto House Restaurant,** located in a sunny, plant-filled courtyard in the center of the hotel, is an inviting place to start the day. The charm factor is multiplied by a number of quaint little shops that peer down from a balcony above. Omelets (four varieties) and the country breakfast (eggs, bacon, hash browns, and toast) are the most popular selections on the menu.

Shopping is the first order of the day. Main Street, with its fancy storefronts and concentration of antiques and collectibles, is a slice of heaven for the romantic at heart. Among the stores in its 5-block span are **The Store Next Door** (110 South Main Street), filled with antique furniture, old wooden trunks, vintage lace clothing, china, and an assortment of memorabilia; **Gary's Antiques** (105 North Main Street), an emporium of American and European antiques and collectibles; **Thomas L. Brisch Bookseller** (238 North Main Street), a specialty shop for used books, especially Western Americana; **Tin-Pan Alley Antiques** (230 North Main Street) with everything from pie safes to vintage Victrolas and a treasury of 78 rpm records; **Ragamuffin Dolls** (115 North Main Street), a great spot for dollhouse enthusiasts; and **Red's Antiques** (232–234 North Main Street), chock full of crocks, jars, wooden wheels, pots, pans, kettles, toys, old cigar boxes, cookie cutters, and the like.

Also take a walk to the **Fulton Brewery Market** at 601 South Prospect Street (about 4 blocks south of the DeSoto House; just west of the U.S. Highway 20 bridge). Well worth a look, this building holds twelve more antique shops selling furniture, quilts, pottery, lanterns, china, prints, etc.

Just a word or two about shopping in Galena: Don't expect to find any great bargains. Merchandise isn't overly inflated, but remember this is a well-touristed area. Also although only a morning is devoted to this endeavor here, you can easily fill an entire day perusing the place. And lastly, even if antiques are not your thing, you'll find enough to keep you busy. Some of the shops sell chic clothing, and there are a number of gift boutiques and art galleries. If all else fails, you can always treat yourself to some delicious homemade ice cream at **The American Old-Fashioned Ice Cream Parlor** (102 North Main Street).

Lunch: **Baker's Oven and Tea Room,** smack dab in the middle of Main Street (200 North Main Street; 815–777–9105), is a cozy country tea room. Muffins, breads, and baked goods are the main event here (the fudge pecan pie is divine). Don't forget to sample the soup, salads, quiche, and sandwiches, however. Dinner is also served here but only on selected nights.

Afternoon

The golf course is an excellent place to be for the balance of the afternoon. **The Eagle Ridge Inn & Resort** (Highway 20 East; 800–892–2269 or 815–777–2444) has three spectacular courses—two championship eighteen-hole and one brand new executive nine-hole course—all designed by Roger Packard. Both of the older courses rank among *Golf Digest's* top resort courses in the world.

Tee time preferences are given to the inn's guests, but if you make a reservation seven days in advance, you won't have any problems on the weekends. Weekday tee times are easier to obtain. Green fees are the same for all—$70 for eighteen holes (including your cart) and $32 for the nine-hole course. Eagle Ridge does offer some "stay and play packages," so check these out if you're interested.

This isn't a course where you'll be able to hit a quick round. Golfers of all skill levels are attracted to Eagle Ridge, so expect a slow play averaging five hours for the eighteen-hole courses and two hours for the nine.

A pro shop with quality merchandise is also at the resort, as is an indoor winter golf center that is open from December through March. Among its offerings are an indoor driving range, video lessons taught by a PGA member ($30 for a half hour), a slew of indoor tournaments (putting and chipping contests), and golf video games.

Dinner: The new Dubuque **Casino Belle** gambling boat offers a dinner excursion that lasts about five hours and leaves from downtown Dubuque, Iowa (20 miles west across the Mississippi River at Third Street and Ice Harbor; 800–426–5591 or 815–777–1660). It is a big riverboat with four levels holding 2,000 passengers. Never mind the size; you'll find yourself standing in a line or two. Reservations are required at least two weeks in advance for the weekend dinner cruises, which leave at 6 P.M. Friday and Sunday and 9 P.M. Saturday. Cost is $39.95 for the cruise and dinner. Plan to bring no more than $200 for fun money; that's Iowa's loss limit per cruise.

Dinner is served during the first few hours of the cruise. The food is adequate but certainly not the reason anyone decides to ride the *Casino Belle*. Served buffet style (except for the salad), entrees are prime rib, chicken, and fish. The voyage also features Las Vegas–type stage shows performed three times throughout the night. Gambling consists of blackjack, craps, roulette, and slot machines.

For those who want to see the big river (to satisfy the Huck Finn side of your personality), the *Casino Belle* heads south to Belleville and back. From the deck you may have the chance to view grassy riverbanks, fishing boats, and—if you're especially lucky—a glorious moon.

During the winter the *Casino Belle* is docked, but there's still plenty of action on board. Parenting note: With advance reservation there's very capable sitter service. The children's room is well stocked with video games, toys, crafts, and snacks.

Lodging: The DeSoto House Hotel.

Day 3

Morning

Breakfast: Many consider the food at the **Farmer's Home Hotel** to be Galena's finest (334 Spring Street; 800–373–3456 or 815–777–3456). The decor is simple, and everything is fresh—including the pork, which is home bred. Only two meals are served. Breakfast is every day from 7:30 A.M. until 11:00 A.M. or until 2:00 P.M. on Friday, Saturday, and Sunday. Dinner is served Friday and Saturday, 5–10 P.M., and Sunday, 5–9 P.M.

Hobo hash is the Farmer's Home signature dish. It's a mixture of diced potatoes, broccoli, and onions with ham or chorizo added. Grilled melted cheddar cheese and a dollop of sour cream top off this favorite. Eggs and toast are also included. Another Farmer's Home specialty is the eggs Benedict challenge. The owners challenge customers to say they've tasted better eggs Benedict somewhere else. If so, the tab's on the owners. So far (they say) they haven't had to fork over any cash. Caution: Breakfast at Farmer's Home is big. The candlelit dinners are said to be very romantic in this 1867 restored hotel. Reservations are strongly recommended for dinner. Off-street parking is provided for restaurant guests, but you can easily walk from the DeSoto Hotel, which is just 4 blocks away.

After breakfast walk north to the far end of Main Street until you reach Diagonal Street. There you'll find the **Dowling House** (220 Diagonal Street; 815–777–1250). Once a trading post, this is the oldest stone house in Galena. A vernacular style home, the house was built in 1826 and has been restored with period furnishings. Allow a half hour to tour. The Dowling House is open daily, 10 A.M. to 5 P.M., Memorial Day–December; 10 A.M. to 4 P.M. on weekends, January–Memorial Day. Admission is $2.50.

Much more elaborate than the Dowling House, the **Belvedere Mansion and Gardens** (1008 Park Avenue; 815–777–0747) has also been completely restored. Built in 1857 for steamboat magnate J. Russel Jones (an ambassador to Belgium), this twenty-two-room Italianate mansion is Galena's largest. The Belvedere is elegantly furnished with Victorian pieces, items from Liberace's estate, and the famous green drapes from the film *Gone with the Wind*. Allow a half hour to tour. Admission is $2.50. Open daily, 11 A.M. to 5 P.M., Memorial Day–October.

The final destination before returning to Chicago is the **Vinegar Hill Historic Lead Mine and Museum** (8885 North Three Pines Road; 815–777–0855). You'll need to drive 6 miles north taking U. S. Highway 20 to Highway 84. The mine is typical of those operating during the early 1800s. The tour lasts a half hour with the first portion above ground in a museum where you can check out ore samples and mining tools, and hear about various lighting techniques. The remaining time is spent underground taking a guided walk. This is a good way to end your trip since it illustrates so much of what you will have seen at the museums. Open daily June through August, 9 A.M. to 5 P.M.; weekends in May, September, and October, 9 A.M. to 5 P.M. Adults, $3.50; students first grade through high school, $1.50; children under 5, free.

Lunch: **The Homestead Restaurant** (at The Eagle Ridge Inn & Resort, Highway 20 East, 815–777–2800). Take Highway 20 east seven miles from downtown Galena. Located just as you enter the Eagle Ridge territory, the Homestead Restaurant sprang to life (in this locale) after the resort's recent fire in January. Deli sandwiches and hamburgers as well as more formal entrees like seafood marinara served over pasta is the fare. Hours: Sunday–Thursday, 7:00 A.M.–9:30 P.M.; Friday and Saturday, 7:00 A.M.–10:30 P.M. Lunch menu items average at $6.95.

Afternoon

Return to Chicago taking U.S. Highway 20 east to I–90.

There's More

Horseback riding. The Shenandoah Riding Center, Highway 20 East; (815) 777–2373. Part of the Eagle Ridge Inn & Resort, the center offers trail rides, lessons, hayrides, and sleighrides. Open daily, weather permitting.

Downhill skiing. Chestnut Mountain Resort, 8700 West Chestnut Road; (800) 397–1320 or (815) 777–1320. Overlooking the Mississippi River 8 miles south of Galena, this ski resort has sixteen runs with a vertical drop of 475 feet. Open 8:30 A.M. to 10:00 P.M. daily, Thanksgiving–St. Patrick's Day.

Cross-country skiing. Eagle Ridge Inn & Resort, Highway 20 East; (800) 892–2269 or (815) 777–2444. Sixty-one kilometers of groomed trails winding through woods and around a lake. There's a snack bar where you can warm up with a hot drink. Open November–March.

Ice skating and sledding. Eagle Ridge Inn & Resort, Highway 20 East; (800) 892–2269 or (815) 777–2444. Lessons available. Open November–March.

Alpine Slide. Chestnut Mountain Resort, 8700 West Chestnut Road, (800) 397–1320 or (815) 777–1320. Tobogganlike track carries wheeled sleds 2,500 feet from a bluff down to the Mississippi. Open daily Memorial Day–Labor Day.

Riverboat rides and sightseeing cruises. Some include meals or overnight packages. In Galena, Jo Daviess County Riverboat Corporation (P.O. Box 132, Galena, IL 61036; 815–777–2648) and River Cruises (P.O. Box 406, Galena, IL 61036; 800–331–1467 or 815–777–1660). In Dubuque, Roberts River Rides (Third Street Ice Harbor, Dubuque, IA 52004; 800–426–5591 or 319–583–1761).

Mallard Duck Hatchery. Whistling Wings, 113 Washington Street, Hanover, IL 61041. The largest mallard duck hatchery in the world, hatching more than 200,000 ducks each year. The retail shop is open 9 A.M.–5 P.M., Monday–Friday, and 9 A.M.–noon on Saturday (815) 591–3512.

Grant Hills Antique Auto Museum, 1 mile east of Galena on U.S. Highway 20; 815–777–2115. Antique and classic automobile displays and memorabilia. Open daily 9 A.M. to 5 P.M., May–October; weekends, November–April. Closed major holidays.

Hiking. Eagle Ridge Inn & Resort (U.S. Highway 20 East; 800–892–2269 or 815–777–2444) and Apple River Canyon State Park (between U.S. Highway 20 and Stagecoach Trail on Canyon Park Road; 815–745–3302).

Camping. Area campsites in Galena include, Palace Campground (U.S. Highway 20 West; 815–777–2466) and Wooded Wonderland (610 South Devil's Ladder Road; 815–777–1223); and in Apple River, Apple River Canyon State Park (8763 East Canyon Road; 815–745–3302).

Special Events

January. Klondike Kapers. Slalom races, freestyle skiing, snow sculptures, fireworks, a torchlight parade, and skydivers. Chestnut Mountain Resort, 8700 West Chestnut Road, Galena.

Mid-May–Late Fall. Farmer's Markets. Held on Saturdays from 8 A.M. to 10 A.M. at the Old Market House Square, Galena.

June. Annual Tour of Historic Homes. Guided tours of privately owned nineteenth-century homes in Galena.

June. Lamplight Tour of Grant Home. Self-guided lamplight tours of U. S. Grant Home State Historic Site.

June. Skills from the Hills. Turn-of-the-century open-air market with farmers' hacks and stands offering produce, flowers, crafts, breads, and pastries served by women in period costume. Held on the brick plaza surrounding the Old Market House State Historic Site.

June. Galena Arts Festival. Fine arts and crafts with continuous music, theater, story-telling, dance, a children's creative corner, and gustatory delights. Held in Grant City Park.

August. Willow Folk Festival. More than 100 folksingers and musicians from throughout the Midwest perform from a hay wagon outside a country church. Stockton.

September. Historical Ice Cream Social. Continuous band music, homemade pies, cakes, desserts, ice cream, and frozen yogurt. Held in Grant City Park.

September. Lamplight Tour of Grant Home. Self-guided tours of U. S. Grant Home State Historic Site.

September. Annual Fall Tour of Homes. Guided tours of privately owned nineteenth-century homes in Galena.

September. Market Days. Open-air market with food, produce, plants, and crafts sold from old farm wagons by people in period costume. Held at Old Market House State Historic Site.

October. Mallardfest. Duck and prime rib dinner, parade, fun runs, live music, food booths, adopt-a-duck program, duck-calling contest, beer garden, arts-and-crafts fair, Ducks Unlimited auction. Held in Hanover.

October. Civil War Encampment. Men and women in period dress re-create a typical campsite of the Civil War era. Held at the Grant Home State Park.

October. Galena County Fair. Old-fashioned harvest festival with arts and crafts, food, games, continuous music, silent auction, face-painting, balloon release, and Galena generals and wives in period costume. Held in Grant City Park.

November. Nouveau Wine Release. Fall vintage is released with great festivity; horse-drawn wagon delivers first bottles to Main Street merchants and restaurants, limited poster signing. Held at Galena Cellars Winery.

November. Country Crafts Weekend. Artists and artisans demonstrate traditional skills in shops throughout Galena's Main Street historic district; includes candle-making, quilting, rosemaling, wreath- and garland-making, weaving, spinning, woodcarving, and cornhusk crafting. Continues into December.

Other Recommended Restaurants and Lodgings

Galena

Aldrich Guest House, 900 Third Street; (815) 777-3323. An 1845 Greek Revival mansion with five guest rooms. The decor is a mix of antiques and reproductions. The innkeeper personally serves breakfast to guests individually. Not suggested for young children. Rates range from $54 to $149 per night; two-night weekend minimum.

Cafe Italia, 301 North Main Street; (815) 777-0033. As the name suggests, Italian cuisine is the specialty here: pizza, soups, and sandwiches. No reservations are taken, so be prepared to stand in line.

Chestnut Mountain Resort, 8700 West Chestnut Road; (800) 397-1320. A full-service, 126-unit resort located 8 miles southeast of Galena on a bluff overlooking the Mississippi River. Children are welcome. Special packages are available. Rates: $55–$95 per night.

Clark's Restaurant, 129 South Main Street; (815) 777-0499. Strictly for lunch, this has a no-frills menu with no-frills prices. Lots of old-fashioned rural charm.

Eagle Ridge Inn & Resort, Highway 20 East; (800) 892-2269 or (815) 777-2444. A full-service resort complex on 6,800 wooded acres. Excellent golf facilities. Although the resort lost its main lodge (including restaurants and pool) to a fire last January, rebuilding is under way and is expected to be completed by this summer. Aside from 60 inn rooms, there are 250 condos, townhomes, and resort dwellings with fireplaces and whirlpools, depending on the units. Children are welcome. Ask about special package deals. Rates range from $100 to $375 per night.

Farmer's Home Hotel, 334 Spring Street; (815) 777-3456 or (800) 373-3456. This nine-room inn was originally a hotel for farmers who couldn't make it to market in Galena and back all in one day. Some twentieth-century amenities have been added such as private baths, color TVs, and an outdoor year-round hot tub. Breakfast is included in price of room. Not suggested for young children. Rates: $65–$115 per night.

Hellman Guest House, 318 Hill Street; (815) 777–3638. A Queen Anne brick mansion built in 1898 with stained glass windows, fine oak paneling, and a turret. The guest rooms are country Victorian. Breakfast is included. Not suggested for young children. Rates: $64–$89 per night; two-night weekend and holiday minimums.

Log Cabin Guest House, 11661 West Chetlain Lane; (815) 777–2845. Four country cabins located about 2 miles from downtown Galena. Three of the guest houses are early log cabins that were disassembled and rebuilt on the premises. The fourth is a former servant's house above a garage. Two of the cabins are reserved for adults only and have a whirlpool in an upstairs loft. Another has old-fashioned rope beds for the kids. Don't look for a kitchen, you won't find one. Rates: $45–$90 per night; two-night weekend minimum.

Market House Tavern, 204 Perry Street; (815) 777–0690. Another good place for lunch. Try the Crab Louis or the Tavernburger.

O'Malley's Cantina, 219 North Main Street; (815) 777–0290. A good lunch spot serving Mexican, Irish, and American cuisine.

Silver Annie's Ltd., 124 North Commerce Street; (815) 777–3131. Just a block off Main Street in a historic limestone building. The menu is Italian, and piano, guitar, and vocal performances are given nightly. Reservations are a must because the dining room is small.

For More Information

Galena/Jo Daviess County Convention & Visitors Bureau, 101 Bouthillier Street, Galena, IL 60136. (800) 747–9377.

Downtown Chicago

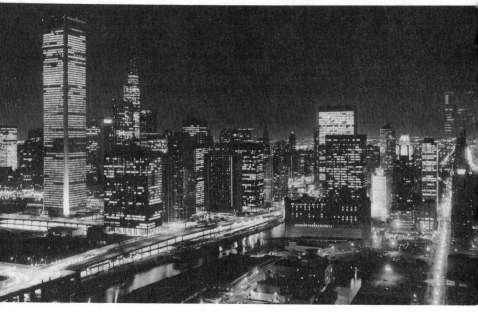

Chicago's glittering skyline

In Your Own Backyard

_____ 1 NIGHT _____

Architecture • Museums • Boat rides • Zoo • Aquarium

Sometimes, the best places are close to home. Chicago attracts tourists from all over the world. It would be silly not to take advantage of the wealth of attractions it has to offer—and without the ride.

In a city as large and diverse as Chicago, coming up with a single weekend is an exercise in decision making. Do you go for one big attraction (Great America), take in an ethnic festival, or attend a professional sports event? Also, there are entire guidebooks devoted to Chicago, so it would be futile to try to duplicate their efforts.

Instead, here are two variations on the in-town getaway. The first is planned with families in mind; the second is more adult-oriented. (Of course, places like The Berghoff are perfectly appropriate for children, that isn't the problem. It's more like whether the Hard Rock Cafe is appropriate for adults—or at least adults who value their hearing.)

You'll find that these itineraries will also come in handy when you're playing tour guide for out-of-towners.

Family Day 1

Morning

Breakfast: **Rock 'n' Roll McDonald's,** 600 North Clark Street; (312) 664–7940. The menu isn't different than any other McDonald's, but the decor is. This is the world's largest, busiest, and most crammed-to-the-rafters-with-'50s stuff McDonald's in the world. You have to see it to understand why it is one of the city's premiere tourist attractions.

After breakfast, head over to the **Wacky Pirate Cruise,** a one-hour trip led by "Buccaneer Bob." The complimentary pirate hats and kazoos are always a big hit. Board at the Mercury Dock, at the southwest corner of the Michigan Avenue bridge on any Friday, Saturday, or Sunday between July 1 and Labor Day. (312) 332–1368. Admission: $7.00.

The next stop is the **Chicago Children's Museum,** 435 East Illinois Street (North Pier). This is a delightful place for kids—pretty amazing for adults, too.

It's the rare spot that can occupy a two-year-old and a ten-year-old. Older kids love the bubbles, the fantasy vehicles (including a very popular ambulance), and the texture tunnels as much as toddlers do. There are plenty of benches for mom and dad to take a breather. Save the Recycle Arts Center for last. This is where kids can stuff bags with tubing, netting, and other thingamajigs, all donated by area manufacturers and guaranteed to jump-start the imagination. Open Tuesday–Friday, 12:30–4:30 P.M.; weekends, 10:00 A.M.–4:30 P.M. Adults, $3.00; children, $2.00; free family night on Thursday, 5:00–8:00 P.M. (312) 527–1000.

Lunch: The kids should get tired and hungry at about the same time, so play it safe and eat right at North Pier. But that doesn't mean you have to settle for the usual food court fare. The **A-1 Beanery** is a top-notch choice, because mom and dad can satisfy their palate (and thirst) with a margarita, chips, and salsa. Also, there are video games and other diversions to pass the time while waiting for food.

If the kids won't wait and you need to go the fast-food route, the food court does have a deli, where you can make some healthy selections, and a grill, where you can get hot dogs, gyros, and fries.

After lunch, it's pleasant to sit outside on the promenade and watch the boats go by. Or there's a lot more shopping to be done. (Don't miss the hologram shop; it is truly mesmerizing.)

If your brood still has a surplus of energy, do a quick nine holes at **City Golf,** located on the first floor of North Pier.

Insider's tip: Before you leave North Pier, be sure to get your parking ticket validated, which will knock off a few bucks—it's not much, but it helps.

Afternoon

Insider's tip: If you missed the Wacky Pirate Cruise, you can pick up a **Landmark cruise** right at North Pier for a ninety-minute trip. If you want to be a spectator to marine life, schedule a stop at the **Shedd Aquarium** (1200 South Lake Shore Drive; 312–939–2438), where you can still get that salt and sea feeling. If you're planning on seeing the Oceanarium, the new home of beluga whales, dolphins, and penguins, just remember to get your tickets in advance. But don't despair if you didn't plan ahead. The aquarium itself is still quite a show. Open daily, 9 A.M.–5 P.M. Admission: $7.00 ($3.00 for aquarium only). Oceanarium tickets can be purchased in advance through Ticketmaster (312–559–0200).

Dinner: You will certainly be a hit if you are willing to queue up at the **Hard Rock Cafe,** 63 West Ontario (312–943–2252). The hamburgers aren't anything special and the din will probably cause minor hearing loss, but any parent who puts this on the agenda immediately sheds his or her geek status.

After dinner, take your kids on a **carriage ride** on Michigan Avenue. Sure, it's meant to be romantic—but when that isn't possible, the next best thing is to go for fun, and a carriage ride fills the bill. The grand finale is a stop at **Buckingham Fountain,** the crown jewel of Grant Park. The color show is from 9 to 11 P.M. and runs from Memorial Day to October 1. (312) 294–4610.

Lodging: **Embassy Suites,** 600 North State Street; (312) 943–3800. Because you get two rooms, you may also steal a little privacy. A full breakfast is included, which, if you have a few kids, can add up to a substantial savings. Rates: $109–$179 per night.

Family Day 2

Morning

Breakfast: Embassy Suites. Or if you're staying somewhere else, **Lou Mitchell's** (563 West Jackson Boulevard) is a Chicago classic.

Whether it's waffles, omelets, or French toast, the portions are large, hot, and delicious. (312) 939–3111.

What better way to see Chicago than from 103 stories up? The **Sears Tower Skydeck Observatory** (233 South Wacker Drive) is a perennial favorite, although most residents only see it when they have out-of-towners in tow. The seventy-second elevator ride is as impressive as the view. Your ticket (adults, $3.75; children, $2.00) includes a multimedia show. On a clear day you can see four states, but if weather is overcast, save your money. Open 9 A.M.–midnight. Phone: (312) 875–9447.

After coming back down to earth, head over to **Lincoln Park Zoo** (200 North Stockton; 312–294–4662) and fraternize with the wildlife. While in the park, you can rent roller skates at Cannon Drive near Fullerton Avenue or paddle a boat in the lagoon.

The five-acre Farm in the Zoo is just what it says. Cows, horses, baby chicks, and lots of other farm animals seem quite content with their urban surroundings. So do the exotic birds in the newly renovated McCormick Bird House. They squawk and fly with wreckless abandon in this tropical habitat.

Lunch: For a midday pick-me-up, take a lunch or an ice cream break at the beautifully restored **Cafe Brauer.** Soups, salads, sandwiches, and other quick-and-easy snacks are available in a vintage setting.

Afternoon

The **Chicago Historical Society,** at Clark Street and North Avenue, often gets overlooked in favor of glitzier museums, but it is an exceptionally good choice—as energy levels wane—because it's very accessible. The exhibit on the Great Chicago Fire is sure to be a hit. Admission: adults, $1.50; children, 50 cents. (312) 642–4844. Open Monday–Saturday, 9:30 A.M.–4:30 P.M.; Sunday, noon–5 P.M.

Adult Day 1

Morning

Breakfast: Continental breakfast, included in the tab, is served on board the **Chicago from the Lake Cruise,** sponsored by the Chicago Architecture Foundation. This ninety-minute ride on the Chicago River highlights some of the glittering jewels of the city's skyline. From June to September 30, cruises depart at 10 A.M. and noon, Wednesday–Sunday; 10 A.M., noon, and 6 P.M. on Monday and Tuesday. Admission: $15. Phone: (312) 527–1977.

If you love architecture, but are a confirmed landlubber, sign up for a **walking tour of the Loop.** Have breakfast at Lou Mitchell's (see above) before the two-hour tour. Loop tours depart daily from the Archicenter, 330 South Dearborn Avenue, at 10 A.M. and 1 P.M. (Sunday at 1 P.M. only) during the summer. (Check for hours during the rest of the year.) The Archicenter also has a tempting design shop and gallery, so leave yourself some browsing time when you return. The tour costs $7.00. For recorded schedule information on all tours, phone (312) 782–1776.

Lunch: **The Berghoff,** 17 West Adams. How can you peruse Loop institutions and not stop at The Berghoff? The modestly priced Chicago cuisine has been around since 1898 and continues to be one of the city's best values, even if the service gets sloppy at times. The weiner schnitzel, creamed spinach, and hearty rye bread, all washed down with The Berghoff's own private label beer (or root beer), is the perfect meal. And do leave room for the strudel. (312) 427–3170.

Afternoon

Walk off lunch by heading north toward **River North,** the heart of Chicago's art district. If you walk 4 blocks north on either Clark or Adams, you'll pass the still-controversial **State of Illinois Center** at 100 West Randolph. This ultramodern glass-and-steel structure by Helmut Jahn is either a masterpiece or a travesty, depending on who you talk to. Pop inside to visit the **State of Illinois Artisan Center,** which features quilts, carvings, textiles, and just about anything else made by the state's best artists.

At River North (Superior Street between Orleans and Franklin), you'll find dozens of galleries showcasing painting, sculpture, and the decorative arts. Some standouts are: **Chiarascuro** and **Gallery Vienna** (both at 750 North Orleans Street), **Objects** (230 West Huron), **Hammer** (200 West Superior Street), and **Mongerson Wunderlich** (704 North Wells Street) for anything Southwest. As you would expect, River North is the place to shop for that one-of-a-kind item or funky jewelry that you could never pick up at the mall. The people-watching is pretty good, too.

Dinner: **Gordon,** 500 North Clark Street. This eclectic restaurant draws a stylish crowd, which is what you'd expect in the artsy part of town. The restaurant has launched the reputations of some of the city's best chefs. Through it all, the kitchen is amazingly consistent and some favorites (the artichoke fritters, for example) endure. The pretheater menu (three courses, $20) is served until 6:30 P.M. and is an excellent value. Phone: (312) 467–9780.

While you can dance at Gordon (after 9 P.M., weekends), the city offers so many late-night choices that you'll want to sample a few other spots. The dance floor is rarely empty at **Yvette Wintergarden,** 311 South Wacker. In fact, diners get up and take a few spins between the soup and the salad—just like they did in the forties. (312) 408–1242. For the quintessential piano bar, the **Gold Star Sardine Bar,** 680 North Lake Shore Drive, hits just the right note. It's clubby and cozy, and you never know when a big name will drop by to do a few sets. (312) 664–4215. Of course, at **The Pump Room,** 1301 North State, it doesn't matter who is playing. This place is so legendary that it is the show. Besides, you can spend an evening just perusing a half century of celebrity photos that line the wall, such as eleven-year-old Liza Minelli, wearing lipstick for the first time, lunching with her Mom. (312) 266–0360.

Lodging: **Four Seasons Hotel,** 900 North Michigan Avenue. While Chicago has many world-class hotels, the Four Seasons is the only one with a five-star, five-diamond ranking from the Mobil Travel Guide and AAA respectively. The furnishings are beautiful and the service is flawless. The health club is one of the most luxe in the city. And tucked into Chicago's most upscale mall, the elevator to Bloomingdale's is quite a ride. (Surprisingly, Four Seasons caters to a family clientele, too, albeit a wealthy one. There are plenty of kids' videos for the VCR in your room, and Fruit Loops are available for breakfast in bed.) Rates: $165 per night. (312) 280–8800.

Adult Day 2

Morning

Breakfast: Have room service bring you up a tray stocked with flaky croissants and beautiful berries.

You can't be on North Michigan Avenue and not shop. It doesn't get any better than this. Marshall Field's, Bloomingdale's, Henri Bendel, Lord and Taylor, Neiman Marcus, and Saks Fifth Avenue are all no more than a couple blocks from your hotel. (Water Tower is the oldest and best known of the Michigan Avenue Malls.) Also, right out your door is Oak Street (between Michigan Avenue and State Street), where Gianni Versace, Sonia Rykiel, and Giorgio Armani are just a few of the names that put the "chic" in Chicago.

Lunch: **Bistro 110,** 110 Pearson. Pass up the franchise offerings at Water Tower and cross the street to this comfortable bistro. The menu is creative, and you can't go wrong with a crusty baguette (which comes with a head of roasted garlic for spreading) and a robust French onion soup. You also won't ever go wrong ordering any of the roasted items from the wood-burning oven. Call (312) 266–3110.

Afternoon

There's not enough time to take on a mega-museum, so scale back with something magnificent, but manageable. The **Terra Museum of American Art,** 666 North Michigan Avenue, fills the bill quite nicely. Works by Sargent, Chase, and Wyeth are exhibited in a soothing, dove-gray interior. (312) 664–3939. Open Wednesday–Saturday, 10 A.M.–5 P.M.; Tuesday, noon–8 P.M. Adults, $4.00; children, $2.50.

End the afternoon by doing something really special: have a full British tea ($12.50). All the finest hotels serve one, but you'll find the scones at the **Mayfair Regent Hotel,** 181 East Lake Shore Drive, the most delectable. Finger sandwiches, cakes, and pastries are also a part of the ritual. (312) 787–8500.

There's More

It is very difficult to sum up Chicago's cultural institutions without giving someone short shrift. Also, there are numerous worthwhile destinations in the suburbs as well. Those apologies aside, here are four that you don't want to miss:

Adler Planetarium, 1300 South Lake Shore Drive; (312) 322–0304. If it's been a while since you've been to the sky shows, you'll find many improvements, thanks to a major addition completed in 1991. A 77-foot escalator now carries visitors from the Universe Theater to the Sky Theater, and the fiber optics in between simulates a journey through the galaxies. Show times (June–Labor Day) are hourly between 11 A.M. and 4 P.M. Children under 6 are not admitted to the shows, but they have one of their own each Saturday and Sunday at 10 A.M.

Art Institute of Chicago, Michigan Avenue at Adams Street; (312) 443–3680. You can easily spend a day at this museum, one of the world's finest, but if you're on a tight schedule, head for the French Impressionist paintings. And if the kids aren't impressed with Degas and Renoir, take them to the Thorne Miniature Rooms, which never fail to enchant.

Field Museum of Natural History, Roosevelt Road at Lake Shore Drive; (312) 922–9410. The Field has made giant strides in recent years to transform itself from a dusty, traditional temple to a more hands-on type of place. The dinosaur skeletons and stuffed animals are always winners. On weekends there are family tours highlighting various exhibits.

Museum of Science and Industry, 57th Street and Lake Shore Drive; (312) 684–1414. Is,there a kid who grew up in Chicago who doesn't have fond memories of the coal mine or the German submarine? While those old favorites are still there (the coal mine opened in 1933), MSI is definitely poised for the twenty-first century. The Crown Space Center is a state-of-the-art approach to space exploration, with the Omnimax theater its crown jewel. If you have your heart set on whatever is being shown on the 76-foot domed screen, be sure to get your tickets in advance. A newly refurbished "Curiosity Place" for kids up to age 16 is a parent's dream, not only because it challenges the imagination but also because it offers such a comfortable place for grown-ups to sit and rest.

Special Events

Where to start? There are more than forty ethnic festivals alone. Here's a selective look at some of the city's major events:

June. Gospel Fest. World's largest free gospel festival. Grant Park Petrillo Music Shell, Columbus Drive and Jackson Boulevard.

June. Blues Festival. National names and local favorites belt out the blues. Grant Park Petrillo Music Shell.

June–August. Grant Park concerts. Bring a blanket and listen to classical, pop, big band, and opera under the stars.

Late June–July 4. Taste of Chicago. Strap on the feed bag. Some seventy restaurants participate, and there's big-name entertainment, to boot. Grant Park.

July. Chicago Air and Water Show. Two days of daredevils in the air and in the water.

August. Gold Coast Art Fair. The granddaddy of art fairs is spread out between Dearborn and Franklin streets, along Huron and Ohio streets.

Other Recommended Restaurants and Lodgings

Summing up Chicago's restaurant scene is next to impossible. Here are six restaurants that should fit almost any occasion.

Best choice when you've won the lottery:

Ambria, 2300 North Lincoln Park West; (312) 472–5959. Chef Gambino Satelino sets the standard of what a luxury restaurant should be. It's all like a dream, from the scallop appetizer with wild-mushroom stuffed cannoli to the airy souffles.

Best choice when you want it to look as though you've been promoted:

Un Grand Cafe, 2300 North Lincoln Park West; (312) 348–8886. This bustling bistro is located across the lobby from Ambria. While it's easily half the price, you'll find the same unstinting quality. The onion soup is the best in town, and the simple dishes such as grilled chicken with crisp, thin fries are always standouts.

Best place for seafood:

Shaw's Crab House, 21 East Hubbard Street; (312) 527–2722. We're always seduced by the seafood house atmosphere here, reminiscent of Joe's Stone Crabs of Miami. At lunch, the abundant bread basket and a bowl of clam chowder can make a most satisfying meal. The accompanying Blue Crab Lounge is the place to head for oysters and other raw-bar items.

Best place to eat when you're visiting the Museum of Science and Industry:

Great museum, horrible food. Turn up your nose at the concessions and head directly across the street to Piccolo Mondo, 1642 East 56th Street; (312) 643–1106. In a corner of the Windemere, a vintage Hyde Park apartment building, is a casual spot that features robust Italian cooking. Pastas, eggplant parmigana, fresh gelati, and a frothy cup of cappucino will make you feel smug.

Best place to eat when you're visiting Shedd Aquarium, Field Museum, or Adler Planetarium:

No other city in the country can boast so many museums on the same block, but while it's a cultural mother lode, it's a culinary wasteland. No matter. You're just minutes from Chinatown, where Emperor's Choice, 2238 South Wentworth (312–225–8800), does an equally fine job with nouvelle-style dishes as with Cantonese classics.

Best inexpensive place for a true Chicago dining experience:

Deep-dish pizza was born in Chicago, but now that you can get it at the Pizza Hut in Aberdeen, South Dakota, it hardly qualifies as distinctive. The Chicago hot dog is a better culinary calling card. Gold Coast Dogs, 418 North State (312–527–1222), offers an outstanding dog, loaded up with fresh toppings. The shakes make a perfect accompaniment. Two other city locations include 2100 North Clark and 325 South Franklin.

Choice lodgings in Chicago include these four:

Ritz-Carlton, Water Tower Place; (312) 266–1000. Everything a lavish hotel should be. The twelfth-floor lobby—complete with fountain—has a real presence. The rooms are beautifully furnished in quiet, understated tones. A number of rooms feature two bathrooms. The restaurant is top-notch, too. Weekend rates start at $155 and can go up to $800.

Mayfair Regent Chicago, 181 East Lake Shore Drive; (312) 787–8500. For decades the Mayfair Regent has built its reputation on Old World elegance. The staff treats you like an honored guest; nothing is too much trouble. Insider's tip: If you're traveling with kids under 16, they'll throw in an adjoining room (if available) for free.

The Drake, Michigan at Lake Shore Drive; (312) 787–2200. For decades, the premier address in Chicago. Ask for a room that faces north to get an optimum view of "the Drive" (as the natives say) and Lake Michigan. The entire place oozes old money. Despite the formality, The Drake hosts a number of events geared for children such as a puppet show in the lobby during the holidays.

Chicago Hilton and Towers, 720 South Michigan Avenue; (312) 922–4400. Massive, ornate, enormous, the Hilton is. This magnificent property is the best place to stay near Grant Park. The lobby (part of a top-to-bottom renovation in 1989) is lovely. Its decor of cool mauves, grays, and marble is echoed in many of the rooms. The pool/health club is arguably the best in the city. Weekend rates start at $85.

For More Information

Chicago Tourism Council, 806 North Michigan Avenue, Chicago, IL 60611. (312) 280–5740.

Wisconsin Escapes

WISCONSIN

Milwaukee

Plankington Arcade at the Grand Avenue Mall

Brewing Up Old World Charm

_____ 2 NIGHTS _____

Architecture • Brewery • Museums • Zoo • Historical sites •
Theater/Opera/Ballet • Professional sports • Ethnic dining •
Hiking/Fishing • Cross-country skiing • Shopping • Swimming

Totally unpretentious and teeming with tradition, Milwaukee, Wisconsin's largest city, is just an hour's drive north of Chicago on Lake Michigan's shore. This is a metropolis with a small-town flair, a place where Old World European influences are striking, but blend harmoniously with the modern day. Peaked roofs, rising church spires, copper gables, and conspicuous clock towers are the protruding landmarks of Milwaukee's beautifully preserved nineteenth- and early twentieth-century Germanic heritage. While Milwaukee's breweries are what the city is best known for, it has plenty of other enticing features that give credence to its Indian-inspired name, "a gathering place by the waters." For starters, it has an elaborate spread of 137 parks, 60 miles of lakefront, ethnic restaurants, cultural attractions, big league sports teams, and one of the nation's finest zoos.

The city's compactness is still another virtue. Milwaukee's central business district is only a mile long and a few blocks wide, so sightseeing is easy on foot. But have no fear, even if you do resort to driving, congestion, as it's known to Chicagoans, is a rare occurrence. Also note that the Milwaukee River divides the downtown area into east and west sections and the city's main east-west thoroughfare is Wisconsin Avenue.

Lastly, Milwaukee is a friendly place. Basically, it's just a cluster of folksy neighborhoods—perfect for a comfortable, easygoing weekend away.

Day 1

Evening

Getting to Milwaukee is easy. Just head north on I-94 (Edens Expressway), following the signs to Milwaukee. As you approach the city, you'll see the shimmering (24-Karat gold leaf) twin domes of St. Stanislaus, the mother church of all Polish-American urban parishes. Soon you'll be on I-43 and in the heart of the city.

Dinner: Friday nights and fish fries go hand in hand in Milwaukee. One of the local favorites is **Turners Bar & Restaurant** (1034 North Fourth Street; 414-273-5590). Not very fancy and located in a 135-year-old gymnastics club, this family-style, all-you-can-eat bargain was friendly, fun, and just plain good. Indulge in deep-fried perch and cod, cole slaw, hearty German potato salad, and fries.

After dinner, head for **Zur Krone** (839 South Second Street; 414-647-1910), a typical German-style Milwaukee neighborhood bar, which stocks more than 200 brands of beer. Sipping from boot-shaped steins is a Zur Krone tradition. (By the way, you'll know you're in close proximity to Zur Krone when you see the famous **Allen Bradley four-faced clock,** which is located on the Bradley factory tower at 1201 South Second Street. It's the world's largest, and when you see its enormous faces illuminated at night, you'll swear you've just seen a close-up view of a full moon.) If you'd like to hear a little jazz before turning in, treat yourself to some smooth and soothing piano sounds at the **Bombay Bicycle Club** at the Marc-Plaza Hotel (509 West Wisconsin Avenue; 414–271–7250). Hours for jazz are from 9 P.M. to 1 A.M.

Lodging: Soak up heady amounts of luxury at the Pfister Hotel (424 East Wisconsin Avenue; 414–273–8222). Born in the final gilded decade of the nineteenth century, the Pfister has been restored to its former splendor. Its lavish lobby, ballroom, and tasteful 307 rooms earned it an international reputation. Two-room suites start at $99 a night and include every amenity—right down to a TV in the marble bathroom. Be sure to book a room in the older part of the hotel, which was redone about two years ago. The result is a perfect marriage of vintage architecture and nineties convenience.

Day 2

Morning

Breakfast: **The Greenery** is the Pfister Hotel's coffee shop and is located on the lobby level. The French toast is nice and plump with powdered sugar dusted on top ($3.85), and the sausage is something you can really sink your teeth into ($3.25). The pancakes (both buttermilk and blueberry) are also rather tempting.

Begin your day by venturing about on foot. A variety of self-guided neighborhood walking tours are available at the **Greater Milwaukee Convention and Visitors Bureau** (510 West Kilbourn Avenue; 800–231–0903), but you may decide to be innovative and explore a few of the sites in your own fashion.

Try heading north on Jefferson Street, past **George Watts & Son,** an exceptional china shop with beautiful displays of china, crystal, silver, and oh-so-lovely objects of art. A little farther up the street is Cathedral Square and the **Skylight Opera Theatre** (813 North Jefferson Street), where the city's musical and operetta productions are performed. Call (414) 271–8815 (box office) or (414) 271–9580 (business office). Performances run from September through May.

Turning toward the river on Kilbourn Avenue, saunter by **Old Saint Mary's Church,** Milwaukee's oldest Catholic church (built in 1846). Within seconds another head turner, **City Hall,** will appear. This copper-domed Flemish Renaissance gem was built in 1895. Free tours can be arranged on weekdays between 8:00 A.M. and 4:45 P.M. when City Hall's doors are open (200 East Wells; 414–278–2221). Once you gain access, even if you forgo the tour, note the ornately carved woodwork and stenciled ceilings in the Common Council chamber and anteroom.

Continue toward the Milwaukee River until you reach the **Performing Arts Center** at 929 North Water Street. Made from brilliant Italian travertine marble, this is the home of the Milwaukee Symphony Orchestra, the Milwaukee Ballet, the Florentine Opera, and the First Stage Theater group. Nearby stands the new red brick and slate-peaked **Milwaukee Center,** which encompasses the Milwaukee Repertory Theatre, the Wyndham Hotel, and the magnificently restored Pabst Theater (144 East Wells Street; 414–278–3665). Free tours are given of this late nineteenth-century, Victorian-style theater on Saturdays at 11:30 A.M. (Allow forty-five minutes.)

Next, head over the river and around Pere Marquette Park before turning south down the cobbled streets of Old World Third Street. In the heart of this old German business district lie some historic 1880s architecture and a few quality delectables. One landmark, **Usinger's Famous Sausage,** is a great place to pick up some knockwurst, bratwurst, and liver sausage munchies for the trip home (1030 North Third Street; 414–276–9100). A few doors down is the **Wisconsin Cheese Mart** (215 West Highland Avenue; 414–272–3544). Here you'll find an incredible selection of cheeses, some even shaped like the state of Wisconsin. The shop has lots of samples, so indulge. Also if you're a collectible type, check out the second floor gift shop at **Mader's** (1037 North Old World Third Street; 414–271–3377), one of Milwaukee's famous German cuisine hot spots. Don't worry if you haven't got time to dine, you can still peruse the shop.

The next stop is the elegant, 4-block-long **Grand Avenue Mall** (275 West Wisconsin Avenue). From its facade, the Mall (a composite of five artfully preserved, turn-of-the-century buildings) bears no resemblance to a newfangled shopping center. Yet sure enough, once you get inside you'll find Marshall Fields, the Boston Store, and loads of other modern shops. The skylights, skywalks, and an exquisite circular stairway leading down to the lower level in the Plankington Arcade (near Marshall Fields) make this an experience you won't soon forget.

At this point you may want to return to pick up your car and take off for the **Marquette University** campus, straight west on Wisconsin Avenue. In the middle of the university is a real treasure—the **St. Joan of Arc Chapel** (14th Street and Wisconsin Avenue). Originally, this medieval French chapel was constructed in the fifteenth century near Lyon, France, where it stood for more than 500 years. Falling into disrepair after the French Revolution, the chapel was eventually transported to a Long Island estate in 1927, where American architect John Russell Pope reconstructed it stone by stone. In the mid-1960s, the chapel was moved and reassembled again at its present site. Near the altar you'll find the stone St. Joan supposedly kissed just before she was executed. Some say it's cooler to the touch than those surrounding it, but you'll have to decide for yourself.

Another campus jewel is the **Patrick and Beatrice Haggerty Museum of Art** (13th and Clybourn streets on the east side of the university's square). Among the permanent exhibits in this intimate museum are Renaissance, Baroque, and modern paintings, as well as sculpture, prints, photography, and examples of decorative art. Call (414) 288–1669. Open Monday–Saturday, 10:00 A.M.–4:30 P.M.; Thursday, 10 A.M.–8 P.M.; Sunday, noon–5 P.M. Free.

Lunch: A west side favorite is **Saz's,** located in the Miller Valley, just minutes away from the Brewery (5539 West State Street; 414–453–2410). The house specialties are barbecued ribs and mozzarella marinara, hunks of mozzarella cheese wrapped as egg rolls.

Afternoon

No traditional tourist can visit Milwaukee without including a trip to a brewery. Tour options are available at several breweries, including the "beer city's" best: **Miller Brewing Company** (4251 West State Street; 414–931–BEER). The free tour (Monday–Saturday, 10:00 A.M. to 3:30 P.M.) starts off with a video presentation on how the operation got started plus some tidbits about the beer-making process. Then it's off to see Miller's mammoth shipping center (the size of five football fields) and the huge copper-topped vats in the brewhouse. The finale, which most consider to be the best part, is a free sampling in the Miller Inn.

To give some equal time to a competitor, journey over to the **Pabst Mansion** (2000 West Wisconsin Avenue; 414–931–0808). This lavish, thirty-seven-room Flemish Renaissance home was built in 1893 for the beer baron himself, Captain Frederick Pabst. Carved wood, stained glass, ornamental ironwork, and terra-cotta are among the handsome accents in this magnificent Victorian landmark. Allow about an hour. Open Monday–Saturday, 10:00 A.M.–3:30 P.M. Sunday, noon–3:30 P.M. Admission: adults, $5.00; children ages 6–17, $2.50.

Mitchell Park Conservatory, affectionately dubbed "the Domes," makes a great afternoon adventure. There's nothing quite like it anywhere, particularly not in Chicago, so make sure you put it on your weekend to-do list. The conservatory is housed in three gigantic domes, each 140 feet wide by 85 feet tall and each with a different climate. The first is a floral garden (the "show dome," where seven themed shows are displayed annually), the second is an arid dome (filled with cacti and other desert plants), and the third is tropical. The conservatory is at 524 South Layton Boulevard. Call (414) 649–9800. Open daily, 9 A.M.–5 P.M. Admission: adults, $2.50; children ages 6–17, $1.00.

Dinner: **Karl Ratzsch's Old World Restaurant** (320 East Mason Street; 414–276–2720) is just a short walk from the Pfister Hotel. This is a Milwaukee classic with a sumptuous menu, impeccable service, and plush Germanic decor (antiques, steins, and hand-painted murals abound). Sauerbraten (marinated roast sirloin with spicy, sweet-sour gravy, at $17.95) and Swabian Schnitzel (veal prepared with sour cream, red wine, and onion, at $20.25) are just two of a long list of house specialties. Dinners are complete (coffee and dessert are extra), and there's even a lighter menu for the after-theater crowd. A wonderful string trio plays nightly, and kids get a trip to the famous treasure chest for candy after they finish their meal. Even though the prices are on the high side, dress is casual.

To make your night complete, return to the Pabst Theater (144 East Wells Street; 414–278–3663) to enjoy a performance of dance or drama or a musical. The Pabst is listed on the National Register of Historic Places. It's a small theater with 1,400 seats and two balconies, so virtually every seat in the house is good. Tickets average around $30 for the prime seats.

Lodging: The Pfister Hotel.

Day 3

Morning

Breakfast: The very popular **Coffee Trader,** 2625 North Downer Avenue; (414) 332–9690. The muffins (especially the blueberry) are divine. Hopple popple (scrambled eggs with kosher salami or ham, diced potatoes, and vegetables) is another foolproof favorite. Ask to be seated by the window (that's where the "cool" crowd sits).

Head west again for the **Milwaukee Public Museum** (800 West Wells Street; 414–278–2702). This is the fourth-largest natural history museum in the country. It even has its own tropical rain forest soaring 19 feet upwards. The museum is also noted for its streets of Old Milwaukee exhibit and a series of outstanding dioramas. Plan to spend at least an hour and a half here. Open 9 A.M. to 5 P.M. daily (11 A.M. to 4 P.M. on holidays). Admission: adults, $4.00; children ages 4–17, $2.00. The museum also has family rates.

Next on the agenda is a trip to the **Milwaukee Art Museum** (750 North Lincoln Memorial Drive; 414–271–9508), overlooking Lake Michigan in the War Memorial Center designed by Eero Saarinen. Exhibits, which include more than 10,000 works of art, range from sculpture and paintings to decorative art and photography. The museum's permanent collection of nineteenth- and twentieth-century European and American art is strong. Don't miss the collection of Haitian art and the Mettlach steins either. Open Tuesday–Saturday, 10 A.M.–5 P.M.; Thursday, noon–9 P.M.; Sunday, noon–5 P.M. Admission: adults, $4.00; seniors and students, $2.00; under age 12 is free. *Lunch:* **Boulevard Inn,** 925 East Wells; (414) 765–1166. Not far from the Art Musuem in the Cudahy Towers and overlooking the lake is the new home of the Boulevard Inn, formerly where Fleur de Lis was located. Continental in flavor (fresh seafood, meat, and poultry), the Boulevard Inn is a great value for its high quality at moderate to expensive prices. A family-owned establishment, this restaurant has years of history. Lunch menu ranges from $6.50 to $8.50.

Afternoon

Round out your day at the spectacular **Milwaukee Zoo** (10001 West Blue Mound Road; 414–771–3040). Ranked among the world's finest, this zoo is really big, with more than 3,000 animals on display in five continental groupings. One of the nicest features of the zoo is its emphasis on natural settings. For example, in the center of the park is a series of predator/prey exhibits where species share nearby resources just as they would in the wild. And the newly remodeled aviary has a generous free flight area where the birds have no barriers from the public. Plan to allot three hours at the very least. Open Monday–Saturday, 9 A.M.–5 P.M.; Sunday, 9 A.M.–6 P.M. Admission is $6.00 for adults, $5.00 for seniors, and $4.00 for children ages 3–12. Prices deflate slightly November through March. Parking is $4.00.

Before heading off for the highway, savor one last Milwaukee treat—frozen custard from **Kopp's.** The burgers are great here, too. Don't look for a place to sit down; this is one of those establishments designed for on-the-go types. The nearest Kopp's location is at 76th and Layton; take Highway 894/45 south to 76th Street and follow to Layton Street.

Note: Return home by picking up Highway 894 east (½ block from Kopp's) and turning south onto I–94.

There's More

Milwaukee County Historical Center, 910 North Old World Third Street; (414) 273–8288. An architectural landmark with exhibits on the city's past and a genealogical research library. Open Monday–Saturday, 9 A.M.–5 P.M.; Sunday, 1–5 P.M. Free.

Discovery World, 818 West Wisconsin Avenue; (414) 765–9966. A hands-on science, economics, and technology museum featuring more than 100 "touch and do" exhibits. Children will love it! Located inside the Public Library. Open Monday–Saturday, 9 A.M.–5 P.M.; Sunday, 11 A.M.–5 P.M. Admission: adults, $3.00; children ages 6–17, $1.50.

Charles Allis Art Museum, 1801 North Prospect Avenue; (414) 278–8295. This elegant Tudor mansion, formerly the home of Charles Allis (the first president of Allis-Chalmers Company), contains a number of collections including the home's original antique furniture, Oriental art objects, French and American nineteenth-century paintings, and Renaissance bronzes. Open Wednesday–Sunday, 1–5 P.M.; Wednesday nights, 7–9 P.M. Admission is $1.00 for adults.

Alfred L. Boerner Botanical Gardens, 5879 South 92nd Street in Whitnall Park; (414) 425–1130. The gardens (both formal and informal) are a lovely respite during the warmer months. The rose garden alone has more than 3,000 plants of 300 varieties. Open mid-April–October, 8 A.M.–sunset. Free.

Whitnall Park (5879 South 92nd Street) is one of the nation's largest municipal parks (660 acres). It includes an eighteen-hole golf course, picnic areas, an environmental education center (the Wehr Nature Center), and botanical gardens. It's also a great spot for cross-country skiing during the winter.

Annunciation Greek Orthodox Church, 9400 West Congress Street, Wauwatosa; (414) 461–9400. The last major building from architect Frank Lloyd Wright's drawing board, this bright blue–domed masterpiece is a magnificent example of Byzantine architecture. Take I–94 west to 76th Street and go north. Tours by appointment Monday–Friday. Admission $1.00.

Olson Planetarium, 1900 East Kenwood Boulevard on the University of Wisconsin campus; (414) 963–4691. Star show and informative lectures by members of the University of Wisconsin–Milwaukee Planetarium staff. A good time for astronomy buffs. Show times: Friday nights (during the school year) at 7:00 P.M. and 8:15 P.M.

Spectator sports. Watch the Milwaukee Brewers play baseball at the Milwaukee County Stadium (201 South 46th Street; 414–933–1818) and the Milwaukee Bucks and the Marquette University Warriors play basketball at the Bradley Center (1001 North Fourth Street; 414–227–0500).

Fishing. Lake Michigan can reward anglers with prize catches of salmon and trout (as big as thirty pounds). Full- and half-day charters are offered by numerous companies including A-1 Sport Charters (414–781–1704) and Banana Split III Lake Michigan Fishing Charters (414–354–3559).

Cross-country skiing. Several local parks provide rentals and lessons, including Brown Deer Park (7835 North Green Bay Avenue), Currie Park (3535 North Mayfair Road), Dretzka Park (12020 West Bradley Road), the Milwaukee County Zoo (10001 West Blue Mound

Road), and Whitnall Park (5879 South 92nd Street). **Old World Wisconsin,** 1 mile south of Milwaukee on Highway 67 in Eagle; (414) 594–2116. This 576-acre outdoor museum consists of more than fifty preserved and furnished buildings erected by nineteenth-century immigrants. Costumed interpreters explain the story of immigration to Wisconsin and each ethnic group's role. A 2½-mile tour is needed to see the entire museum. Bring your most comfortable walking shoes. Allow a minimum of five hours. Open daily, 10 A.M.–5 P.M. in July and August. Hours in May and June and September and October: Monday–Friday, 10 A.M.–4 P.M.; Saturday and Sunday, 10 A.M.–5 P.M. Admission: adults, $6.00; seniors, $4.80; children ages 5–17, $2.50. Family rates available.

Special Events

June. Polish Fest. Continuous polka music, dancing, international polka contest, beauty pageant, ethnic foods, and historical and cultural demonstrations. Held on the lakefront at the Summerfest grounds.

June. Greater Milwaukee Air & Water Show. Power boat racing, air show performances, boat shows, military fly-overs, and static displays. Held on the lakefront.

June–July. Summerfest. The world's largest outdoor music festival with comedy, food, and sports activities. It includes eleven stages and booths from more than thirty area restaurants. Held on the lakefront.

July. Great Circus Parade. Bands, costumed units, animals, and a unique collection of horse-drawn wagons from the Circus World Museum (at Kilbourn and Wisconsin avenues, the heart of the downtown area).

July. Festa Italiana. Four-day Italian festival with eight stages of entertainment, plenty of Italian delicacies, cultural exhibits, fireworks, and a traditional mass and procession. Held at the Henry W. Maier Festival Park, 200 North Harbor Drive.

July. German Fest. Nonstop German music and entertainment, folk dancing, cultural presentations, souvenirs, fireworks, food, and beverages. Held at the Summerfest grounds.

August. Wisconsin State Fair. Entertainment on 20 stages, blue-ribbon livestock, 500 exhibits, 200 food concessions, 150 carnival rides and games. Held at the State Fair Park in West Allis, a fifteen-minute drive from downtown.

August. Milwaukee à la Carte. Milwaukee's premiere food fest with more than thirty restaurants serving sample-sized gourmet portions. Held at the Milwaukee County Zoo.

August. Mexican Fiesta. Wisconsin's largest Hispanic festival, with world record jalapeño contest, Midwest lowriders exhibition, national and international entertainment. Held at the lakefront.

September. Oktoberfest. Authentic fall festival featuring brass bands, Bavarian folk dancers, yodelers, music, dancing, German food and beer. Held at Old Heidelberg Park in Glendale, a fifteen-minute drive north of downtown.

Late November. Christmas Parade. Bands, floats, live animals, clowns, radio and TV personalities, and Santa parade on Wisconsin Avenue near Grand Avenue shopping mall to the lakefront.

December. Old World Holiday Market. Month-long holiday celebration reminiscent of Old World villages and their holiday customs. Traditional tree-lighting ceremony and fireworks. Held at the European outdoor market in Red Arrow Park, near the Performing Arts Center.

Other Recommended Restaurants and Lodgings

Milwaukee

Astor Hotel, 924 East Juneau Avenue; (414) 271–4220. One of the loveliest Milwaukee hotels. Designed in the grand tradition, the Astor is well located on a slightly residential, tree-lined street. Accommodations are plush and full of amenities. Rates range from $84 to $114 per night.

Cafe Knickerbocker, 1030 East Juneau Avenue; (414) 272–0011. Without mincing words, the food here is excellent. You'll find a large assortment of wonderful menu items like grilled marlin and grilled duck breast pepper oil shrimp sauté.

Conejito's Place, 539 West Virginia; (414) 278–9106. Not in the nicest neighborhood, but the food (Mexican) is excellent and very cheap. The mood can be a little raucous, but it's all part of the fun. Try the chicken mole and the guacamole and chips. This is a lunch or early dinner choice.

Elsa's on the Park, 833 North Jefferson Street; (414) 765–0615. Fancy hamburgers make this place special. The pork chop sandwiches and buffalo wings also get two thumbs up. Atmosphere is casual.

The English Room, 424 East Wisconsin Avenue, in the Pfister Hotel; (414) 273–8222. Known for its fine continental cuisine, The English Room is considered one of Milwaukee's best restaurants. The atmosphere, which is enhanced by an original nineteenth-century art collection, is very elegant and very formal. Despite the name, the fare is very French.

John Ernst Cafe, 600 East Ogden Avenue; (414) 273–1878. Plainer than Karl Ratzsch's, but still one of the city's finest purveyors of German cuisine. Family-owned and -operated for three generations, the Ernst Cafe is Milwaukee's oldest restaurant. Music nightly.

Ken Elliot's, 158 East Juneau Avenue; (414) 274–7204. Very popular and very hip, Elliot's serves lighter fare that's mostly American. The Santa Fe Sampler (grilled and marinated pork, chicken, and beef with tomatoes, peppers, olives, and mushrooms on a bed of corn) is among the most popular items.

Mader's German Restaurant, 1037 North Old World Third Street; (414) 271–3377. A lot of old-world charm here. Medieval suits of armor and antiques are the decor accents. Considered by many to be Milwaukee's best German restaurant.

Marc Plaza Hotel, 509 West Wisconsin Avenue; (414) 271–7250. Located away from the lake, this is Milwaukee's largest hotel, with 500 rooms. Built more than sixty-five years ago, the Marc Plaza is noted for its comfort and service. Rates range from $110 to $145 per night.

Park East Hotel, 916 East State Street; (414) 276–8800. Almost on the lakefront (across from Juneau Park), the Park East is another choice pick for the traveler with discriminating taste. This hotel is contemporary in feel. Rates range from $55 to $65 per night.

The Safe House, 779 North Front Street; (414) 271–2007. Don't be fooled by the sign out front: INTERNATIONAL EXPORTS LIMITED. Yes, you've arrived at the right place. The Safe House, a spy's hideout, is a favorite Milwaukee nightclub. Secret doors, an ejection seat, a CIA phone booth, and a collection of spy gear are a few clues of what you'll find inside (after you give the password, of course).

Sanford's, 1547 North Jackson Street; (414) 276–9608. Tiny and elegant, Sanford's is very chic and somewhat new. Reservations are a must! Cuisine is French-nouvelle American.

Wyndham Milwaukee Center, 139 East Kilbourn Avenue; (414) 276–8686. If you like theater, you can't get any closer. The Wyndham is part of the Milwaukee Center and the city's new "theater district." Accommodations are luxurious, and you'll find lots of amenities including a health club. Rates range from $133 to $153 per night.

Bayside

Pandl's in Bayside, 8825 North Lake Drive; (414) 352–1430. Another family-owned spot, this elegant supper club is located in a county landmark building. Food specialties include German pancake whitefish, walleye, and roast duck. The homemade soups are tasty, too. Bayside is north of downtown Milwaukee; take I-43 north.

For More Information

Greater Milwaukee Convention and Visitors Bureau, 510 West Kilbourn Avenue, Milwaukee, WI 53203. Call (414) 273–3950 or (800) 231–0903, or call the *Events Fun Line* (a daily updated message tape) at (414) 799–1177.

Metropolitan Milwaukee Association of Commerce, 756 North Milwaukee Street, Milwaukee, WI 53202. (414) 278–4100.

Milwaukee Minority Chamber of Commerce, 2821 North Fourth Street, Milwaukee, WI 53203. (414) 264–4111.

Lake Geneva

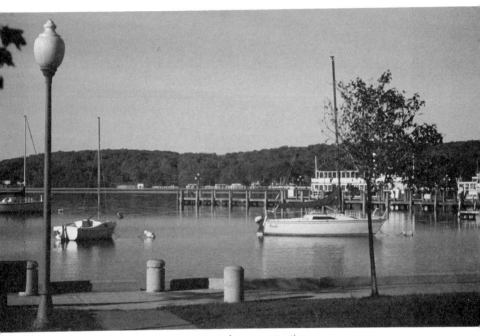

The lovely lake is still this resort town's number-one attraction.

Luxury and the Lake

_____ 2 NIGHTS _____
Antiques · Boating · Fishing · Shopping · Skiing · Golf

If you're the kind of traveler who doesn't like to shave on the week-end, you may perceive Lake Geneva to be too tony for your tastes. But that elitist air is as much part of the area's history as the lake itself. As far back as the 1870s, Chicago's chewing-gum, meat-packing, and retailing barons turned this into a playground of the rich by practicing competitive mansion building.

Today a lot of the formality of Lake Geneva is gone. There are still a few places that require jackets and ties at dinner, but for the most part you'll find an equitable mix of suburban families and stylish young professionals.

Lake Geneva is just one resort community situated on the 26 miles of shoreline that rim this picturesque, spring-fed lake. The two others are Fontana and Williams Bay, but visitors tend to refer to the entire area as "Lake Geneva."

You'll find a wealth of accommodations, from sprawling resorts to rustic cabins and cottages—but that doesn't mean you can count on a vacancy. With the lake being the absolute center of activity, it should come as no surprise that the area is positively packed during summer weekends. If long lines and bumper-to-bumper traffic doesn't sound like your idea of a vacation, try booking a post–Labor Day weekend.

In the fall the lake positively shimmers against reds, oranges, and golds. Even in the dead of winter, Lake Geneva is warm and hospitable, thanks to a concentration of resorts that cater to skiers, snowmobilers, and sailors. That's right: during the last few years, ice sailing has become popular among the die-hards who can't bear to put their boat in dry dock. Sailboats are mounted onto large skates and glide atop the frozen lake at speeds as high as 60 miles per hour. Those brave enough to try it claim it is an invigorating experience; others may find that curling up with a good book near the hotel hearth provides all the activity one needs.

Best of all, Lake Geneva is just 75 miles away—and if traffic cooperates, you can leave the Loop by six and be sipping a glass of chablis by eight.

Day 1

Evening

Bring your weekend bag to work, so you can make a quick getaway Friday evening. Take I–94 north to Highway 50 west, which takes you right into Lake Geneva.

Dinner: The **Grandview Restaurant,** Geneva Inn, 804 South Lake Shore Drive; (414) 248–5680. The chef does a splendid job with fish, and the salmon is as good as anything you'll find in the Pacific Northwest. The service is polished, and the atmosphere is romantic, especially if you snare a table overlooking the lake or sit out on the terrace. Even if you don't want a full-blown meal, at least stop by for a nightcap. Ice cream drinks are the house specialty, and the piano bar adds just the right touch. Prices for entrees are in the $12–$20 range.

Lodging: Go no farther than up the stairs to unwind from a rough week. While the **Geneva Inn,** which opened in 1990, is expensive, it offers the charm of a country inn with the service of a luxury hotel.

The rooms are beautifully furnished in an English country motif and the lake views from your balcony are spectacular. Some rooms have whirlpools, all have VCRs. Rates range from $145 to $275 per night. Phone (414) 248–5680.

Day 2

Morning

Breakfast: Continental breakfast is included at the Geneva Inn.

Do what everyone else does—enjoy the lake. The best way to do that is by being smack in the middle of it. The **Geneva Lake Cruise Line** offers sightseeing tours on restored turn-of-the-century paddle-wheelers, the perfect vessels for viewing the elegant Victorian estates. Tours range from one to three hours and some include lunch or dinner. Some also offer Sunday champagne brunches or feature Dixieland jazz.

Another interesting way to cruise the lake is aboard *Walworth II,* one of the last operating marine mail services in the United States. During the 2½-hour loop around the lake, the mail carrier periodically leaps off the moving boat, dashes to the mailbox, and jumps back into the boat without missing a beat. Besides agility, the carrier needs a sense of history, as well. He or she points out landmarks and other local lore in between leaps. The mailboat operates between May and September 15; other cruises, through the end of October. Prices: adults, $13.95; students age 13–16, $11.20; children age 4–12, $7.25; children under 4 ride free. Board at the Riviera Docks at the foot of Broad Street. Be sure to bring a camera. Phone (414) 248–6206 or (800) 558–5911.

Lunch: Right near the Riviera Docks is **Popeye's Gallery** (811 Wrigley Drive; (414) 248–4361. Its menu is a rather eclectic mix of sandwiches, salads, and Greek and Mexican fare. You can also dine outdoors—the best way to enjoy this casual restaurant's prime location.

Afternoon

Since you're so close, you can always return to the beach. The **Lake Geneva Municipal Beach** is right across the street. (**Fontana and Williams Bay Municipal Beaches** also rate a recommendation and are the only two beaches that have lifeguards. Fontana is on the west side of the lake, and Williams Bay is on the north.) You can rent just about anything from a yacht to a jetski. If hipness is important, try boogie boarding, which is similar to waterskiing, except you're strapped to a small surfboard.

More serious, perhaps, but no less stimulating is a trip to **Yerkes**

Observatory (373 West Geneva Street, Williams Bay, 5 miles west of Lake Geneva). This research outpost of the University of Chicago was built in 1897 and houses the world's largest refracting telescope. It is open only on Saturdays. From June through September, tours are offered at 1:30 P.M., 2:15 P.M., and 3:00 P.M.; from October through May, tours depart at 10 A.M. and 11 A.M. For more information phone (414) 245–5555. Free.

If the only science you're interested in is the science of economics, then head over to the main shopping streets of Main and Broad. You'll find the usual souvenir and T-shirt emporiums, but there are some finds as well. An off-price mini-mall, called **Fancy Fare,** contains several quality stores including a JH Collectible outlet that offers bona fide bargains.

Bibliophiles should check out the **Breadloaf Book Shop** (253 Broad Street; 414–248–9446), and **Allison Wonderland** has a terrific toy selection (720 Main Street; 414–248–6500). If you have time to see only one gallery, make it **The O Gallery** (623 Main Street; 414–248–3612), which represents more than 100 artists. Those who believe you can never have too much jewelry should check out **Starfire** (159 Broad Street; 414–248–3878).

Grazers will note that the entire area is a landmine of bakeries, ice cream parlors, and candy stores. For chocolate, try **Kilwin's** at the corner of Main and Broad (414–248–4400), and for ice cream, try **Annie's** at 712 Main Street (414–248–1933). In the summer, locals swear by the peppermint, but in the winter, the house specialty seems to be chili.

You will also find numerous antique stores. Try the Lake Geneva Antique Mall (829 William Street; 414–248–6345). And on the other side of the lake in Walworth is the Square Antique Mall, located just west of the Village Square, which displays wares from fifty dealers (414–275–9858).

Dinner: **The Red Geranium,** Highway 50 east; (414) 248–3637. This restaurant is mentioned repeatedly as one of the area's best and most consistent. Seafood (especially fresh tuna, salmon, and lobster) and steaks dominate here. Everything is cooked on an open hearth, and it's fun to watch the chefs at work. Entrees, which come with soup, salad, potato, and vegetable, average about $16. Dress is casual and there is also a children's menu.

After dinner watch the "world's fastest greyhounds" compete at the **Geneva Lakes Kennel Club,** one of four dog tracks that opened in 1990 in Wisconsin. Races, which are held from early June to late November, are fun even if you stay away from the win, place, or show windows. Weekend races start at 1:00 P.M. and 7:30 P.M., and it will cost you just a buck to get in and another buck to park. If you're unsure that this is an appropriate place to take children, rest assured that in terms of atmosphere these tracks more closely resemble a suburban shopping mall than anything Damon Runyon would have thought up. The tracks are located at the intersection of I–43 and Highway 50, in Delavan. Call (414) 728–8000.

Lodging: Geneva Inn.

Day 3

Morning

Breakfast: Two choices, depending on how you like your Sunday mornings. Try **Millie's Restaurants and Shopping Village** (South Shore Drive and County Highway 0, south of Delavan) for Swedish pancakes, caramel rolls, and other traditional breakfast favorites. Phone (414) 728–2434.

If it isn't Sunday for you without a gut-busting brunch and a Bloody Mary, however, try the **Interlaken Resort** on Highway 50 (414–248–9121) with its endless smorgasbord of hot entrees.

If you've opted for Delavan and you have kids, check out the **Clown Hall of Fame** at 212 East Walworth Avenue (414–728–9075). You can drop in on a class on juggling, makeup, or costuming. There's lots of circus memorabilia, but if it's a show you're after, note that performances only take place on Saturday. Museum hours are Monday–Saturday, 9 A.M.–5 P.M. in the summer; 10 A.M.–4 P.M. in the winter. Admission: adults, $3.50; children, $2.50; kids under 3, free.

If you're staying in Lake Geneva and have had enough of sun and surf, take a drive through the country. You'll soon discover that Walworth County is horse country, with more than a dozen stables and ranches in the area. You'll also find that horse-related activities take place the year round, with fall's hayride becoming winter's sleigh ride. A few that cater to the littlest cowboys include **Geneva Lakes** (414–245–0650) and **Wolline Stables** (414–723–4484).

Lunch: Trying to squeeze in one more meal? Try **Kirsch's** at the French Country Inn (Highway 4, just off Highway 50 west; 414–245–5220). Kirsch's is a charming spot to have a lovely lunch while looking out over Lake Como. Try a basket of homemade corn muffins with the warm scallop salad—a first-rate combination of greens, vinaigrette, and large sea scallops. Consider the reasonable prices (most entrees are under $10) a bonus.

Afternoon

Start to wend your way back to Chicago, going south on Highway 12. Just over the Illinois/Wisconsin border is the tiny town of **Rich-**

mond, which has more than two dozen antique shops—in fact, as far as anyone can tell, Richmond is nothing but antique shops. Depending on your schedule you can spend an hour or a day here.

Dinner: If you want to eat dinner before you get home, try **Elder's Mill** (5604 Mill Street, Richmond; 815–678–2841). Harold Elder, former chef at Un Grand Cafe and the Pump Room in Chicago, brings casual, bistro dining to the country. Open Tuesday–Sunday at 5 P.M.

There's More

Ballooning. Sunbird Balloons Inc. offers a view of the entire area that would be hard to duplicate with more traditional transportation. You also travel in style; the balloon comes stocked with champagne, a throwback to the days when the balloonists offered a peace offering to farmers for landing on their property. $150 for an hour-long ride. Phone (414) 251–0909.

Boating. There are numerous marinas and boat rentals. Here are just a few: Marina Bay Boat Rentals, Lake Geneva (414–248–4477); Gage Marine, Lake Geneva (800–558–5911); Gordy's Lakefront Marine, Fontana (414–275–2163); Carlson's Boat Livery, Williams Bay (414–245–5066); Jerry's, Fontana (414–275–5222).

Fishing. Lake Geneva produces primarily lake trout. Any of the above marinas will also rent fishing boats or help arrange fishing charters.

Golf. Since Lake Geneva has always been a playground for the rich, good golf courses abound. Americana Lake Geneva Resort (414–248–8811) is the largest, with thirty-six holes, followed by Alpine Valley Resort in nearby East Troy, with twenty-seven holes. Other highly recommended courses include Abbey Springs Country Club in Fontana (414–275–6111) and George Williams College in Williams Bay (414–248–8811).

Hiking. The 26-mile path around the lake is a hiker's dream for all seasons. The fact that you are never more than three feet from the water accounts for its popularity. However, doing the whole circuit generally consumes nine or ten hours. Another alternative is to do a walk-and-cruise tour. Buy your boat ticket at the Riviera boat docks and take the 8-mile footpath to Williams Bay. Board the *Belle of the Lake* there and cruise back for the best of both worlds. For reservations call Geneva Lake Cruise Line, (414) 245–2628.

Skiing. It's not Aspen, but Lake Geneva is about the closest area to Chicago where ski bums have at least a few options. The vertical drops are on the smallish side, but you'll find an interesting mix of trails and decent amenities, such as restaurants, rentals, and repair.

Alpine Valley, 3 miles south of East Troy, has twelve runs, with a vertical drop of 388 feet (414–642–7374). Wilmot Mountain, 1 mile south of Wilmot, has a vertical drop of 230 feet (414–862–2301). Americana in Lake Geneva has thirteen runs, with a vertical drop of 211 feet (414–248–8811).

Special Events

May. Chocolate Festival. Nestlé is the biggest employer in Burlington, so it stands to reason that people would want to celebrate its very existence with music, clowns, petting zoo, and of course, chocolate concoctions of all kinds. Burlington.

August. Venetian Night. Decorated boats, entertainment, food. Lake Geneva.

December. Children's Christmas Parade. Lake Geneva.

Other Recommended Restaurants and Lodgings

Delavan

Lake Lawn Lodge, Highway 50; (414) 728–5511. Lake Lawn Lodge can keep you busy in even the worst weather. Activities include miniature golf, horseback riding, ice skating, and just about anything else you can think of. It's probably the only resort that can boast of having a petting zoo. A bonus for weary parents: A children's program (for ages 3–12) features games, hikes, crafts, and more, year-round. Rates range from $115 to $275 per night.

Fontana

The Abbey Resort & Fontana Spa, Highway 67; (414) 275–6811. The accommodations—especially the townhouses—and recreational facilities have always been of good quality at this resort, but the kitchen lags far behind. Full marina, tennis courts, championship golf course, indoor/outdoor pools, and spa. Rates range from $60 to $135 per night.

Lake Geneva

Anthony's Steak House, Highway 50 just west of town; (414) 248–1818. Steaks may be in the title, but this is the best place to go for a real Wisconsin Friday night fish fry. It's all you can eat, with tasty side dishes of cole slaw and potato pancakes. Cost is just $7.25.

Cafe Calamari, Highway 67 and Geneva Street, Williams Bay; (414)

245–9665. Pastas and seafood are the specialties at this new restaurant on the lake. The ambience is of an authentic Italian cafe, and the cuisine lives up to the billing. Homemade focaccia are baked daily on the premises, while cannoli and Italian ices will delight your sweet tooth.

Elizabethan Inn, 463 Wrigley Drive; (414) 248–9131. Only 3 blocks from downtown and providing an unobstructed view of the lake and its own pier, the Elizabethan Inn is actually two buildings—the main house and the renovated stable. The stable, called Kimberly House, is a better choice, if for no other reason than all rooms have private baths. The rooms are handsomely furnished, with quilts, dolls, and four-poster beds. Full breakfast included. Rates: $85 per night, half-price on second night.

French Country Inn, Highway 4 just off Highway 50 west; (414) 245–5220. Another popular spot for those who want privacy and luxury. Off the beaten track on smaller Como Lake (3 miles west of Lake Geneva), the French Country Inn is picturesque without being pretentious. The inlaid floor previously occupied the foyer of the Danish Pavilion at the 1893 World Columbian Exposition in Chicago. It was dismantled, board by board, and brought north—with spectacular results. Rooms have a country French motif. Rates range from $125 to $145 per night and include a full breakfast and afternoon tea (sherry and pastries).

Harpoon Willie's. Right next door to Cafe Calamari (and owned by the same folks); (414) 245–6906. Sandwiches with homemade shakes and malts. Antique nautical decor, which you'd expect, given the big boating crowd it attracts. Open late.

Interlaken Resort, Highway 50; (414) 248–9121. A full-service resort that offers all amenities, from exercise room to rental boats. This is a popular choice with families. Rates range from $50 to $135 per night.

For More Information

Geneva Lakes Area Chamber of Commerce, 201 Wrigley Drive, Lake Geneva, WI 53147. (414) 248–4416.

Madison and Spring Green

One of many badgers in the Wisconsin state capitol

A Capital Adventure

_____ 2 NIGHTS _____

Government seat · Museums (art and historic) · Prehistoric caves · Zoo ·
University of Wisconsin · Bicycling · Watersports · Golfing/Fishing ·
Arboretum · Shopping · Theater · Architecture · Fine dining ·
Botanical gardens · Microbrewery

If you're a nautical type, then Madison will lure you to its shores.
"Madtown," as some affectionately refer to Wisconsin's water-laden

state capital, is set on four freshwater lakes spanning more than 18,000 acres combined. An 8-block wide isthmus formed by the two larger lakes, Mendota and Monona, is the heart of the city. This is the home of Madison's most commanding feature: the capitol, a splendorous sight during the day, but even more so at night when its 2,500-ton dome radiates the sky with a magnificent glow.

Madison is also the stomping ground for 44,000 students during the academic year. The University of Wisconsin's main campus stretches along the hilly south shore of Lake Mendota.

Always a bastion of liberalism, Madison had a front-row seat for the turbulence of the sixties and seventies. Even well into the eighties, pockets of hippies still found refuge in the campus environment. Today the rebelliousness has mellowed, and a warm, friendly, easygoing atmosphere pervades.

From an ethnic standpoint, the savvy-minded will delight at Madison's mix of cultures. Nowhere is this melange more distinct than in the food department. Eating is an adventure, running the gamut from American cooking to foreign fare (Greek, Italian, Chinese, Mexican, German, and virtually any other cuisine your palate craves).

Don't be surprised by the magnitude of things to see and do in Madison and its surrounding area. In fact, you'll be tempted to schedule your next weekend excursion before heading home. Centrally located, Madison is a convenient base to travel to the Dairy State's calendar-art countryside and historic (and prehistoric) attractions. Furthermore, Madison is a recreational haven all year round. One word of caution, however, during football season, unless you're a Badger fan, stay away on Saturdays. Motels and restaurants are booked for miles when the team is in town.

Day 1

Morning

The drive to Madison can be a quick 2½-hour trip. From downtown Chicago take I–90 northwest to Madison; from the northern suburbs take I–94 north to Milwaukee, bypass the city on I–894 west, which will eventually feed back into I–94 for the remainder of the journey.

On the other hand, you can choose a more ambitious alternative and do some local sightseeing. If you opt for this version, an early start (around six o'clock) is highly recommended.

Breakfast: Heading northwest on I–90, make a brief stop in Rockford (one hour out of Chicago) at the **Clock Tower coffee shop,** located in a resort bearing the same name. Here, you'll find an ample menu with everything from waffles to omelets to Swedish pancakes served with lingonberries. The coffee shop is located at the junction of I–90 and U.S. Highway 20 (7801 East State Street; 815–398–6000).

Continue your drive on I–90, turning west on the Beltline Highway (U.S. Highways 12 and 18) just outside Madison. Stay on Highway 18, also known as U.S. Highway 151, to Blue Mounds (about a 1½-hour drive from Rockford). The first stop, the **Cave of the Mounds,** is a magical maze of underground caverns considered the most significant caves in the upper Midwest. This geological jewel is a registered National Natural Landmark. Its colorful, iciclelike stalactites and stalagmites glisten so tantalizingly you'll be tempted to touch. But don't, or at least save your curiosity for the samples provided solely for that purpose. Your appreciation for the place will soar when you hear that the main cavern's earliest rock formations began more than a million years ago. You'll also develop an acute appreciation for light. The guides get a kick out of repeatedly extinguishing the lights and showing you the true definition of darkness.

Although a hot summer day is the ideal time to visit the Cave of the Mounds (the temperature remains at a cool fifty degrees, so bring a sweater), tours are given daily mid-March through mid-November and on Saturdays and Sundays during the winter. They last about forty-five minutes. Cost is $6.00 for adults, $5.00 for seniors, and $3.00 for the kids. Phone (608) 437–3038.

Not far (only a thirty-minute drive farther west on U.S. Highway 18 and north on Highway 23) is **The House on the Rock,** billed as Wisconsin's number one tourist attraction. Some might argue that it's the most peculiar as well.

A monument to obsession, The House on the Rock was originally built in the 1940s as a country retreat by its now-deceased owner Alex Jordan. The grottolike house, an architectural wonder built in and atop a 60-foot-high chimney of rock, is only a mere trifle compared to the labyrinth of bizarre collections that await in a series of adjoining dimly lit museums. Prepare yourself for a brush with the twilight zone and slip into some comfortable shoes; you'll be doing a lot of walking.

Once you get past the first hour of your three-hour (self-guided) tour, you'll be doing a lot of marveling, too. This is a place of superlatives including the world's largest carousel, the world's largest fireplace, the world's largest theater organ console, and the world's largest collection of Bauer and Koble stained-glass lamps.

Especially memorable is The Music of Yesterday Museum, which houses an extensive collection of animated, automated musical machines as well as the gigantic carousel illuminated with more than 20,000 lights. Also worthy of remaining in the deep recesses of your memory bank is the Organ Building. Some say Jordan considered this to be his pièce de résistance. Here lies the renowned theater organ console that has fifteen manuals and hundreds of stops. Twenty-nine of The House of the Rock's fifty-two grand pianos are wired to the console. You'll feel like you're in a dream (or perhaps a nightmare) when you enter this cavernous chamber that gleams with copper (500,000 pounds are in the room). Catwalks zigzag, bridges that go nowhere abound, and spiral staircases will lead you to a photographer's deck. If you have an affinity for dolls, the Dollhouse Building is a must. A mammoth collection of dollhouses, ranging in architectural styles (colonial to contemporary), are furnished in minute detail.

The best time to visit The House is in the morning. Crowds seem to triple in the afternoons. Also because The House on the Rock relies heavily on natural lighting, an overcast, rainy day can greatly diminish your outing. Hours are 8 A.M. to dusk, April through October; tickets are sold until 2½ hours before closing. Admission is $15 for adults, less for children. Phone (608) 935–3639.

Lunch: **The Spring Green Restaurant,** a twenty-minute drive north from The House on the Rock and located at Highway 23 and County C, is the only restaurant designed by Frank Lloyd Wright. Nestled among the trees and overlooking the Wisconsin River, the restaurant's earth-red roof and antennalike spire are conspicuous. Interior furnishings are also Wright inspired. The views are splendid, actually much better than the food. You'll be able to fill up, however, on the very "American" menu, even if you're a vegetarian. Try the fresh fish and salad entrees. Lunch is served between 11 A.M. and 3 P.M. Prices range from $4.50 to $11.00. Phone (608) 588–2571. Open April–December.

Afternoon

Don't linger too long over a late lunch because 4 P.M. is the last tour of the day at **Frank Lloyd Wright's Hillside Home School at Taliesin** (go east on County C and south on Highway 23). Tours start at 9 A.M. daily mid-April through October and are given every hour on the hour.

Wright was born just 30 miles from Spring Green and spent much of his childhood in the area working on his uncle's farm. He chose this community as the site for his home, Taliesin (the name means "shining brow" in Welsh), and for his architectural school. Also located on the grounds of Taliesin are several other Wright structures: the Hillside Home School, Midway Farms, Romeo and Juliet Windmill, and a house called Tan-y-deri, which he built for his sister Jane. Today Taliesin is the summer and fall headquarters of the Frank Lloyd Wright Foundation. Architects trained in the Wright tradition still practice here.

Allow at least an hour for the tour, which includes the school, a small theater, living and dining rooms, drafting studios, and two galleries containing Wright-designed furniture, artwork from his extensive Oriental collection, and models of Wright buildings. Admission is

$6.00 for adults and $3.00 for children under 12. Pricier walking tours of the grounds ($15) are given mid-June through September, Monday–Saturday at 10:30 A.M. Phone (608) 588–2511.

You might also want to take a quick peek at **Unity Chapel** (go south on Highway 23 and east on County Road T). Designed by Chicago architect Joseph Silsbee in 1886, the chapel was built by Wright's mother's family. You'll be able to get a glimpse of Wright's former grave in the family cemetery, but that's all that remains. Although Wright was originally buried here in 1959, his third wife, Olgivanna, who hated Wisconsin, had him moved to his final resting ground in Arizona in 1985.

Also in the vicinity is the open-air **American Players Theatre,** set on seventy-one acres of the beautiful pastoral environs. The APT, which performs only Shakespeare and other classics, is recognized for having one of the nation's finest professional repertory companies. Matinee and evening shows (with more than 100 performances per season) run from mid-June to early October. Attire is casual, so don't dress up. If you do call ahead and order tickets, arrive a little early so you can stroll the amphitheater. And don't forget the insect repellent. Tickets range from $13.50 to $21.50. Phone (608) 588–7401.

Dinner: Head for **Keyes West,** formerly known as Carodonnes, in Black Earth. Go north on Highway 23 to Highway 14 and go east to Highway 78 south (1221 Mills Street; 608–767–2501). This restaurant was a meat market in earlier days, and many of the accoutrements are still in place, such as antique meat hooks that hang from the ceiling. Take a look at the bar; it was converted from the market's meat locker. Specials change nightly, but the prime rib ($10.95) is especially recommended. Oh, and don't let the carnivorous past fool you; Keyes West also serves up great fish and poultry dishes, and the homemade Hershey bar pie is a delicious finishing touch ($3.00).

Lodging: After dinner, get back on Highway 14 and go east to Madison. **The Edgewater Hotel** (666 Wisconsin Avenue; 608–256–9071), is everything its name suggests and more. Just a few short blocks from the Memorial Union and Capitol Square (where the Capitol is situated), this hotel is intimate (only 117 rooms) and within walking distance to all downtown Madison activity. Lakefront rooms ($110 per night), which are a bit more pricey than the lakeview rooms ($85–$95), give a breathtaking panoramic view of Lake Mendota.

Day 2

Morning

Breakfast: **The Admiralty,** which overlooks the Edgewater Hotel's pier. The restaurant won Madison's 1991 best service award, so expect to be treated royally.

Begin your day at the **Henry Vilas Park Zoo,** on the banks of Lake Wingra and the Wingra Lagoon (702 South Randall Avenue; 608–258–1460). Admission is free and so is parking. As zoos go, this one is relatively small, but still very enjoyable. You can watch the animals, stroll to the beach, and if you've brought the kids along, you'll welcome the nearby playground. On Sundays, you can indulge them in free camel rides too (10:30 A.M.). The zoo's primates are a favorite among the natives as are the felines. If you happen to still be hanging around at 1 P.M. on Sunday, you can also check out the lions at feeding time. The zoo is open from 9:30 A.M. to 8:00 P.M., May through August; 9:30 A.M. to 5:00 P.M., the remainder of the year.

Next take a walk, just 5 blocks away, to **Budget Bicycle Center** (1230 Regent Street; 608–251–8413) to rent some wheels. A reconditioned five- or ten-speed rents for $7.00 a day. If you prefer a mountain bike ($9.50) or a racing tandem ($25), try **Yellow Jersey** (419 State Street; 608–257–4737). First, take a quick spin to the **University Arboretum** (1207 Seminole Highway near Budget Bicycle Center) to see its impressive and clearly labeled collection of the area's natural flora and fauna. Free nature lectures and walking tours are also given most weekends at the arboretum's McKay Center.

After spending a short time cycling around, you won't be surprised that Madison was voted one of the ten best bicycling cities in the country. The Greater Madison Convention and Visitors Bureau developed "Madison Daytrippers," a whimsical eight-tour salute to the Beatles that will take you through the "Long and Winding Road" of lush hills and valleys synonymous with the Wisconsin countryside. Or you can stay within the city limits and cycle around Lake Monona, a 12-mile ride. Just a note of local history: Rock-and-roller Otis Redding died when his plane crashed into Lake Monona on December 10, 1967, only three days after he recorded his biggest hit, "Dock of the Bay." A memorial to Redding is located on the lake's shore in Law Park off John Nolen Drive.

At the north end of Lake Monona, pedal into the **Olbrich Gardens** (3330 Atwood Avenue) to see its all-American-rose garden. During the summer months, it's not uncommon to see a wedding in this romantic spot.

Lunch: Before returning your bikes, ride back to campus and relax at one of the university favorites—the **Rathskeller,** located inside the Memorial Union (800 Langdon Street). Although the Rathskeller is nothing the students write home about, its fare of hamburgers, brats, milkshakes, and beer (served cafeteria style) is inexpensive and transportable to the union's popular outdoor terrace overlooking Lake

Mendota. This is one of Madison's best spots to find discussions on politics or philosophy, or just to do some serious people watching. While you're at the union, you can almost always join in a game of pool or table tennis, and the collection of video games rivals the best arcade.

Note: Walking tours of the university depart from the second floor information desk at 1 P.M. Tuesday and Saturday or by special group appointment. Phone (608) 262–2511.

Afternoon

Visiting the **State Historical Museum** (30 North Carroll Street on Capitol Square; 608–262–7700) is a good way to spend a Sunday afternoon. Closed on Mondays, museum hours are Tuesday–Saturday, 10 A.M. to 5 P.M., and Sunday, noon to 5 P.M. Admission is free. You'll be pleasantly surprised that there's nothing musty about this museum. It won't take you more than an hour to meander through the exhibits on Wisconsin history (from the prehistoric Indian culture to contemporary social issues). But remember to save some time for the gift shop. It is better than most and has some exceptionally designed Indian crafts.

Dinner: **Quivey's Grove** is a twenty-minute drive southwest from downtown Madison (6261 Nesbitt Road; 608–273–4900). Consisting of a stone farmhouse and stable built in 1855, this site is listed on the National Register of Historic Places. Dining is very intimate, as you'll find each room of the house contains no more than five tables. Cheese, butter, and other dairy products are used generously, and all baking and cooking are done the old-fashioned way—"from scratch." Sample the chicken bond ($14.75)—chicken breast stuffed with smoked duck and Wisconsin Swiss cheese and served on a bed of wild rice; polish it off with turtle pie ($3.50). Dinner entrees range from $12.50 to $18.50, including soup or salad.

Lodging: The Edgewater Hotel.

Day 3

Morning

Breakfast: **Ovens of Brittany,** 305 State Street; 608–257–7000. Originally a bakery that grew into a restaurant, Ovens of Brittany is best known for the Brittany bun, a huge cinnamon roll sans the frosting. In deference to those trying to be trim, the bakery has also come up with a smaller version. Muffins, scones, and breads of all varieties are other specialties of the house. This is a Madison tradition that should not be missed!

A trip to the **state capitol,** just down the street on Capitol Square, is a must. Free tours are given daily on the hour: Monday–Saturday, 9 A.M. to 3 P.M.; Sunday, 1 to 3 P.M. (608–266–0382); they begin at the rotunda information desk. Allow one hour to tour the rotunda, governor's conference room, the Wisconsin Supreme Court, and the senate and assembly chambers. You'll also hear a commentary on the artwork in the various rooms. Don't forget to look up at the capitol's ornate ceiling or, when outside, to catch the glint of gold perched atop its white granite dome. That bit of gold (actually gold leaf) is a sculpture that's topped the capitol since 1914.

State Street is really a great street in Madison. You'll enjoy roaming this 8-block pedestrian mall. The capitol sits at one end and the University of Wisconsin campus is at the other. This is the emotional heart of Madison, and you'll find everything from ethnic restaurants, campus bars, and T-shirt emporiums to coffee shops, art galleries, bookstores, and theaters.

The Madison Civic Center (211 State Street; 608–266–6550), is a restored movie theater that houses the 2,200-seat Oscar Mayer Theatre and the smaller, more intimate Isthmus Playhouse (330 seats). Tours of the theater spaces and facilities must be scheduled two to three weeks in advance. The **Madison Art Center** is also located at the same address. Its galleries contain changing exhibits of modern and contemporary art. Open Tuesday–Thursday, 11 A.M.–5 P.M.; Friday, 11 A.M.–9 P.M.; Saturday, 10 A.M.–5 P.M.; Sunday, 1–5 P.M. Closed Mondays. Admission free. Phone (608) 257–0158.

Lunch: **The Parthenon Gyros Restaurant,** (316 State Street; 608–251–6311). This is a Madison hot spot. Gyros and french fries are the preferred fare, and onions are served generously, so you may want to go easy depending on how well you know your traveling companion.

Afternoon

Time for dessert and another Madison tradition—ice cream from **Babcock Hall** (1605 Linden Drive; 608–262–3046). This is the campus dairy plant where ice cream, yogurt, and cheese are manufactured. The milk is produced on a working dairy farm around the corner. If you walk upstairs to Babcock's second floor viewing window, you'll be able to watch all the action. Babcock's scoops are generous. Flavors (about a dozen) are changed daily. Hours are Monday–Friday, 9:30 A.M. to 5:00 P.M.; Saturday, 9:30 A.M. to noon.

One last stop before heading home—the **Elvehjem Museum of Art** (800 University Avenue; 608–263–2246). Designed by architect Harry Weese, the Elvehjem is said to be one of the largest university art museums in the country. The permanent collection includes more than 13,000 artworks dating from 2300 B.C. to the present. Egyptian tomb sculpture, Russian icons, American and European paintings, sculpture, prints, and drawings, as well as Asian art and a 35-foot-high dinosaur skeleton are some of the highlights. Admission is free. Tours are offered if you call between two and six weeks ahead. Open Monday–Saturday, 9:00 A.M. to 4:45 P.M.; Sunday, 11:00 A.M. to 4:45 P.M.

There's More

Farmer's Market. One of the Midwest's finest, this is held at Capitol Square in conjunction with other festivities on Saturday mornings, 6 A.M.–2 P.M., late April–early November. Get there early!
Capital Brewery, Gift Haus & Beer Garden (7734 Terrace Avenue, Middleton; 608–836–7100). This traditional small German-style brewery opened in 1986 and specializes in lager beers. To get to Middleton from downtown Madison, go west on Highway 14 (University Avenue) and north on Highway 12. It's a fifteen-minute drive. Forty-five-minute tours of the working microbrewery (a very small brewery) are offered mid-May through mid-September. Tours start at 1 P.M., Monday–Thursday; 1:00 P.M. and 3:30 P.M., Friday; 1 P.M., 3 P.M., and 4 P.M., Saturday. During the summer season, the Beer Garden is open from noon to 8 P.M.
Watersports. To rent canoes, paddleboats, aqua cycles, kayaks, sailboats, sailboards, and waterbikes, try Nauti-gal (5360 Westport Road; 608–244–4464); Rutabaga (820 South Park Street; 608–256–4303); or Wingra Canoe and Sailing Center (824 Knickerbocker Street; 608–233–5332).
Golf. Two of the area's championship courses are the Springs Golf Course (3 miles south of Spring Green at Highway C and Golf Course Road; 608–588–7707), rated one of the top seventy-five public courses in the country by *Golf Digest*; and the newly opened University of Wisconsin eighteen-hole course, converted from farmland, at the intersection of highways M and PD (608–845–7700).
Fishing. Picnic Point on Lake Mendota is a preferred spot on campus grounds to fish and picnic.
Ice skating. During winter months, the lagoon at Henry Vilas Park, 1400 Drake Street, offers skating. Warming house.
Cross-country skiing. The UW Arboretum (1207 Seminole Highway; 608–263–7888) is one of the most popular places. Other good trails can be found at Blue Mound State Park at Blue Mounds (608–437–5711) and Governor Nelson State Park, located on the north side of Lake Mendota, 5140 County Highway M (608–831–3005).
Madison Art Center (211 State Street, in the Madison Civic Center; 608–257–0158). Galleries contain changing exhibits of modern and

contemporary art. Open Tuesday–Thursday, 11 A.M.–5 P.M.; Friday, 11 A.M.–9 P.M.; Saturday, 10 A.M.–5 P.M.; Sunday, 1–5 P.M. Free.

Madison Children's Museum, near Capitol Square at 100 State Street; (608) 256–6445. A real hands-on experience for the younger set (ages 1–13) and a real lifesaver on a rainy day. Open Tuesday–Saturday, 10 A.M.–5 P.M.; Sunday, 1–5 P.M. Admission is $1.50.

Geology Museum, 1215 West Dayton Street (first floor of UW's Weeks Hall). Rocks, fossils, and a giant mastodon, the trademark of this museum, can be seen Monday–Friday, 8:30 A.M.–4:30 P.M. and Saturday, 9 A.M.–1 P.M. Free. Phone (608) 262–2399.

U.S. Forest Products Laboratory, Gifford Pinchot Drive and North Walnut Street; (608–231–9200). Established in 1910 by the U.S. Department of Agriculture and the university, this institution, which investigates the efficient use of forest products, was the first of its kind in the world. Tours Monday–Thursday, 2 P.M. Free.

Hot Air Balloons. Sunrise and sunset rides spring to fall. Reservations required eight weeks in advance. Departures from 4512 East Washington (across from East Town Mall). One hour rides cost $185; half-hour express rides, $125. Phone (608) 241–4000.

Whad Ya'Know Radio Show. Saturday morning comedy/quiz radio show with host Michael Feldman. Write ahead for free tickets. Send a stamped self-addressed envelope to: Whad Ya'Know Radio Show, 821 University Avenue, Madison, WI 53706 with show date and number of tickets you're requesting. Last minute remaining tickets are often available. Lines start early for seats; doors open at 9 A.M. for the 10 A.M. show (Parliamentary Room, UW's Vilas Halls; 608–263–4141).

Special Events

Early May. Capitol City Jazz Fest. Jazz jam attracting bands from throughout the United States. Held at Holiday Inn Southeast, intersection I–90 and highways 12 and 18.

July. Song of Norway. Musical production "Song of Norway" performed outdoors under the stars at Cave of the Mounds, in Blue Mounds.

July. Art Fair On the Square and Art Fair Off the Square. Hundreds of artists show works at Capitol Square and surrounding area.

July. Dane County Fair. Livestock judging, carnival, entertainment, and sampling of the area's best cream puffs. Dane County Exposition Center (highways 12 and 18 and John Nolan Drive).

August. Middleton Good Neighbor Festival. Carnival, parade, art show, entertainment, and a classic German beer garden. Fireman's Park, Clark and Lee streets, Middleton.

September. Taste of Madison. Madison's finest fare, plus entertainment. Capitol Square.
November. Holiday Parade. Santa and bands march at Capitol Square.

Other Recommended Restaurants and Lodgings

Madison

Annie's Hill House, 2117 Sheridan Drive; (608) 244–2224. Traditional bed-and-breakfast, reasonably priced ($65 to $85 per night). No restaurant.

Blue Marlin, 101 North Hamilton Street (just off Capitol Square); (608) 255–2255. Informal and affordable. Seafood is the specialty of the house; try the grilled yellowfin tuna or the namesake blue marlin.

The Concourse and Governor's Club, 1 West Dayton Street; (608) 257–6000. Just steps from the Capitol Square and State Street Mall, this dual hotel offers luxurious executive suites at the Governor's Club and better-than-average accommodations at The Concourse. Rates range from $49 to $135 per night. Indoor pool.

Crandall's at the Depot, 640 West Washington; (608) 255–6070. Renovated 1940s depot serving American favorites.

Essen Haus-German Restaurant, 514 East Wilson; (608) 255–4674. Oktoberfest atmosphere, German cuisine.

Gino's, 540 State Street; (608) 257–9022. Specializes in veal, pastas, and stuffed pizza.

Inn on the Park Hotel, 22 South Carroll Street; (608) 257–8811. Some of the city's best views of the Capitol. (Rates range from $71 to $78 per night.) Indoor pool.

L'Escargot, 2784 Fish Hatchery Road; (608) 273–2666. A gourmet's delight. Intimate continental restaurant applauded by the critics.

L'Etoile, 25 North Pinckney; (608) 251–0500. Airy loft dining room with breathtaking view of Capitol Square. Named one of the top U.S. restaurants by *Food Arts* magazine.

Mansion Hill, 424 North Pinckney Street; (608) 255–3999. Enchanting but pricey historic bed-and-breakfast renovated from a magnificent twenty-one-room mansion. Rates range from $100 to $250 per night. No restaurant.

Mariner's Inn, 5339 Lighthouse Bay Drive (off Highway M); (608) 244–8418. On the waterfront. Specialties of this Madison favorite are steaks, red snapper, whitefish, and lobster.

Sheraton Inn & Conference Center, 706 John Nolen Drive; (608)

251–2300. Although not as well located as other accommodations, this hotel is quite comfortable and reasonably priced ($84 to $91 per night). For an extra $10 per night, you can get a room upgrade that includes a full breakfast well worth the money. Indoor pool.

For More Information

Greater Madison Convention and Visitors Bureau, 615 East Washington, Madison, WI 53703. (608) 25–LAKES or 800–373–6376.

Madison Chamber of Commerce, 615 East Washington, P.O. Box 71, Madison, WI 53701-0071. (608) 256–8348.

Middleton Chamber of Commerce, 7507 Hubbard Avenue, P.O. Box 553, Middleton, WI 53562. (608) 831–5696.

Spring Green Area Chamber of Commerce, Box 3, Spring Green, WI 53588. (608) 588–2042.

Wisconsin Dells

Hidden pockets of tranquillity in the Dells

Carnival Along the Cliffs

_____ 2 NIGHTS _____

Theme parks • Boat tours • Miniature golf • Circus museum • Watershows •
Indian ceremonials • Railway museum • Watersports • Horseback riding •
Fishing • Golfing • Camping • Natural formations

The Wisconsin Dells is for the young and the young at heart. This is
magnificent country, where natural formations of carved sandstone
cliffs climb for miles along a serpentine channel cut by the Wisconsin

River. A scenic beauty it is, but make no mistake: the Dells is also the land of cotton candy, go-carts, haunted houses, gigantic waterparks, moccasins, and miniature golf. In short, the Wisconsin Dells is a rambunctious carnival set against a stunning backdrop, beckoning tourists to try its wares and have a wonderfully good time.

Although the Dells, both Upper and Lower, are literally the wellsprings of activity in this children's paradise, most of the area's seventy-plus attractions spill over into nearby Lake Delton and along the town's two main strips: Broadway (downtown Dells) and Highway 12. A seasonal spot (May through mid-October), the Wisconsin Dells doesn't really get rolling until mid-June when the crowds start pouring in. And they do. Summer in the Dells is somewhat akin to bees swarming a honeycomb.

The winter months may seem pretty sparse in comparison, but don't rule out this locale as a cold-weather retreat. Snowmobiling and cross-country and downhill skiing are all for the taking at Devil's Lake and Mirror Lake State Parks during the Dells' off-season.

While picturesque scenery and hokey entertainment are Dells' staples, don't expect much in the way of fancy cuisine. American fare served in "all you can eat" style is the norm as are kiddie menus (which can be found in abundance). Oh, and one last pointer about this amusement haven: the Dells can be pricey. Discount tickets to various attractions or package deals are available, but when you come right down to it, there's no getting away cheap on this getaway weekend. The Wisconsin Dells can be a heck-of-a-lot-of-fun, but it will cost you.

Day 1

Afternoon

Dinner: **Ella's Kosher Deli & Ice Cream Parlor** (3 miles west of I–90/94 on Highway 151, 2902 East Washington Avenue; 608–241–5291). Take a quick stop along the way at Ella's, an oversized ice cream parlor and perfect place for the kids. The menu is Kosher, and the deli sandwiches are divine. Ice-cream cones and milkshakes are another must. Make sure to look up—a fascinating menagerie of mechanized characters, ranging from Bart Simpson to Mickey Mouse, perform amazing feats overhead. Don't forget to take a ride on the giant carousel out front, which operates May through October. Prices run from $3.00 to $6.50.

Roughly a 200-mile (3½-hour) drive from Chicago, the Wisconsin Dells won't seem nearly as far away when a splash of evening entertainment awaits at your journey's end. Take I–90 or I–94 north to Madison. They merge east of the city. Continue heading northwest to

U.S. Highway 12 and arrive just in time for the 8:30 P.M. "Tommy Bartlett Laser-Rama Ski, Sky and Stage Show" (Highway 12 at 560 Wisconsin Dells Parkway; 608–254–2525).

Bartlett, a veritable Dells institution, was a 1930s radio prodigy in Milwaukee and Chicago before becoming the vacation town's aquatic and air show impresario in the fifties. The show, which is performed rain or shine, plays three times daily (1:00 P.M., 4:30 P.M., and 8:30 P.M.) at an outdoor amphitheater on the shores of Lake Delton. The best seats tend to be in the middle, but if you enjoy being part of the action, try for the front-row seats.

Waterskiing, Tahitian drum dancers (who hula with the audience), an acrobatic act atop 60-foot-high poles, and a juggling joker are among the entertaining entourage. Although the night show can almost be a bit too long for children, this performance does have a colorful Laser-Rama light finale. If you have a hankering to participate, miniflashlights (sold for $3.00 a piece) will do the trick.

Even though the theater is quite large (4,500 seats), you should order tickets in advance (especially if you drive up for the night show). Tickets range from $8.45 to $13.45. Children under 6 years old (who sit on your lap) are free. The show runs late Memorial Day through Labor Day.

Lodging: **The Monte Carlo Resort Motel** on Lake Delton (350 East Hiawatha Drive; 608–254–8761) is within walking distance of Tommy Bartlett's. Kitchenettes (for those who prefer to save a few bucks and fix a meal or two of their own) are available. A heated swimming pool, tennis courts, and a small beach are other motel amenities. Just in case you were thinking of bringing Fido, don't. No pets allowed. Motel room rates range from $64 to $85 a night. Cottages and apartments can be rented on a weekly basis at $650.

Day 2

Morning

Breakfast: Travel into downtown Baraboo—about a twenty-minute drive—for a stop at a local favorite, **Kristina's** (113 Third Street; 608–356–3430). Take Highway 12 south and Highway 33 east. **Baraboo,** which is built around a square, is the county seat as well as the original winter home of the Ringling Brothers' Circus (from 1884 to 1918). The Sauk County Court House, other municipal and civic buildings, a few historic circus sites, retail shops, and Kristina's are all easily identifiable. Kristina's serves a big breakfast, and at nearly half the price of a comparable early morning eye opener in the Dells. Belgian waffles, ham and eggs, and omelets are a sampling of the selection.

Just 3 blocks southeast of Kristina's (take Third Street east, turning south on Ash Street, and east again on Water Street) is the renowned **Circus World Museum** (426 Water Street; 608–356–0800). For anyone who has even the slightest curiosity about the circus, the museum is a rewarding adventure into the realm of the big-top.

Live performances (three times daily), magic shows, circus parades, demonstrations of historic circus operations, concerts, and exhibits will absorb you. Plan on spending at least four hours here, and don't be surprised if you wind up hanging around for the entire day. In fact, you might find this museum to be the highlight of your weekend trip.

Make sure to catch one of the live shows. You'll see all the typicals: animal acts, high-wire walks, and a few flying-trapeze artists. All performances take place in a single ring, so there's no competition for your attention. The elaborate collection of circus wagons is also impressive. Ornate with three-dimensional statues and characters, some of these gaudy antique wagons are real works of art. It's not hard to imagine how they captivated the crowds while traveling from town to town.

The Circus World Museum is open from mid-May to mid-September from 9 A.M. to 6 P.M. Hours are extended to a 10 P.M. closing from July 20 to August 24, but exhibit facilities are open year-round. Admission is $8.95 for adults, $7.95 for seniors, and $5.50 for children ages 3 to 12.

Lunch: The Circus World Museum. Children will enjoy the ever-popular circus fare: hot dogs, hamburgers, pizza. Eat outdoors picnic-style.

Afternoon

Head for the **Mid-Continent Railroad Museum,** 5 miles west in North Freedom (take Highway 12 to Highway 136, then head 2¼ miles southwest on County PF). A 9-mile ride on an early twentieth-century train pulled by a vintage steam locomotive is the highlight here. What better way to get a glimpse of the countryside? The ride is exceptionally beautiful when the autumn colors are at their height, during the first two weekends of October.

The museum, run by volunteers who have restored dozens of antique engines and railcars, also includes an 1894 depot, a wooden water tower, locomotives, railroad cars, and equipment displays. Allow two hours for your visit.

Museum hours are 9:30 A.M. to 5:00 P.M. daily. Train rides depart at 10:30 A.M., 12:30 P.M., 2:00 P.M., and 3:30 P.M., mid-May to early September. Only weekend rides are given during September and October. A winter ride also runs the third weekend in February. Tickets cost $6.00 for adults, $5.00 for seniors, and $3.00 for children ages 3–15. Phone (608) 522–4261.

Dinner: Retrace your steps back to Highway 12 and return to the

Dells. Once there, head downtown to **Monk's Bar & Grill** (220 Broadway; 608–254–2955) for hamburgers, the house specialty. Part of the fun is watching the burgers frying in the front window. The other part is knowing that your bill won't punch too big a hole in your pockets. Don't forget to order the fresh-cut fries.

No trip to the Dells would be complete without a boat ride. After arriving at that conclusion, you'll need to decide which direction you want to take—namely, Upper or Lower. The Upper Dells tour (above the dam) lasts 2½ hours (adults $10.50; half-price for kids ages 6–11). It features two shore landings and an opportunity to see the famous Dells' dog (the trademark of the place) leap over a rocky cliff to Stand Rock, a historic meeting ground of the Midwestern Indian tribes. The last Upper Dells boat ride of the night (7:45 P.M.) also includes the Indian Ceremonial at Stand Rock ($12.25 per person). Boats leave the Upper Dells Landing in downtown Dells (11 Broadway; 608–254–8555 and 608–253–1561).

The two-hour evening show at Stand Rock is filled with Winnebago dances, traditions, and costumes. This might get a little long for young ones, but after the program's over, children will find the sing-along back on the boat (led by the first mate) to be lots of fun. It is possible to attend the ceremony without taking the boat ride (608–254–6774). You can drive to Stand Rock and cut back on the cost ($10.50 for reserved seating; $8.50 for general admission).

Lower Dells tours (below the dam) cost a little less than those to the Upper Dells (adults $6.85; same deal for the kids) but only last one hour, are nonstop, and are less scenic. Combination tours are also available.

Lodging: The Monte Carlo Resort Motel.

Day 3

Morning

Breakfast: In the mood for a hearty breakfast? Begin your day at **Paul Bunyan's Lumberjack Meals** (411 Highway 13; 608–254–8717). The place looks like an 1890s logging camp in a humongous log cabin. Food (everything from sugar doughnuts and pancakes to eggs, sausage links, and hash brown potatoes) is unlimited and served at the very long tables. That's right; you'll be seated with your neighbors. Getting to know them and their eating habits is an integral part of the Bunyan ambience. The wait is never more than ten minutes. Don't look for a menu, because you won't find one; they don't exist. Breakfast is served 7 A.M. to noon, May through September. Cost for adults is $5.29; for children, 45 cents times their age.

Doing the Ducks is considered an absolute must at the Dells. It's hard to tell who enjoys these amphibious World War II assault crafts more, adults or children. Basically, this is another boat ride (7½ miles on the Wisconsin River, Dell Creek, and Lake Delton). Yet these transports will also take you roaring through the woods. Remember not to wear nice shoes when you do the Ducks and be wary of putting purses or other parcels on the floor (they'll get wet!). Start the ride at Highway 12 and Highway 23 (608–254–8751) or at 1550 Wisconsin Dells Parkway (608–254–6080). One-hour rides cost $10.00 for adults and $5.00 for kids ages 6–12. Open daily 9 A.M.–6 P.M., May through early October.

Next stop is **Pirates' Cove Adventure Golf** for a few rounds of miniature golf (at the intersection of highways 12-13-16-23, exit 87, I–90/94; (608–254–7500). All in all, there are seventy-two holes on the numerous courses that seem to go on endlessly. The park overlooks the Wisconsin River, and you'll find ponds and cascading waterfalls spread generously throughout.

A leisurely stroll in the downtown Dells along Broadway is another must. It won't take you long before you begin wondering whether the term "tourist trap" was coined here. Nonetheless, it's all part of the Dells experience. Besides, you'll find plenty to stick your nose into: game arcades, a wax museum, a haunted mansion, and shops that sell cotton candy, taffy, fudge, cheese, moccasins, old-time photos, blown glass, T-shirts, Indian mementos, and more.

Lunch: **Upper Crust,** 232 Broadway; (608) 253–6001. Situated on the second floor with a big glass window, this restaurant will give you a good view of the goings-on along the downtown strip. Pan pizza is the main meal here, so sink your teeth in and enjoy. Open April through October.

Afternoon

Big Chief Go-Kart World bills itself as the nation's largest go-cart complex, and it very well may be. All ages will find a track to match their skills. You'll find lots of curves and multiple levels of track at Big Chief. The complex is located on Highway A off Highway 12. Phone (608) 254–2490.

If you're not exhausted yet, take a trip to **Noah's Ark,** a spectacular sixty-acre water park featuring two wave pools, twenty-five water slides, four kiddie water play areas, bumper boats, and virtually any other water attraction imaginable. You'll also find Can-Am race cars (stands for Canadian-American), an eighteen-hole miniature golf course, eleven restaurants, and nineteen picnic pavilions. Allow four hours, but realistically you can spend an entire day here.

Noah's Ark is located at highways 12 and 23. It is open daily from 9

A.M. to 8 P.M., late May through early September. Phone (608) 254–6351. Admission: $15.95 adult or child; under age 2, free. Inner tube rental is $2.50 or $5.00, plus a 50-cent or $1.00 deposit.

Dinner: **Ishnala Supper Club** (Ishnala Road in Lake Delton) is one of the most serene and secluded spots in the area. The natural setting, overlooking Mirror Lake, is so tranquil and so beautiful that it makes the perfect ending to a weekend at the Dells. The hubbub is left behind; reservations aren't taken for parties less than eight, however, and the wait can at times be long. Nevertheless, the menu matches the scenery, and you'll be glad you decided to stay. Steaks, prime rib, fresh seafood, and lobster tail are the suggested choices. This isn't inexpensive dining, but your meal here will be most memorable. Phone (608) 253–1771.

There's More

Wisconsin Opry, Highway 12 at exit 92; (608) 254–7951. Country music performed by local and national professional talent. Nightly at 8 P.M., Memorial Day through Labor Day.

Winnebago Indian Museum, 3889 River Road; (608) 254–2268. Started in 1953 as a basket stand on an old stagecoach trail, the museum features Native American relics, Indian crafts, and souvenir trinkets. Open April through early January.

Ripley's Believe It or Not, downtown at 115 Broadway; (608) 253–7556. Displays of the bizarre and unusual including a genuine shrunken head from the Amazon region and videos of other strange Ripley discoveries. Open May through October.

Storybook Gardens, 1500 Wisconsin Dells Parkway; (608) 253–2391. Animated and live fairy-tale characters, a petting zoo, the Safari Sam stage show, merry-go-round rides, and guided tours of the gardens given aboard a miniature train. Open late May through Labor Day.

Lost Canyon Tours, 720 Canyon Road, Lake Delton; (608) 253–2781 or (608) 254–8757. Horse-drawn carriage rides down a mile of cliff-walled gorges. Tours operate mid-May through September.

International Crane Foundation, Shady Lane Road, Baraboo; (608) 356–9462. (Take Highway 12 to Baraboo, then go 1¼ miles east on Shady Lane Road.) A center for the study, propagation, and preservation of endangered cranes. Open May through October.

Sauk County Historical Museum, 531 Fourth Avenue, Baraboo; (608) 356–1001. Displays of American Indian and pioneer relics, Civil War equipment, household furnishings, toys, textiles, and memorabilia inside a 1906 mansion. Open mid-May through mid-September.

Museum of Norman Rockwell Art, 227 South Park Street, Reedsburg; (608) 524–2123. One of the nation's largest collections of Rockwell art. Late May through early September, open daily 10 A.M.–6 P.M.; by appointment only for the remainder of the year.
Devil's Lake State Park, Highway 123, Baraboo; (608) 356–8301. Devil's Lake is bounded on three sides by the quartzite cliffs of the Baraboo Range. Sailboard, rowboat, snorkel, and fishing equipment rentals are available. This is also the site of ancient Indian mounds. Naturalist programs and exhibits explaining the glacial phenomena of the area are provided. Open daily from 6 A.M. to 11 P.M.
Fishing. Beaver Springs Trout Farm on Trout Road (608–254–2735) and B & H Trout Farm at 3640 Highway 13 (608–254–7280). Catch rainbow trout from spring-fed ponds. Sold by the inch. April through November.
Watersports. Lake Delton: Lake Delton Water Sports on Highway 12 (608–254–8702); Wisconsin Dells: Aqua Sports-Port Vista Marina on Lake Delton (608–253–2561); Holiday Shores Campground and Resort at 3900 River Road (608–254–2717); Point Bluff Resort at 3199 County Z (608–253–6181); River's Edge Resort at 1196 Highway A (608–254–7707); Schleef's Boat Rental at 1141 East Hiawatha Drive (608–254–7707); Yogi Bear's Jellystone Campresort on Mirror Lake (608–254–2034). All have canoe, pontoon boat, paddleboat, shuttle, sailboat, sailboard, skiboat, waverunner, and parasailing rentals.
Horseback riding. Wisconsin Dells: Christmas Mountain Ranch, S944 Christmas Mountain Road, (608) 254–3935; OK Corral Riding Stable, Highway 16, (608) 254–2811. Lyndon Station: Dell View Riding Stable, Highway 2, (608) 666–2300; Little Heaven Frontier Ranch, N783 highways 12 and 16, (800) 22–DELLS or (608) 254–8149. Scenic trail riding, May through November.
Golf. Coldwater Canyon Golf Course (4065 River Road, Wisconsin Dells; 608–254–8489). Nine-hole facility; lessons including package plans offered by the International Golf Academy (608–254–6361). Or try the brand new eighteen-hole Trappers Turn Golf Course (highways 12 and 16, Wisconsin Dells; 608–253–7000).

Special Events

February. Wisconsin Sled Dog Championships and Christmas Mountain Winter Carnival. Sled-dog racing, weight-pulling championships, sleigh rides, entertainment, chili-cooking contest, cross-country and downhill skiing. Five miles west of the Wisconsin Dells on Highway H, Christmas Mountain Village.
May. Auto Show. Car showcase for auto buffs includes antiques,

street machines, and classics. Also features antique flea market, swap meet, and "Parade of Cars." Held at Bowman's Park in downtown Wisconsin Dells.

May. Dells Balloon Rally. Hot air–balloon weekend competition at I–90/94 and Highway 12 (exit 92) and Wisconsin Dells High School Athletic Field.

June. Heritage Days Celebration. Arts and crafts fair, ice cream social, tours of historic Jonathon Bowman Home at Bowman Park in downtown Dells.

September. Wo-Zha-Wa Days Fall Festival. Autumn Celebration with arts and crafts fair, antique flea market, street carnival, food, entertainment, and parade. Downtown Dells.

October. Autumn Color Tours. Authentic steam train tours amid brilliant hues of autumn. Held the first two weekends in October at the Mid-Continent Railway Museum, North Freedom.

November. Dells Jazz Festival. Jazz bands converge at the Holiday Inn, Inn of the Dells, and the Dell View Resort.

Other Recommended Restaurants and Lodgings

Wisconsin Dells

Bahama Bay Resort, 131 Canyon Road on Lake Delton; (608) 254–2584. Deluxe suites with microwave, fridge, stove top, dishware, and more in a beautiful setting. Rooms also come with whirlpools if you choose. The outdoor pool has a waterfall, and there's a boating dock too. Peak season rates range from $119 to $159 per night.

Chula Vista Resort, 4031 North River Road; (800) 38–VISTA. One of the more luxurious accommodations in the area. Lush suites with Jacuzzis, two-person bathtubs, and big-screen TVs. Indoor/outdoor pools, health club, tennis courts, Las Vegas–type nightclub. Secluded on fifty-five pine-studded acres along the Wisconsin River. During peak season, rates range from $89 to $225 per night.

Dell View Resort, 501 East Adams; (800) 87–DELLS or (608) 253–1261. Although this lodging has been around since the roaring twenties, everything is modern and very comfortable. Situated on 180 acres, it includes an 18-hole championship golf course, indoor and outdoor pools, Jacuzzi, tennis, and a live comedy showcase during the summer months. Whirlpool suites are available. Peak season rates range from $70 to $120 per night.

Field's Steak 'N Stein, Highway 13; (608) 254–4841. A local favorite that serves prime rib, steaks, and seafood.

The Polynesian Suite Hotel, Highway 13 at exit 87; (608) 254–2883. With its Polynesian theme, this hotel is geared more for the kids. A great waterslide, a hidden cave, and kiddie play areas can be found as can nice indoor and outdoor pools for the adults. Peak season rates range from $115 to $210 per night.

Lake Delton

House of Embers, Highway 12, (608) 253–6411. A family-owned restaurant with classic American cuisine, especially known for hickory-smoked ribs. For intimate dining ask for the Omar Shariff room (a private booth for two).

Jimmy's Del-Bar, Highway 12; (608) 253–1861. Seafood and steaks are the specialties here. Atmosphere is casual. Reservations aren't required, but they are definitely recommended. Desserts are homemade and include tantalizing chocolate torte, pecan pie, key lime pie, and cheesecake.

For More Information

Baraboo Chamber of Commerce, 124 Second Street, Baraboo, WI 53913. (608) 356–8333.

Wisconsin Dells Visitor and Convention Bureau, 701 Superior Street, P.O. Box 390, Wisconsin Dells, WI 53965-0390. (800) 22–DELLS or (608) 254–8088.

Platteville and Mineral Point

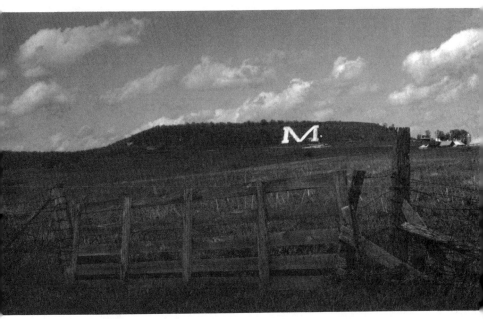

M is for mining at the state university's school of engineering in Platteville.

Bear Hunting in Wisconsin
with a Side of Swiss

_____ 2 NIGHTS _____

Football summer camp • Antiques • Arts and crafts •
Camping • Hiking • Museums • Festivals • Cheese tours

Every year from about the end of July through mid-August, the favorite sport in Platteville is Bear watching.

For rabid fans, Platteville is sheer heaven. Here, on the University
of Wisconsin's Platteville campus, is where the Chicago Bears have
trained since 1984.

The primary objective of the hordes of fans is to catch the twice-daily scrimmages. That's easy. Just pull up a lawn chair or a blanket. The hard part is getting accommodations.

The best advice is to book ahead. It used to be that a Platteville visit could be delightfully spontaneous, but no more. Each year, the crowds get bigger and a weekend takes more and more planning. If you are aced out, either consider a midweek getaway, use a more distant town as your base of operations, or consider the camping alternative.

Even if you're not a Bears fan, you don't have to spend the weekend hibernating. There are some other diversions in Platteville. Or even better, you can parlay a Bears weekend into something more.

Platteville is situated amid the hills and valleys of southern Wisconsin, and you can take side trips to Mineral Point, which has some top-notch crafts shopping; New Glarus, known as America's Little Switzerland; and Monroe, cheese capital of the Dairy State. All are easy drives from one another. The area bleeds into Madison and its environs (Wisconsin Escape Three), and Platteville's location makes even out-of-state forays accessible. (Galena and Dubuque are a mere thirty minutes away; see Illinois Escape Five).

Day 1

Morning

Take I–90 west to Rockford and hook up with U.S. Highway 20 west to Galena.

Lunch: **Silver Annie's Ltd.,** 124 North Commerce Street in Galena. Phone (815) 777–3131. Good for sandwiches, salads, and Italian specialties.

Afternoon

Take Highway 151 north to Platteville, about a half-hour's drive. Head right to the stadium, where afternoon scrimmage starts at about 2 P.M. Hang around after all the knees and ankles have been unwrapped and you may even get an autograph.

Dinner: **Timbers Supper Club,** Highways 151 and 80–81; (608) 348–2406. Known for its sprawling sirloins, it has surprisingly good seafood as well. Baking done on premises. Like everywhere else, the lines can get long during Bears camp. Eat early or late to avoid the crunch. Moderate.

There are two primary ways to occupy your evening hours in Platteville and they could not be at more extreme ends of the entertainment spectrum.

The first is hanging out at one of the many drinking establishments on Mineral Street. Places like Freddie's Bar, Jobie's Tap, and The Patio

Lounge not only give you a ready forum for your own preseason analysis, but you also have a pretty good chance of catching the players downing a few beers.

The second option is the **Wisconsin Shakespeare Festival,** which runs from early July to early August. Said one Shakespeare fan: "The quality is equal to that of Spring Green (home of the highly acclaimed American Players Theatre). The only difference is that you're seated in an indoor theater with cushions and air-conditioning." Call the university box office for the schedule: (608) 342–1298.

Lodging: **The Governor Dodge/Best Western Motor Inn,** Highway 151 near junction with Highway 80; (608) 348–2301. The amenities include an indoor pool, a sauna, and cable TV. The Bears' practice field is 5 blocks away. Rates range from $48 to $56 per night.

Day 2

Morning

Breakfast: Governor Dodge Coffee Shop.

No doubt those who are interested in football are already queuing up for the morning scrimmage. But if you have kids whose fascination with linebackers is dwindling, try the **Mining Museum** and **Rollo Jamison Museum,** 405 East Main Street. The big hit here is descending the ninety or so steps into the Bevans Lead Mine, circa 1845, and riding the iron-ore cars around the museum grounds. At the Rollo Jamison Museum, you can view carriages, farm implements, and other turn-of-the-century artifacts. Admission to both: adults, $3.50; children, $1.50. Open daily, 9 A.M.–4 P.M., Memorial Day through Labor Day. Check hours during the rest of the year. Phone (608) 348–3301.

After all that mining stuff, get the lead out with an afternoon in Mineral Point, just about twenty minutes north on Highway 151. This region is known as the Uplands, because it was the only area not covered by glaciers. Like Platteville, Mineral Point's history is tied to mining, but today it is known as a center for arts and crafts.

Lunch: If you'd like to experience a real small-town diner, save your midday meal for the **Red Rooster,** 158 High Street; (608–987–9936). This is Mineral Point's main street. Don't miss an opportunity to try a Cornish pasty (rhymes with "nasty" but it's really quite a delicious turnover, stuffed with meat and potatoes). The homemade pies are blue-ribbon quality, and the prices are equally old-fashioned.

Afternoon

Check out **Pendarvis,** 114 Shake Rag Street. This group of six carefully restored stone and log houses were originally built by Cornish miners in the 1840s. A few blocks away is **Shake Rag Valley,** which consists of restored businesses and homes of artisans. The name comes from the custom of women shaking dishrags from the doorway as a signal to their husbands in the mines that the noon meal was ready. Open from May to October only. Phone (608) 987–2122. Adults, $4.00; children, $1.50; family rate, $10.00.

Down the road is the **Looms,** a former stone brewery that has been converted to a place where local weavers demonstrate their craft. In addition, their beautiful hand-woven art is for sale, usually at much lower prices than what you would find in the city. Phone (608) 987–2277.

There are numerous antique stores and galleries on High Street. Start at the top of High Street at the **Mineral Point Antiques Center,** which houses seventeen dealers. Artisans on High Street that are particularly worth noting include Bruce Howdle (architectural pottery), Jennifer Sharp (watercolors) and her husband, John (Western wood carvings), and Jill Engels (stained glass). The Mineral Point Artisans Guild publishes a map showing the various galleries and studios.

Dinner: **Chesterfield Inn,** 20 Commerce Street, Mineral Point; (608) 987–3682. This 1834 Cornish stone stagecoach-house-turned-restaurant features Cornish specialties, as well as standard American fare. In the summer, it's delightful to dine on the patio. Moderate.

After dinner, return to your base at the Governor Dodge Motor Inn in Platteville.

Day 3

Morning

Breakfast: If you return to Mineral Point, the Red Rooster is a very popular gathering spot for breakfast, and it's open every day.

Travel another twenty minutes north from Mineral Point and see Spring Green, site of The House on the Rock, Wisconsin's number-one tourist attraction.

Bargain-hunter's alert: **Land's End** (men's and women's wear) is headquartered in Dodgeville, just north of Mineral Point. The prices are better than what you'll find at Chicago outlets.

Head to **New Glarus** in time for lunch, which is fortuitous timing because New Glarus is the perfect town for people who love to eat. Known as "America's Little Switzerland," the town lives up to its culinary heritage, from cheese to chocolate. Indeed, many of the residents still speak Swiss.

Lunch: **New Glarus Hotel,** 100 Sixth Avenue, looks like a gingerbread castle with flowers overflowing from every balcony and window box. Don't miss the roesti (hash browns swimming in cheese and butter). Other traditional fare includes fondue, which really hits the spot when there's a chill in the air. If you're here on a weekend night, you can also work up quite a sweat dancing to the lively polka band. Phone (608) 527-5244. Moderate.

Afternoon

After lunch, browse some of the shops that specialize in old-world goods. Snatch up lace from **Swiss Miss Lace Factory** (which you can tour during the week), sausages from **Ruef's Meat Market,** and music boxes and clocks from just about everywhere.

No matter that you just ate lunch. If you have time for only one stop, make it the **New Glarus Bakery & Tea Room,** 534 First Street. During the holiday season there are people who come all the way from Chicago just to buy the stollen—a moist dense bread studded with almonds and raisins. Baking begins November and continues until Christmas. Phone (608) 527-2916.

A more touristlike experience can be had at the **Swiss Historic Village,** 612 Seventh Avenue. The Swiss immigrant experience is retold by friendly guides who lead you through original and replica buildings. Open May–October; (608) 527-2317.

The **Chalet of the Golden Fleece,** an authentic mountain-style chalet is the other significant museum. The chalet contains Swiss antiques and collectibles. It is located at 618 Second Street. Open May–October. Phone (608) 527-2614.

En route home, continue south on Highway 69 to Monroe, where you'll find yourself in prime cheesehead territory. In this small town alone, four factories offer tours. The biggest is **Zim's** (657 Second Street; 608-325-7808). Free tours are offered between 8 A.M. and noon (other times by prearranged request). Even if you don't hook up with a tour, you'll certainly have a good time stocking up on all varieties at the retail store.

There's More

Cycling. Military Ridge State Trail, which goes between Dodgeville and Verona, is particularly scenic. The 39-mile trail, developed on an abandoned Northwestern Railroad line, has a gentle grade of only 2 percent. For a guide, call (608) 935-2315. In New Glarus, try the 23-mile Sugar River State Trail, which runs to Brodhead; phone (608) 935-2315.

Camping. Closest site to the Bears is Mound View Park, Platteville's city campground (with electricity and shower facilities). Also, check out the two state parks, Blue Mound (outside Mt. Horeb) and Governor

Dodge (near Dodgeville, about 15 miles south of Spring Green).

Cross-country skiing. Military Ridge or Governor Dodge State Park, which is the second largest state park and has exceptionally well-groomed trails. (But be on the lookout for wild turkeys.)

Downhill skiing. Tyrol Ski Basin, 5 miles west of Mt. Horeb. Ten runs; longest run: 1,700 feet; vertical drop: 386 feet. Rentals, instruction, lodge. Phone (608) 437–4135.

Fishing. Blackhawk Lake (crappie, blue gill). Also small streams in the area are known for bass and trout. Best course is Locoma in East Dubuque, about twenty minutes away.

Golf. Edelweiss Chalet Golf Course, Edelweiss Road. This lush course is Green County's only public eighteen-hole course. Phone (608) 527–2315.

Hiking. Military Ridge State Trail and Governor Dodge State Park.

Horseback riding. Governor Dodge State Park offers extensive bridle paths.

Special Events

August. Flavors of Old Cornwall. Demonstrations by costumed guides as they cook Old World favorites. Mineral Point.

September. Wilhelm Tell Drama and Festival. English version of the famous drama in outdoor setting. New Glarus. (608) 527–2095.

September. Monroe Cheese Days. Farm and factory tours. Cow-milking contests. Dances, food, parade. Monroe.

Other Recommended Lodgings

Mineral Point

The Duke House, 618 Maiden Street; (608) 987–2821. This Colonial house has three rooms furnished with antique beds and other collectibles. Tea and wine are served in the afternoon. Rates range from $30 to $40, which includes homemade coffee cake for breakfast. Shared bath.

The Wilson House Inn, 110 Dodge Street; (608) 987–3600. 1853 red-brick Federal mansion. Four rooms, some with private baths. Full breakfast included. Rates: $45–$60.

New Glarus

Chalet Landhaus, 801 Highway 69; (608) 527–5234. A comfortable but Spartan hotel. Some rooms with whirlpool baths. Good for cyclists because of proximity to Sugar River bike trail. Rates: $42–$80.

Platteville

Mound View Motel, 1455 East U.S. Highway 151; (608) 348–9518. Downscale from the Governor Dodge, but clean and convenient.

For More Information

Mineral Point Chamber of Commerce, 237 High Street, Mineral Point, WI 53565. (608) 987–3201.

New Glarus Tourism, P.O. Box 713, New Glarus, WI 53574. (608) 527–2095.

Platteville Chamber of Commerce, 97 East Main Street, Platteville, WI 53818. (608) 348–8888.

Oshkosh and Horicon Marsh

Exact replica of Lindberg's *Spirit of St. Louis* at the EAA Air Adventure Museum

Come Fly with Me

_____ 2 NIGHTS _____

Aviation · Fishing · Hiking · Outlet shops · Museums · Geese migration

For one week every year, this quiet community—otherwise known for overalls—has the busiest airport in the world. That fact may not sound too appealing to travelers weary of O'Hare, but if you love aviation and it's late July, you don't want to be anywhere but Oshkosh.

The Experimental Aircraft Association (EAA) Fly-In and convention is the world's largest aviation event, attracting more than 800,000 people and 15,000 planes. Visitors peruse row upon row of aircraft ranging from antique classics to warbirds to NASA's latest technology. If talking "wingspan" and "cruising altitude" isn't your idea of a good time, stick around. A highlight of each day's activity is the airshow, when various sizes and configurations of aircraft make fly-bys over Wittman Field. Thousands of spectators crane their necks to get a better view of wingwalkers and daredevil pilots performing aerial stunts on such aircraft as Hawker Hurricanes and deHaviland Mosquitos. The show starts at 4 P.M. every day during the Fly-In except Sunday, when it starts at 3 P.M.

Less awesome but just as important to aviation junkies are the forums and workshops, which have brought in such name speakers as Chuck Yeager and Wally Schirra.

Even if you can't schedule a visit during the Fly-In, it's possible to experience some of the city's aviation fever anytime at the EAA Air Adventure Museum.

If you're not into aviation, you won't be grounded. Oshkosh is also home to two other exceptional attractions: the Oshkosh Public Museum and the Paine Art Center and Arboretum. Add some excellent fishing and off-price shopping, and you have a weekend that offers something for everybody.

Day 1

Morning

Plan on a three-hour drive to Oshkosh. Head north on I–94 to Highway 41. About 40 miles outside of Milwaukee, go west on Highway 33. This route will take you through **Horicon Marsh,** where 31,000 federally protected acres serve as a wildlife refuge—the largest in the United States. Each fall, tourists flock here, too, eager to breathe in the crisp, cool air and to enjoy the fiery hues of red and gold. But mostly they come to listen to the call of geese overhead.

Starting in late September and through October, tens of thousands of migrating Canada geese use the marsh as a layover on their way south. There are so many that the sky will actually blacken. (Be prepared to stop; everybody rubbernecks.) For a really good look, take a pontoon ride with **Blue Heron Tours,** on Highway 33, right near the bridge. Or, if you'd rather be your own captain, you can rent a canoe. Tours are daily from Memorial Day to Labor Day and on weekends only during September and October. (414) 485–2942.

Lunch: Pack a lunch at home and enjoy it here at Horicon Marsh, amid the cattails and the marsh grass. If you'd rather stop here on the way home, the sunsets are legendary.

Afternoon

Continue on Highway 26 north through Waupun. Downtown is a rugged **statue of Chief John Big Tree,** the Indian who was the model for the buffalo nickel. At Fond du Lac, 26 hooks up with Highway 41; then it's smooth sailing to Oshkosh.

After you arrive in Oshkosh, you might want to spend the rest of the afternoon bargain-hunting in the town's outlet stores. Check out the **Manufacturer's Marketplace,** 3001 Washburn (off Highway 41), located just across from the Air Adventure Museum. Brand name outlet stores include Royal Doulton, Dansk, Oshkosh B'Gosh, and J.H. Collectibles. Elsewhere, there is additional off-price shopping at Carolina Designs (627 Bay Shore Drive), the factory outlet for Lenox candles, soaps, and accessories. The Company Store (901 South Main Street) is an outlet for down comforters, outerwear, and pillows.

Dinner: One of Oshkosh's most popular restaurants, **Butch's Anchor Inn** (225 West Twentieth Street) has been the place to go for seafood since the early seventies. It features a nautical atmosphere, including piranhas in the fish tanks. Entrees range from $11 to $17. Reservations recommended. (414) 236–5360.

Lodging: **Pioneer Inn,** 1000 Pioneer Drive (on Kini Island). The Pioneer is situated on Lake Winnebago, which puts it a little farther away from the center of things, but gives it an edge in atmosphere. Extras include indoor and outdoor pools, whirlpool, tennis courts, miniature golf, and marina facilities. Rooms are well furnished and some suites are available. Prices range from $68 to $85 per night. (414) 233–1980.

Day 2

Morning

Breakfast: The Pioneer has an excellent coffee shop, with the obligatory Wisconsin sausage to go with an omelet.

Start your day at the **EAA Air Adventure Museum** (3000 Poberezny Road, just off Highway 41 at Highway 44). It houses more than ninety planes—the largest private collection of aircraft in the world. In addition, there are several mini-theaters throughout the museum, including one designed especially for future flyers under twelve years old, and a gift shop that the kids will go crazy for. Open daily (closed New Year's Day, Easter, Thanksgiving, and Christmas), 8:30 A.M.–5:00 P.M.; Sunday, 11 A.M.–5 P.M. Adults, $5.00; kids, $4.00; family rate, $15.00. (414) 426–4800.

Lunch: From the museum, travel about five minutes north to **Field's Restaurant,** on the corner of Ninth and Knapp streets. Actually, this funky little spot will fit in just about anywhere in your schedule. Not only can you get breakfast all day, but you can also choose from a good selection of salads and other healthy fare for lunch or a casual dinner. The ice cream shop scoops up a wicked hot fudge sundae (in addition to thirty-seven other flavors). And, just for good measure, there's a tour of the adjacent cheese shop, which stocks some sixty varieties. Open until 11 P.M. daily, until 11:30 P.M. on weekends. (414) 231–9975.

Afternoon

Take in the **Paine Art Center and Arboretum** (1410 Algoma Boulevard). A truly lovely Tudor Revival, the Paine Art Center and Arboretum was designed in the 1920s as the baronial residence of Oshkosh lumber mogul Nathan Paine. Construction was halted during the Depression but was resumed in the 1940s. Finally, in 1946, the Paines donated the home to the city, without ever having lived there themselves.

Today the public can enjoy the magnificent paintings, beautiful tapestries, and decorative arts, all displayed in period rooms representing the sixteenth through the nineteenth centuries. The five-acre arboretum changes with the seasons. Open Tuesday–Saturday, 10:00 A.M.–4:30 P.M.; Sunday, 1:00–4:30 P.M. A donation is requested. (414) 235–4530.

Dinner: The **Granary Restaurant,** 50 West Sixth Street, is a historic (1883) stone mill that has been converted into a very amiable restaurant. Prime rib is the specialty of the house, but there are always some seafood selections on the menu. The restaurant also has a children's menu, as well as a decent wine list. (414) 233–3929. Moderate.

Lodging: Pioneer Inn.

Day 3

Morning

Breakfast: Pioneer Coffee Shop.

Complete your visit to the trio of museums with **Oshkosh Public Museum,** just a stone's throw from the Paine (1331 Algoma Boulevard). The most popular attraction is easily the Apostles Clock, which sends twelve figures rotating every hour on the hour. Another favorite is the exhibit of stuffed animals (as in taxidermy, not toys). Its woodland settings are amazingly lifelike.

On the grounds adjacent to the museum are a replica train depot and fire station. Historians take note: The museum's reference library and archives, consisting of an impressive collection of manuscripts, photographs, maps, and other material, are available to the public, by appointment. The museum is open Tuesday–Saturday, 9 A.M.–5 P.M.; Sunday, 1–5 P.M. Free. (414) 236–5150.

Before returning home, take a slight detour and head north on Highway 44 for about twenty minutes to **Neenah** to fit in the **Bergstrom Mahler Museum** (165 North Park Avenue; 414–722–4658). The museum's collection of 1,700 glass paperweights is considered by some to be even more encompassing than the Art Institute's. Donation. Open Tuesday–Friday, 10:00 A.M.–4:30 P.M.; weekends, 1:00–4:30 P.M. Downtown Neenah also has some cute shops that are worth browsing.

There's More

Grand Opera House, 100 High Avenue; (414) 236–5290. This was the place for entertainment between Minneapolis and Chicago. Built in 1883, the Grand attracted some great touring stars, including Will Rogers and Sarah Bernhardt. It prospered through the early twentieth century, but in the 1940s it was converted to a movie theater and began to deteriorate. Thanks to some civic-minded folks, it has been restored to its original elegance and is now a fully functional center for performing arts. Private tours last about sixty to ninety minutes; call for an appointment.

Camping. Circle R Campground, 5703 Knapp Street; (414) 235–8909. Also features free shuttle service during Fly-In.

High Cliff State Park, High Cliff Road, Menasha; (414) 989–1106. About thirty minutes north of Oshkosh (on Highway 55), near Neenah, is High Cliff, long a favorite for its stone bluffs. Besides camping, the park has facilities for horseback riding, hiking, cross-country skiing, and snowmobiling.

Fishing. Oshkosh is situated on Lake Winnebago, the largest inland lake in the state, and fishing is a big part of life in the city. While fishing is a year-round activity, peak season is May 5–June 3. Good for walleye, perch, and white bass. Licenses may be obtained at local sporting goods stores and many bars. Also, with an abundance of marinas, boat rentals are easy and affordable.

Boating/Marinas. Fox River Marina (501 South Main Street; 414–235–2340), Gehrke's Marine Supply (1102 North Main Street; 414–235–3337).

Golf. Oshkosh has four eighteen-hole courses: Far-Vu (4985 Van Dyne Road; 414–231–2631); Lakeshore Municipal (2175 Punhoqua Road; 414–236–5090), Utica (3350 Knott Road; 414–233–4446), and Westhaven (1400 Westhaven Drive; 414–233-4640).

Special Events

Late July–early August. EAA International Fly-In Convention (see pg. 102). Whittman Regional Airport, 20th Avenue at Oregon Street. (414) 426–4800.

September (first Saturday after Labor Day). E.K. Petrie's Indian Artifact and Antique Sale. Oshkosh Public Museum grounds. (414) 236–5150.

Other Recommended Restaurants and Lodgings

Oshkosh

Great Wall Restaurant, 700 North Koeller Road; (414) 231–1828. The lunch buffet is a very good bargain.

Holiday Inn Holidome, U.S. Highway 41 at Ninth Avenue; (414) 233–1511. This is an upscale property with lots of amenities, including pool, whirlpool, and sauna. $52–$85 per night.

Hunan, 323 North Main Street; (414) 235–0122. Special lunch buffet and Sunday night dinner buffet. Ample selection of Szechuan entrees as well.

Lara's Tortilla Flats, 715 North Main Street; (414) 233–4400. Very good tacos, enchiladas, and burritos. Large selection of Mexican beers.

Marco's Italian Gardens, 2605 Jackson Drive; (414) 236–5376. Straightforward Italian food, served in a garden atmosphere. The owners also operate the nearby Vitale's.

Oshkosh Hilton and Convention Centre, 1 Main Street; (414) 231–5000. Located in the heart of downtown near the Fox River. All rooms overlook the water. Pool, whirlpool, gameroom. Rates: $45–$80 per night.

For More Information

Oshkosh Convention and Tourism Bureau, 2 North Main Street, Oshkosh, WI 54903. (414) 236–5250.

Kohler

The American Club in Kohler entices weary travelers with luxury amenities.

Plumbing and Pampering

——————————————— 2 NIGHTS ———————————————

Spa · Hiking · Hunting · Fishing · Golf ·
Wildlife refuge · Art galleries · Antiques · Crafts

Kohler—known for bathroom fixtures—doesn't sound like it would be a particularly sumptuous place to spend a weekend. But most people leap at the chance to spend even a single night at The American Club, recognized as one of the finest hotels in the country and the primary reason people make the trek to this small town near Sheboygan. Since 1986 The American Club has earned the prestigious AAA five-diamond award, a claim that can be made by only one other hotel in the Midwest (the Four Seasons in Chicago). It also ranked as the seventh-best resort in the country by the ultrasophisticated readers of *Condé Nast Traveler.*

Kohler is less than a three-hour drive from the big city, but it feels as if it's a world away. Built in 1918 to provide housing for the European immigrants who came to Kohler to work, the club was listed on the National Register of Historic Places in 1978. Two years later, it was completely renovated as a luxury resort.

Since this is the town that bills itself as the plumbing capital of the United States, you'd expect your room to have a nice bathroom, but are you ready for one with a greenhouse and a whirlpool? When you've reached the point of "prune," slip into the fluffy terrycloth robes that are provided for your stay. (They're also available for purchase.) Also impressive is the quality of the other furnishings, from crystal chandeliers to Oriental rugs to down comforters.

Day 1

Morning

The three-hour trip to Kohler is an easy one along I–94 to I–43. A stop in picturesque **Cedarburg,** about 17 miles north of Milwaukee, is an excellent idea, since check-in time at The American Club is not until midafternoon.

The attraction in Cedarburg is the town itself, which has been designated a National Historic District. The venerable limestone mill, the church spires, the horse-drawn carriages that clip-clop through the streets in the summer all make this a charming destination, but it almost didn't happen. Some twenty years ago, Cedarburg Woolen Mill, built circa 1864, was scheduled for demolition. A visionary city council saved it from the wrecker's ball, and it now is known as the **Cedar Creek Settlement,** a collection of thirty shops, boutiques, restaurants, and galleries. One of the tenants, the **Stone Mill Winery** (N70 W6340 Bridge Road; 414–377–8020), offers a forty-five minute free tour that includes sampling. Don't miss the upstairs, where you'll find more artisans. The pottery is especially attractive.

If you haven't had your craft fix, the **Brewery Works** (W62 N718 Riveredge Drive; 414–377–7220) is home to more artists, this time in a converted 1843 brewery.

You'll find a thriving business district, dominated by antique shops.

Washington Avenue Antiques (china, jewelry, furniture) and **Grandpa's Barn Antiques** (where merchandise is displayed in roomlike settings) are among the best. You don't need to be a rock hound to enjoy **The Gem House,** which has more than 100,000 pounds of rocks for sale. We didn't have the time, but you can really get a feel for the district by taking a self-guided walking tour. (Maps are available from the Cedarburg Visitor Information Center in City Hall, W6 N645 Washington Avenue; 414–377–9620.)

Lunch: **Victor's,** in the heart of downtown Cedarburg, is a very classy lunch spot, where entrees are closer to julienne of veal frangelico (the house specialty) than a burger and fries. Prices range from $6.00–$10.00 (414) 375–1777.

There are some other very good lunch options that are more casual, but if you really want something low-key, consider stopping at **Covered Bridge Park** (junction of I–43 and Highway 60 at Five Corners) for a picnic. Not only are there excellent picnic facilities at water's edge, but the park also is the site of the last covered bridge in Wisconsin.

Afternoon

Continue traveling north on I–43. Take exit 126 to **The American Club** in Kohler.

Attention to detail is what gives the American Club an international reputation, which comes at a price—even by Chicago standards. All rooms have whirlpool baths and European comforters and are appointed with hand-crafted woodwork and furniture. But rooms in categories 3 and 4 are more spacious, with amenities such as sitting areas, wet bars, and oversized whirlpools. Category 5 is the most deluxe, with a patio area, for example.

If those extras are important to you, splurge on a more expensive room. If you don't spend that much time in your room but are eager to try everything from the game preserve to the racquet club, save the money. (All guests have the same access to the facilities, regardless of their accommodations.) Room rates range from $122 to $292 per night (slightly less November–April). Special weekend packages for two start at about $330 to $780, with varying meals and services included. (414) 457–8000 or (800) 344–2838.

Dinner: If you are feeling flush, dine at the **Immigrant,** which is the resort's most elegant restaurant. Prices start at about $20 and go up from there—and it's strictly a la carte. Again, the extras, which include monogrammed silver, palate cleansers of lemon sorbet served in crystal flutes, and impeccable service (two servers per table), help justify the freight. This is beef country, and the London broil is excellent. Sautéed shrimp is also a winner. If you still have some room left on the credit card, tell 'em to roll the pastry cart your way. Jacket and reservations required. In fact, this is such a popular spot, if you have your heart set on dining here, book a table as soon as you arrive at the resort.

Day 2

Morning

Breakfast: In the **Wisconsin Room,** the hotel's classic dining room, you can load up on the all-you-can-eat buffet. At $16.95, it's not cheap but will keep you going all day.

You'll need it for the 2½-mile tour of the **Kohler Company,** 101 Upper Road; (414) 457–4441. How often do you get to see how toilets are made?

Settings in the 36,000-square foot exhibition hall range from the traditional to the futuristic. The free tour takes a little more than two hours, and if you really want to see optimum activity, avoid Fridays, when many of the craftspeople have the day off. You must be fourteen years old, and reservations are required. Tours leave at 8:30 A.M. weekdays.

If you're more interested in the finished product rather than the process, head over to the **Design Center,** where you can see many room vignettes featuring state-of-the-art kitchens and baths. The center is open daily and admission is free. (414) 457–3699.

Across the street from the Design Center is **The Shops at Woodlake,** an inviting shopping complex. Worth seeking out is **Artspace,** which is a gallery of the John Michael Kohler Art Center. You'll find a very well-edited selection of porcelain, earthenware, jewelry, and glass. (The hotel provides complimentary transportation for guests on request.)

Lunch: Ready to eat? Depending on your mood, the shopping center offers two good dining options: **Cucina** and **Woodlake Market.** Cucina features moderately priced Italian cuisine. Enjoy al fresco lakeside dining in season and carryout service year-round. (414) 452–3888. Woodlake is a New York–style deli, with a very impressive selection of meats, cheeses, and gourmet foods. With a few tables and a dessert shop, this is just right for an impromptu snack. (414) 457–6570.

Afternoon

Depending on the season, hike (or cross-country ski) the 30 miles of wilderness trails at **River Wildlife,** a private game preserve for hotel guests only. Fishing (salmon is the catch of the day), canoeing, and hunting (pheasant) are also available for the outdoor enthusiast. In balmy weather this is an ideal spot for a picnic, or stop at **Log**

Cabin Lodge for lunch daily or dinner on weekends. Here you can glimpse deer strolling right up to the dining room windows.

Speaking of fairways, the golf course at **Blackwolf Run,** 111 West Riverside Drive, is considered a real challenge. Designed by Peter Dye, it was rated the best new public course in 1988 by *Golf Digest.*

You could always move your fitness indoors and schedule a visit to the **Sports Core** (on the resort grounds) where you can play a few sets of tennis, join in an aerobics class, or swim laps. The 2.2-mile jogging trail meanders through wildflowers (walkers welcome, too). Follow your regimen with some much-needed pampering at the salon. You'll be greeted with a cup of herbal tea that is just the beginning of a hedonistic experience that can include facials, manicures, massages, and a hairstyling. Don't worry if you have kids in tow; a child care center is right on the premises.

Dinner: If you want to try a more casual restaurant in the complex, the **Horse & Plow** is a glorified tavern, with pub fare such as hamburgers. Inexpensive.

After dinner, stop by the **Greenhouse,** a glassed-in gazebo that serves desserts, ice cream, and liqueurs.

Day 3

Morning

Breakfast: Wisconsin Room.

The American Club may be the most famous place in the area, but it's certainly not the only one on the map.

Take Highway 23 about 15 miles west to the town of Greenbush and the **Old Wade House and Wisconsin Carriage Museum.** Built in 1853 as a stagecoach inn, the Old Wade House was a stop on the trail between Sheboygan and Fond du Lac. The home is completely furnished in period antiques and open for tours, which also take in a smokehouse, blacksmith shop, and maple-sugaring cabin. The adjacent carriage museum features more than 100 carriages, wagons, and sleighs from the nineteenth and early twentieth centuries. Open daily, 9 A.M.–5 P.M.; May–October. Admission: adults, $4.00; children, $1.50; family rate, $10.00. Ticket sales end one hour before closing. (414) 526–3271.

Return east on 23, past Kohler, and into Sheboygan, home of the **John Michael Kohler Arts Center** (608 New York Avenue; 414–458–6144). This former family mansion has been transformed into a gallery of contemporary American arts. Open daily, noon–5 P.M.

The **Sheboygan County Museum** is at 3110 Erie Avenue. Built in 1848, it is another home-turned-museum. Each room has a theme, such as children's toys or antique farm machinery. And, this being Wisconsin, there's a fitting homage to a nineteenth-century cheese factory. (414) 458–1103. Open April–October, Tuesday–Saturday, 10 A.M.–5 P.M.; Sunday, 1–5 P.M. Admission: adults, $2.00; children, $1.00.

Lunch: You can't leave Sheboygan without having a "brat," slathered with mustard, and a brew. Try **Randall's Sports Emporium,** 539 Riverfront Drive, which also offers a view of the shoreline. In true Wisconsin style, the beer selection is staggering. For dessert try the frozen custard, which changes daily. (414) 457–9050.

There's More

Sheboygan Indian Mound Park, Twelfth Street and Panther Avenue, Sheboygan. This park contains eighteen of the original thirty-four effigy burial mounds of early Woodland Indians, circa A.D. 500–1000. The park has a self-guided mound and trail tour.

Kohler-Andrae State Park, 1520 Old Park Road (off City Road KK), 7 miles south of Sheboygan; (414) 452–3457. A lovely stretch of dunes and beach, as well as the **Sanderling Nature Center.** Camping and riding trails are also available.

Waelderhaus, West Riverside Drive, Kohler; (414) 452–4079. A reproduction of a home in Bregenzerwald, Austria, where the Kohler family originated is open for tours.

Special Events

Early March. Antique Weekend features fine antiques on display, as well as clinics and forums conducted by experts in various fields. At The American Club.

June. Strawberry Festival. Strawberry desserts, contest, and all-you-can-eat strawberry pancake breakfast. Cedarburg.

July. Sousa Concert. Annual concert features the very same forty-eight-star American flag used when John Philip Sousa made his concert debut here in 1919. At The American Club.

July. Outdoor Arts Festival. The John Michael Kohler Arts Center holds an arts and crafts show, featuring 125 juried artists. Sheboygan.

August. Bratwurst Day. Carnival, entertainment. Sheboygan.

Early November. Wisconsin Holiday Market includes arts and crafts to kick off the holiday season. At The American Club.

November. Christmas in the Country. Wisconsin crafts, decorations. Cedarburg.

Other Recommended Restaurants and Lodgings

Cedarburg

Barth's at the Bridge, 194 Columbia Drive; (414) 377–0660. Regional American cooking (homemade soups, ribs, delectable desserts) served in an early American setting of candlelit rooms and antique clocks. Children's menu.

Stagecoach Inn, W61 N520 Washington Avenue; (414) 375–0208. These twelve rooms are not as luxe as the Washington House (below), but filled with the same charm and graciousness. Some rooms have whirlpools. The inn also features a pub, a chocolate shop, and a bookstore. Continental breakfast features warm, flaky croissants. Rates: $55–$85 per night.

Washington House Inn, W62 N573 Washington Avenue; (414) 375–3550. Lovers of Victoriana should put this B&B on their must list. The 1886 "cream city brick" building right in the heart of the historic district is terrifically cozy. Some of the twenty-nine rooms have fireplaces, some have whirlpool baths, all have antiques, down-filled comforters, and fresh flowers. Rates range from $60 to $130 and include an afternoon wine-and-cheese social hour and breakfast.

Plymouth

52 Stafford, 52 Stafford Street; (414) 893–0552. This is one of those inns that makes it onto everybody's "best" lists, so as long as you're so close (about 15 miles west of Sheboygan), you may want to add an extra night to your weekend just to see what all the fuss is about. The imported brass chandeliers, cherry hardwoods, and leaded glass makes this Irish guest house a place to behold. There are twenty rooms, but the real center of activity is the bar, where Guiness Stout flows freely. The rates of $85 per night include continental breakfast.

For More Information

Cedarburg Visitors Information Center, W63 N645 Washington Avenue, Cedarburg, WI 53012. (414) 377–9620.

Sheboygan Area Convention and Visitors Bureau, 631 New York Avenue, Sheboygan, WI 53081. (414) 457–9495.

Door County

Door County's exhilarating lakeshore

Cape Cod of the Midwest

_____ 3 NIGHTS _____

Biking • Boating • Hiking • Galleries/Shopping •
Theater/Concerts • Fishing • Artists colony

You can easily spend a month in Door County, the finger of land that juts out from Wisconsin into Lake Michigan and Green Bay, so trying to distill the experience into a weekend is a formidable task.

With some 250 miles of shoreline (ranging from smooth beaches to rugged limestone), five state parks, and more antique shops and gift boutiques than you could ever visit, it's no surprise that this has been one of the most popular spots in the Midwest for more than a century. After all, how many counties have not one maritime museum, but two? That's but one indication of just how strongly Door County has always depended on water for its livelihood—from fishing to shipbuilding.

Such geography has always been a magnet for artists, eager to capture its serene beauty on canvas. Then came the galleries and vacationers, and before you knew it, traffic was bumper-to-bumper on

Highway 42 every weekend from June until Labor Day. Yet Door County has somehow managed to retain its small-town charm.

From Chicago, it's a long ride (about 250 miles), so if you don't want to spend your entire weekend driving, save this trip for a three-day weekend. One good way to pick up an extra day at no additional cost is to come during the off season, when bargains abound. Door County has a wealth of wonderful little inns that seem especially cozy when the weather turns chilly. Nordic skiers can take advantage of more than 100 miles of cross-country ski and snowmobile trails.

While there is a lot to see and do, the peninsula is only 18 miles across at its widest point, which makes getting around easy. (Highway 42 goes up the Green Bay side; Highway 57 goes up the Lake Michigan side.) The string of towns that run along the thumb each have their own personality, from Sturgeon Bay, the entry point for the county, to Washington Island, America's first permanent Icelandic settlement, accessible only by ferry.

Day 1

Morning

Start your drive north on I–94, which turns into I–43, and take exit 76 into Manitowoc, about a three-hour drive from Chicago.

Lunch: Head over to **Beerntsen's,** 108 North Eighth Street, which has been a fixture in downtown Manitowoc since 1932. Soups and sandwiches are available, but the real business here is superb home-made candies and ice cream. If you long for an old-time soda fountain experience, then this is a must.

You can travel even further back in time at the **Manitowoc Maritime Museum** (75 Maritime Drive; 414–684–0218), which celebrates a century of nautical life. The highlight is the USS *Cobia,* a full-scale World War II submarine, which is moored outside the museum. The 311-foot-long vessel had a distinguished war record, sinking thirteen Japanese ships. Admission is $3.25. The submarine is open only from May to October.

Get back on Highway 43, which turns into Highway 42 around Sturgeon Bay. Continue on 42 until you reach **Fish Creek.** Stop at **Ray's Cherry Hut,** Door County's oldest farm market, to stock up on goodies to take back to the room. What started as a humble produce stand is now a gourmet emporium stocked with cheeses, honey, jams, Nueske's bacon (regarded by some people as the ultimate) and twenty-three varieties of apples. During cherry season you can pick your own. (414) 868–3406.

While you're in Fish Creek, check out some of the stores. (Everything is on Highway 42 unless otherwise noted.) The more unusual offerings include **Fish Creek Kite Company** (414–868–3769) just north of town, which offers a kaleidoscope of kite shapes and colors. **Spielman's Wood Works** is owned by Pat Spielman, the author of about twenty-five how-to books. At his shop you'll find everything from mailboxes to outdoor furniture. Also stop by **Murray's Irish House** (414–868–3528) for beautiful sweaters, jewelry, and other gifts from the Emerald Isle.

Dinner: **Sister Bay Bowl,** about a block from the hotel where you'll be staying (504 North Bay Shore Drive), doesn't look like much, but it is known for its succulent prime rib. If you arrive on Friday night, you'll see the crowds queuing up for the fish fry. It's casual, it's fun, and it's just perfect after a day of driving. You can always wind up the evening by bowling a line or two. Open daily year-round, except for January through March, when it's open weekends only. (414) 854–2841. Moderate.

Lodging: **Helms 4 Seasons Motel,** just off Highway 42 in Sister Bay. Located right on the water. Cable TV; some units have fireplaces. A room with a screened porch—where you can watch the sun dip into Green Bay—will greatly add to your enjoyment. Rates: $55–$97 per night. (414) 854–2356.

Day 2

Morning

Breakfast: **Al Johnson's,** on Highway 42 in Sister Bay, is a tradition in Door County. The history stretches back to the 1940s, when Johnson first opened a small lunch counter. Today it's a large complex that includes a boutique, a duck pond, and the trademark goats grazing on the roof. Al Johnson's is busy all day long, but at breakfast you can sink your fork into some Swedish pancakes and lingonberries. (414) 854–2626.

After breakfast you'll be ready for some physical activity. There are dozens of companies that will rent anything from a paddleboat to a 38-foot yacht. You might want to try sailboarding at Windsurf Door County, right across from the public beach in Ephraim.

If you'd rather just relax, hit any of the public beaches on the Bay side.

Afternoon

Pack up a picnic lunch and explore **Peninsula State Park.** The 3,700-plus acres located between Fish Creek and Ephraim extend northward into the waters of Green Bay. A large percentage of the park is untamed, so you can almost count on seeing a deer or two, especially from the 10 miles of bicycle paths (bikes can be rented at the park entrance) or 20 miles of hiking trails. There are 467 campsites, and a lush eighteen-hole golf course as well. For great photographs and a spectacular view, climb the 100 steps to the top of Eagle Tower. *Dinner:* **Casey's Inn,** Highway 42, Egg Harbor. The atmosphere says "tavern," but the food is much better than that with such upscale entrees as veal scallopine and veal Oskar. Entrees start at about $12.

If you're visiting between late June through mid-October, don't miss **The Peninsula Players** in Fish Creek, the oldest professional resident summer theater in the country. The repertoire runs toward Broadway classics and the casts–professionals culled from New York, Los Angeles, and Chicago—are almost always first-rate. That it plays in a lovely setting, just steps from the Green Bay shoreline, merely makes a good experience even better. Sell-outs are not uncommon, so if you have your heart set on theater, it's best to get your tickets in advance. Mid-June through mid-October. (414) 868–3287.

Lodging: Helms 4 Seasons Motel.

Day 3

Morning

Breakfast: **White Gull Inn** in Fish Creek for fresh coffee cake and the best corned beef hash you've ever had. (414) 868–3517.

If you still feel like getting close to nature, there are four more state parks to explore. **Newport State Park** (414–854–2500), near Ellison Bay, is the second largest, with 2,200 acres and 13 miles of coastline. **Potawatomi,** named after the Indian tribe that populated the peninsula, is known for its "Ancient Shores" Nature Trail. This trail follows the edge of glacial Lakes Algonquin and Nipissing, which cut shorelines still visible 60 feet above the present level of Green Bay. Here, you'll find the county's only downhill skiing (414–743–8869). **Whitefish Dunes** is the smallest of the county's parks (686 acres) and the only one that does not allow camping (414–823–2400). **Rock Island State Park** (414–847–2235) is the most primitive of the bunch. It may be reached by ferry from Gills Rock or Washington Island. The waves can be choppy and the winds can be wicked, so all but the most experienced sailors should leave the transportation to somebody else.

Lunch: **Village Cafe,** Egg Harbor. A cheery, homey coffee shop that makes great omelets. Inexpensive.

Afternoon

Some people are die-hard shoppers who don't consider it a real vacation unless they return home with an armload of packages. Others would rather get a root canal than be dragged around from store to store on vacation. Even if you fall into the second camp, there are a few more shops that you really should squeeze in.

The juxtaposition of fine English collectibles in an eighty-year-old barn is just part of the cachet at **Chelsea Antiques,** located 2 miles south of Sister Bay on Highway 57. The names of various rooms (Chicken Coop, Country Loft, Milking Room) are as colorful as the merchandise. There's a huge variety here, from silver sugar tongs to a pine armoire. It's next door to **Tannenbaum** (10002 Highway 57; 414–854–5004). For people who truly want Christmas in July, this is the place to be. The shop stocks a huge selection of ornaments, wreaths, and other seasonal decorations. In December, St. Nick himself pays a visit.

Of the clothing stores, the most interesting is **Ek Tradet,** a resale shop in Ellison Bay. This must be where all the North Shore ladies take their clothes; all we saw were designer labels.

Dinner: If you're a first-time visitor to Door County, you must attend a fish boil. A fish boil is to Door County what a luau is to Hawaii. It may not be the best food you've ever had, but it's part of the experience. Whitefish, potatoes, and onions are thrown into a big pot and boiled outside over an open fire (bring your camera). The dessert is always cherry or apple pie a la mode. There are several places that "do" fish boils. **White Gull Inn** in Fish Creek serves it on Wednesday, Friday, Saturday, and Sunday evenings. Reservations are essential (414–868–3517). The **Viking Restaurant,** which is Door County's longest-running fish boil, serves nightly from mid-May through October. (414) 854–2998. Prices at each range from $10 to $13.

Lodging: Helms 4 Seasons Motel.

Breakfast: Back to Al Johnson's to sustain yourself for the long ride home. On the way out of town, you might want to stop at Ray's Cherry Hut again to pick up some herring (they pickle their own).

There's More

Birch Creek Music Center, 3 miles east of Egg Harbor on County Road E; (414) 868–3763. This dairy farm-turned-performing arts center sponsors an annual summer concert series. From mid-June through mid-August the center offers a wide variety of music—Strauss to Sousa, Big Band to Steel Band.

The Clearing, Ellison Bay; (414) 854–4088. Established in 1935 by noted Chicago landscaper Jens Jensen, the Clearing is an art school, but it's also for seekers of solitude. Even if you don't have an artistic bone in your body, stop by for the sheer peace.

Peninsula Art School, just off Highway 42 on County Road F, Fish

Creek; (414) 868–3455. The Peninsula Art School has attracted serious and amateur artists ever since it opened its doors in the early 1950s. Anyone can sign up for a class, but perhaps the most accessible forum is the Saturday morning sketch sessions. It's open to anyone who wishes to draw from a model and likes the camaraderie of artists.

Door County Museum, Fourth Street and Michigan Avenue, Sturgeon Bay; (414) 743–8139. Some 5,000 artifacts depict Door County's past. The "Pioneer Fire Company" faithfully re-creates a turn-of-the-century fire department. Open May–October.

Door County Maritime Museum, Gills Rock. Full-size fish tug, which visitors may board, is the highlight; other nautical memorabilia. Open daily, July and August. Weekend only hours May, June, September, and October.

Sturgeon Bay Maritime Museum, Sunset Park, Sturgeon Bay. More tribute to fishing and shipbuilding, including several ship sections and a sea captain's office. Open daily, Memorial Day to mid-October.

Chief Oshkosh Museum, 7631 Egg Harbor Road, Egg Harbor; (414) 868–3240. Dedicated to the memory of Chief Roy Oshkosh of the Menominee Indians. Artifacts and possessions of the late chief, including his hand-painted buffalo robe, are on display.

Thumb Fun Park, Highway 42 between Ephraim and Fish Creek; (414) 868–3418. Rides and attractions including Wilderness Railroad and Haunted Mansions. Open Memorial Day to Labor Day.

Fishing. Door County offers outstanding perch, walleye, large lake trout, and salmon fishing throughout the year. For a twenty-four-hour fishing report, call the Door County fishing hot line at (414) 743–7046. You can get a list of charter fishing captains from the Chamber of Commerce (414–743–4456).

Sailing. Again, lots of charter services and sailing schools. For lessons, even landlubbers swear by Sailboats Inc. (800–826–7010 outside Wisconsin). Others worth noting are Bay Breeze Sailing Charters (414–743–1333), Classic Yacht Charters (414–743–7200), and Door County Sailing (414–854–2124).

Golf. There are six courses in the area, including a very good eighteen-hole course in Peninsula State Park; (414) 854–5791. At the southern end of the county, try Cherry Hills, on Highway 42 just north of Sturgeon Bay; (414) 743–3240.

Miniature golf. Pirate's Cove, Highway 42, Sister Bay. (414) 854–4929.

Special Events

May. Maifest. Horsepulling, arts, antiques, 10K run, rides, entertainment. Jacksonport.

June. Old Peninsula Day. Arts, crafts, historic walk, food. Fish Creek.

June. Fyr Bal Festival. Scandinavian festival in Ephraim. Art fair, bonfires on beach, fish boil.

July. House & Garden Festival. Tour of selected homes throughout the county. Phone (414) 743–4456 for tickets.

August. Door County Fair. Exhibits, rides, and games in Sturgeon Bay.

August. Venetian Night Boat Parade. Sailboat races, dance, fireworks, food. Sturgeon Bay.

September. Door County Century Weekend. Bike rides of 30, 50, 75, or 100 miles take place throughout the county. Fish boil, entertainment.

Other Recommended
Restaurants and Lodgings

Ellison Bay

Griffin Inn, 11976 Mink River Road; (414) 854–4306. Nestled on five acres dotted with sugar maples, this inn typifies the gracious country retreat, from the gazebo on the front lawn to the handmade quilts on the beds. Ten rooms share two and one-half baths; the cottages have private baths. Rates: $56–$66.

Ephraim

Eagle Harbor Inn & Cottages, 9914 Water Street; (414) 854–2121. This white-clapboard inn, lovingly furnished with antiques, is that rare inn that welcomes kids. (You can tell by the swingsets.) Nine guest rooms with private baths, twelve cabins. Full breakfast included. Rates range from $60 to $100 for a cottage; $65 to $95 for a double.

Fish Creek

Thorp House & Inn, 4135 Bluff Road; (414) 868–2444. The word on this meticulously restored country Victorian is getting around. Four guest rooms and six cottages, along with some wonderful common areas, such as a parlor with stone fireplace and a front porch with a view of the bay. Breakfast includes homemade scones. Not recommended for children. Rates: $70 to $115 per room; $325 to $625 for a two-bedroom cottage for one week. During winter, open on weekends only.

Sturgeon Bay

French Country Inn, 3052 Spruce Lane; (414) 854–4001. Lace curtains, period furniture, and lazy ceiling fans can be found at this

European-style bed-and-breakfast. Each of the seven rooms has a pleasant view of the gardens. Take breakfast either in front of the fireplace or on the porch. Rates: $45–$65.

The Inn at Cedar Crossing, 336 Louisiana Street; (414) 743–4200. Tucked into Sturgeon Bay's historic downtown, this is country Victorian living at its most gracious. The lobby, with its pressed tin ceiling and crackling fire in the fireplace, instantly welcomes you. Nine rooms are tastefully appointed and some have double whirlpools. Breakfast includes from-scratch muffins, fresh fruit, granola, and coffee. Rates: $65 to $110 per night.

The Scofield House (908 Michigan Street; 414–743–7727. Magnificent Queen Anne–style home filled with antiques, stained glass, and an abundance of Victoriana. Four rooms have oversized whirlpool tubs. For true decadence reserve the 800-square-foot "Room at the Top," with five skylights, double whirlpool, fireplace, and wet bar. Enjoy breakfast on the gazebo. Rates: $65–$175.

Whistling Swan, 4192 Main Street; (414) 868–3442. The atmosphere is one of spaciousness and luxury (fresh flowers, gleaming wood floors, baby grand piano). Seven decorated rooms and suites, all with private baths. Even if you're not a guest here, you'll want to stop at the Whistling Swan Shoppe, which carries top-of-the-line linens, Crabtree & Evelyn bath products, and other amenities. Rates: $90–$120 per night.

White Gull Inn, 4225 Main Street; (414) 868–3517. Step into the White Gull and you might as well be stepping back to the nineteenth century. Note the wood-burning fireplace, the period wallpapers, fabrics, and furniture. No wonder it's a fixture on many "best" lists. Rates: $65–$105; cottage (sleeps up to 8), $120–$195.

White Lace Inn, 16 North Fifth Avenue; (414) 743–1105. This fifteen-room Victorian is undeniably romantic and is always mentioned on "10 best inns" lists. It's actually three historic houses connected by a red brick path that winds through lovely grounds. Breakfast (included) is homemade baked goods with Scandinavian fruit soup. Rates range from $78 to $135 per night.

For More Information

Door County Chamber of Commerce, Box 406, Sturgeon, WI 54235. (414) 743–4456.

Indiana Escapes

INDIANA

Michigan City

The Indiana National Lakeshore boasts one of the best beaches in the Midwest.

Doin' Dunes Country

_____ 1 NIGHT _____

Antiques · Shopping · Fishing · Boating ·
U-pick produce · Golf · Hiking · Cross-country skiing

As you travel through northwest Indiana, it's hard to believe that beyond the grime of the steel mills lies as unspoiled and untamed a landscape as you'll find anywhere in the Midwest. The Indiana Dunes National Lakeshore, which covers 13,000 acres on the southern shore of Lake Michigan, is one of the region's jewels. Carl Sandburg wrote "The dunes are to the Midwest what the Grand Canyon is to Arizona and Yosemite is to California. They constitute a signature of time and eternity."

The area is easily accessible (not much more than an hour from downtown) and not overly touristed. No two people "do" the Dunes in exactly the same way, so personal discoveries abound for anyone willing to turn off the interstate.

Unlike other weekend trips where everything is usually confined to one quaint little town, this trip can spread over three counties (Lake,

Porter, and LaPorte). For this trip we've made Michigan City our base of operations. But you could just as easily opt for Crown Point or Valparaiso (see "There's More").

The first order of business is to zero in on what kind of weekend it's going to be. Hanging out at the beach? Hiking? Outlet shopping? Antiquing? Berry picking? Festival? Once you've determined the focus, the other considerations (lodging, restaurants) will fall into place.

Day 1

Morning

Hit the road (I–94) early and you should be at your final destination, Michigan City, by afternoon—and that's with a few stops at some of the area's prime antique malls. One of the advantages of leaving Saturday morning instead of Friday night is that you avoid the horrendous traffic as everyone else heads out of town. If the tie-ups are interminable, get off at Highway 65 and go north until you reach U.S. Highway 12; then continue traveling east. It's the route people traveled before the days of the superhighways.

Now back to those antiques. Northwest Indiana still has terrific bargains—especially in furniture—because it doesn't get the huge influx of tourists of other areas, such as Galena and Lake Geneva. Indeed, judging by the number of tour buses from far-flung states, northwest Indiana's reputation as a mother lode of antiques is better known outside the Midwest.

Turn off I–94 at Highway 49 and travel 1 mile south to **Chesterton** for a stop at **Yesterday's Treasures** (700 West Broadway; 219–926–2268). This antique mall has 130 dealers. Other spots for collectors (all within a few minutes) include **The Schoolhouse Shop** (278 East 1500 N, 1 block north of Highway 20), where the setting—a late nineteenth-century schoolhouse—is as appealing as the wares. Also worth your time are **Carol's Antiques** (214 South Calumet); **Emma's Antiques** (428 South Calumet); **Kathy's Antiques,** at Indian Oak Mall (Highway 49, just south of I–94); **Rainbotique** (corner of 15th and Lincoln streets); and **Russ & Barb** (Third Street at Lincoln Avenue). For questions on hours or directions, call (219) 926–1400 or (219) 926–4757.

One other unusual stop is the **Oz Museum** (109 East 950 N; 219–926–7048). Every September, Chesterton plays host to the Wizard of Oz Festival, which attracts fans from all over the country. Events include Oz trivia contests and personal appearances by the surviving Munchkins. But even if you're not visiting at festival time, you can still follow the Yellow Brick Road to the museum, which features lots of fascinating memorabilia. Open 10 A.M. to 5 P.M. Free.

Lunch: **Katie's Ice Cream Parlor,** 225 South Calumet. Order a sandwich and a soda and get back change from your five-dollar bill.

Afternoon

Get back to I–94 and travel the short distance to Michigan City, largest city in LaPorte County.

Make this your designated shopping day and forge ahead to **Lighthouse Place,** 601 Wabash Street. With eighty factory outlet stores featuring such brand names as Ralph Lauren, Chaus, Dansk, Eddie Bauer, Anne Klein, and Jaymar, this is a shopper's paradise. (219) 879–6506.

Head over to the **Barker Mansion,** 631 Washington Street. This opulent thirty-eight-room Victorian estate was home to millionaire industrialist John Barker. You'll admire the rare woods, sleek marble, and lush gardens any time of the year, but at Christmas the home is decorated and especially worth your time. Guided tours during the summer: Monday–Friday at 10:00 A.M., 11:30 A.M., and 1:00 P.M.; Saturday and Sunday at noon and 2 P.M. Check hours during the off-season. Admission is $2.00. Phone (219) 873–1520.

Dinner: **Old Heidelberg,** 110 West Ninth Street; (219) 879–8726. This restaurant is located less than 4 blocks from Lighthouse Place. German specialties include a fine wiener schnitzel and apple strudel. Prices start at $10.

After dinner check out **Canterbury Theatre,** adjacent to the restaurant. Built in 1867, this former church is home to the Festival Players Guild, which performs mostly musicals and classics. For a schedule, call (219) 874–4269.

Or you can join the thousands of folks armed with blankets and mosquito repellent to watch the **Laser Light Show,** which takes place nightly, from late June to Labor Day, at the lakefront. The NIPSCO tower is the canvas for animated graphics combined with 20,000 beams of light, all choreographed to a wide range of music, from Bach to rock. Admission: adults, $4.00; children, $2.00. For information call (219) 872–5055.

Lodging: **Creekwood Inn,** County Road 600 W and Highways 35/20, Michigan City. (Take exit 40 B from I–94, then take first street on left, then turn left to the inn.) The Creekwood has a casual but elegant atmosphere. The 33-acre wooded setting, complete with a meandering creek (hence the name), can be enjoyed from the inn's patio or screened porch. Classical music adds to the feeling of tranquility. All rooms have their own bath. Rates range from $90–$150 (suite). Phone (219) 872–8357.

Day 2

Morning

Breakfast: A continental breakfast of delicious muffins and other baked goods is included with the cost of the room at the Creekwood Inn. A full breakfast is available for an extra charge. Pack a lunch from **5th Street Deli** (431 Washington Street; 219–872–5204) and head to the Dunes. If you are farther south, near Merrillville, **Cafe Venezia** (405 West 81st Avenue) is the region's most authentic Italian grocery (see Other Recommended Restaurants).

By the way, when people say they're going to the dunes, you have to determine if it's the National Lakeshore or Dunes State Park that they're talking about.

What's the difference? **Dunes State Park** is in Chesterton and is a part of the larger Indiana Dunes National Lakeshore. It's tamer, but still lovely, offering a fine swimming beach, cross-country skiing and hiking trails, picnic area, and camping. Of the ten marked trails winding through the Indiana Dunes State Park, the longest and most interesting are trails numbers 9 and 10. Call (219) 926–1390 for information or to check water conditions.

Afternoon

Lunch: Open your picnic basket, enjoy the beautiful surroundings, and maybe even let the waves lull you into an afternoon snooze.

The **Indiana Dunes National Lakeshore** is about a half hour closer to Chicago. (Take I–65 to U.S. Highway 20; west on 20 to Lake Street and go north. It is larger and offers nature study, bike/horseback riding trails, one of the best beaches in the Midwest, ranger-led hikes, and picnic areas. (The visitors center is a good place to get oriented.)

Here, you can climb 135-foot-tall **Mount Baldy,** which offers a fine view of Chicago's skyline. Farther east, you can visit the **Bailly Homestead,** a Victorian farmhouse, and **Chellberg Farm,** a working nineteenth-century farm. There are horses, goats, and chickens to entertain the little ones. Both are part of the National Lakeshore park and the site of the popular Maple Sugar Time Program each March, when you can tap for syrup. Hours vary with the season. A $2.50 fee per car is charged.

A word of caution: The walk from the parking lot to the beach can be quite a trek, so if you have young children, you may want to bring a stroller. So you don't have to travel home in wet swimsuits, change in the bathhouse. To check on special programs or water conditions, call (219) 926–7561.

Dinner: The **Miller Bakery Cafe,** 555 South Lake Street, Gary (about a block north of U.S. Highway 12, just over the railroad tracks). This intimate restaurant, with exposed brick and well-chosen antiques, is as good as anything on the Near North Side at one-third the price. Specialties include fabulous soups (don't miss the Mediterranean tomato), seafood (crab cakes and salmon ravioli), and a decadent flourless chocolate torte. Open Tuesday–Saturday. Prices start at $5.00 per entree for lunch, $12.00 for dinner. While you don't need to dress up, you'd feel uncomfortable if you stopped here in beachwear. Not recommended for young children. Reservations essential on weekend nights. Phone (219) 928–2229.

Take I–94 west back to Chicago.

There's More

Antiques. Coachman Antique Mall, 500 Lincolnway, LaPorte. 23,000 square feet of antiques.

Valparaiso Antique Mall, 212 East Lincoln Way, Valparaiso; (219) 465–1869. Not as large as Coachman, this mall is housed on two floors of a former car dealership. Approximately thirty dealers sell an eclectic mix of wares ranging from late nineteenth century furniture to 1950s advertising memorabilia. European, Asian, and American pieces can be found. Open Monday–Saturday, 10 A.M.–5 P.M.; Sunday, noon–5 P.M.

Art. The Art Barn, 695 North 400 E, Valparaiso; (219) 462–9009. The gallery exhibits the work of local and national artists. Also known for their Saturday morning children's art class.

Hesston Steam Museum, County Road 1000 N, Hesston; (219) 872–7405. It's small, but younger kids enjoy this unusual outdoor museum with one of the most varied collections of operating steam equipment in the United States. A highlight is a steam engine ride through the surrounding forest, which goes nicely with the fresh-pressed apple cider sold on the premises. Open weekends only from Memorial Day to Labor Day; Sundays only in September and October.

Lake County Courthouse, Courthouse Square, Crown Point. John Dillinger escaped from here. Valentino was married here as was Ronald Reagan (the first time). Today this 1879 courthouse is home to about a dozen shops.

LaPorte County Museum, County Complex, LaPorte; (219) 326–6808. Considered to own the best collection of antique firearms in the country.

Old Lighthouse Museum, Washington Park; (219) 872–6133. Indiana's only lighthouse, built in 1858, features exhibits on marine lore. Open daily 1–4 P.M., except Mondays and holidays.

Kingsbury Fish and Wildlife Area, 5344 South Hupp Road, La-

Porte; (219) 393–3612. This 6,000-acre hunting and fishing preserve offers nature trails, target shooting, birdwatching, and very good mushroom hunting.

Washington Park Zoo. Michigan City lakefront; (219) 873–1510. One of Indiana's oldest zoos. Small (260 animals), but just the right size for the young set.

Portage Charter Fishing Fleet Inc. Can accommodate individuals as well as groups. (219) 464–0918.

Golf. Northwest Indiana has some excellent courses. In fact, many Chicagoans, finding long lines at their home courses, drive here for tee-off time. With some thirty courses in the area, check with the tourism offices listed below.

Horseback riding. Red Arrow Stables, 3848 Academy Road, Michigan City; (219) 872–2114.

Horse Country of Galena, 2525 East 850 North, LaPorte; (219) 778–4625.

Bicycling. Rent-a-Wreck, 1402 East Michigan Boulevard, Michigan City; (219) 879–7325.

U-pick orchards. LaPorte County alone is home to about thirty orchards and berry farms. Crops include blueberries, strawberries, apples, cherries, and peaches. For current harvest information, call (219) 872–5055 or (800) 634–2650.

Elsewhere in the region, spots include Anderson in Valparaiso (430 East U.S. Highway 6; 219–464–4936), Garwood in LaPorte (5911 West County Road 50; 219–362–4385), Anderson in Chesterton (98 East U.S. Highway 20; 219–926–3141), and Johnson's in Hobart (8960 East Ridge; 219–962–1169).

Special Events

July. Porter County Fair. Carnival, entertainment, agriculture. Porter County Fairgrounds, Valparaiso.

August. Chesterton Art Fair. The same artists that you'll find at the Gold Coast or Old Town Art fairs without the crowds. Chesterton; (219) 926–4711.

August. Lake County Fair. Arts, crafts, carnival midway, horse shoe, entertainment. Lake County Fairgrounds, Crown Point.

August. Augustfest. National music acts, ethnic food, rides. Wolfe Lake Park, Hammond.

September. Michigan City holds the first and largest Oktoberfest celebration in the region on Labor Day Weekend. Rides, food, arts and crafts booths. (219) 874–8927.

September. Valparaiso Popcorn Festival. The home of Orville Redenbacher goes all out with entertainment, food, and arts and crafts.

September. Wizard of Oz Festival. Tribute to the MGM classic. Parade, food, contests. Chesterton.

Other Recommended Restaurants and Lodgings

Chesterton

Indian Oak Inn and Spa, 558 Indian Boundary Road; (219) 926–2200. Indoor pool, private balcony. All spa services (facials, massages, etc.) are extra. Rates: $64–$120 (generally, rooms on lake side are more expensive than woods side).

Hammond

Phil Smidt and Son, 1205 North Calumet; (219) 659–0025. The epitome of the Calumet Region restaurant. Generations have been making a special trip for the golden, butter-drenched perch and the frogs' legs. If you're hungry, it's well worth the few extra bucks for the all-you-can-eat option.

Merrillville

Cafe Venezia, 405 West 81st Avenue (Ross Plaza). Don't be scared off by the suburban strip mall. This is probably the only spot in the entire region where you can get serious Italian cuisine. Pastas are exceptional, as are the Italian pastries. At the adjacent grocery store, you can pick up the great beginnings (meats, cheeses, breads) of a picnic. Also, given its proximity to the Star Plaza, it's worth remembering when you want to bring a snack back to your room.

Star Plaza Theatre and Resort, I–65 at U.S. Highway 30; (219) 769–6311. A little bit of Vegas comes to the Midwest. A good choice if you're looking for a resort experience. Two pools, whirlpool, children's indoor playground. The theater attracts big name entertainment and frequently offers great room deals when you buy show tickets. Call for a schedule.

Michigan City

Michigan City Holiday Inn, 5820 South Franklin Street; (219) 879–0311. Best choice if you want to stay near Lighthouse Place, but want a hotel with the amenities of pool and sauna.

Valparaiso

Restaurant Don Quijote, 119 East Lincolnway; (219) 462–7976. The tapas are excellent, as is the paella—or anything with seafood, for that matter.

Strongbow Inn, 2405 U.S. Highway 30 East; (219) 462–3311. People come here from all over to get turkey with all the trimmings (stuffing, sweet potatoes, cranberries). Family owned since 1940, it's perfect for when you crave a traditional Thanksgiving dinner, even if it's in July.

For More Information

Lake County Tourism Bureau, 5800 Broadway, Suite S, Merrillville, IN 46410. (219) 980–1617.

LaPorte County Convention and Visitors Bureau, 1503 South Meer Road, Michigan City, IN 46360. (219) 872–5055 or (800) 634–2650.

Porter County Tourism Bureau, 528 Indian Oak Mall, Chesterton, IN 46304. (219) 926–2255 or (800) 283–TOUR.

South Bend

Notre Dame's Sacred Heart Church

Home of the Irish

_____ 2 NIGHTS _____

Football · Cycling · Golf · Sightseeing ·
Antiques/Flea markets · Amish village

How you feel about South Bend has a lot to do with how you feel about Notre Dame. If you rank it right up there with God and country, it's like heaven on earth. If you couldn't care less about the Fighting Irish, it's just another notch on the Midwest's Rust Belt.

Each fall thousands of visitors from all over the country converge on South Bend to view the perennial gridiron powerhouse. The usual routine for Chicagoans is to make the 90-mile trip for the game and return home the same day. Even people who positively bleed blue and gold will tell you that once you get off campus, the list of diversions in the area is a short one.

But if you add side trips to Amish Acres in Nappanee, there are more than enough activities to make for a fulfilling weekend. If you're more interested in farm life than field goals, you can reverse the emphasis and make the Amish country your base of operations.

A precaution: Don't think you can make a spur-of-the-moment decision to stay over in South Bend after the game. (Hotels are full any weekend the Irish are at home.) If you're not visiting on a Saturday, consider adding "Amish Country" (Indiana Escape Three) to your itinerary. But never on Sunday—the area virtually closes down.

Day 1

Evening

Make the drive to South Bend on I-90 on a Friday evening, so you can be well rested for Saturday's activities and you won't have the pressure of arriving in time for kick-off.

Dinner: One advantage to arriving the night before is that reservations at the **Carriage House,** 24460 Adams Road, which many people consider to be South Bend's finest restaurant, are easier to get on a Friday. The cuisine—from appetizer (crab strudel topped with caviar) to entree (roast duck adorned with cranberries) to dessert (puff pastry with chocolate mousse)—is as serious as you'll find anywhere in the area. Entrees fall in the $15 to $18 range, with a wine list that goes from nominal to stratospheric. Reservations a must. Phone (219) 272-9220.

Lodging: **South Bend Marriott,** 123 North Saint Joseph Street. The accommodations in South Bend are surprisingly limited, considering that it's home to a world-class university. The South Bend Marriott, a five-minute drive from the university, is generally regarded as the best place to stay, but the furnishings have really seen better days. The reasonable price ($65 per night), central location, and the indoor pool/Jacuzzi helped compensate for the lackluster showing, however. Phone (219) 234-2000.

Day 2

Morning

Breakfast: Start your day at **Bibler's,** 1430 North Ironwood, which is near the stadium and similar to The Original Pancake House or

Walker Brothers in Chicago. The apple pancake is just as decadent, the orange juice is just as fresh, and the coffee is just as piping hot as it is back home. And the lines are shorter—providing you beat the pregame crowd on Saturday and after-church crowd on Sunday. Phone (219) 232–3220.

Afternoon

After the game, let everyone make a beeline to the parking lot. Then you can explore the 1,250-acre campus without the crowds. Two popular sights are particularly conducive to peace and quiet: the **Grotto of Our Lady of Lourdes** (which is a replica of the one in the French Pyrenees) and the **Sacred Heart Church,** which reopened in 1990 after an extensive renovation. The church boasts one of the finest collections of nineteenth-century French stained-glass windows.

From the church proceed to the **Snite Museum of Art,** which owns more than 17,000 works, from early African art to twentieth-century works. Open Tuesday–Saturday, 10 A.M.–4 P.M.; Sunday 1–4 P.M. Free. If you're interested in a student-conducted tour of the campus, call (219) 239–7367.

If you spent four (or more) years on campus and know its nooks and crannies intimately, head to the **Studebaker Museum** (Century Center, 120 South Joseph Street). This is more than just a shrine to a now-defunct model of car; it provides a look at the critical formative years of America's auto industry as well. Open Monday–Friday, 10 A.M.–4:30 P.M.; Saturday, 10 A.M.–4 P.M.; Sunday, noon–4 P.M. Admission: adults, $3.50; children, $1.50. Admission covers archives center (see below).

The museum does a good job of tracing the company's history from the blacksmith shop—where brothers Clem and Henry turned out their first buggy in 1852—to the last Avanti, which rolled off the line in 1964. (Perhaps the car's fate was sealed when the powers that be chose Mr. Ed as its spokesman?) In between are some 100 carriages (including the one that Abraham Lincoln rode to Ford's Theatre), cars, and trucks, all buffed to a high-gloss. The **Studebaker Archives Center,** 525 South Main Street, provides even more detail.

If the weather is balmy, take advantage of South Bend's excellent county parks. Potowatomi Park (on Greenlawn, ¼ mile south of Jefferson Avenue) houses some one hundred animals in its petting zoo. (219) 284–9800.

Dinner: About this time, you'll be searching for a good place to eat. If you're still dressed for a football game, then head to **Bruno's,** 2610 Prairie Avenue, which serves up a great thin-crust pizza. Also, if you must choose between a kiss and the garlic bread, opt for the latter. There will be other kisses, but fabulous garlic bread is much less certain. Phone (219) 288–3320. Inexpensive.

After dinner, you can find a number of college bars. If you're looking for more than just a brew, check out **Center Street,** 100 Center Street, in nearby Mishawaka, where there's also jazz and blues on tap.
Lodging: South Bend Marriott.

Day 3

Morning

Breakfast: Bibler's.
Make sure your route home takes you south on Highway 19 to U.S. Highway 6, so you can stop at **Amish Acres** in Nappanee, an 80-acre preserved and restored Amish farm. It is open to the public from May until the end of December. This is not the sort of place that would work as a lone destination, but it is just fine as a detour.

If you ignore the frankly commercial qualities and instead regard it as an opportunity to stock up on jams, jellies, sausages, and other foodstuffs, you won't be disappointed. A buggy ride through picturesque woods isn't a bad way to spend a crisp, autumn afternoon, either.

The pricing structure is a bit confusing. Depending on what options you want, the tab can range from about $20 for the "total experience" (forty-five-minute house and farm tour, twenty-minute documentary, buggy ride, and dinner) to free if all you do is hit the shops.

Lunch: Stay at Amish Acres to enjoy the Thresher's Dinner, which is served family style and includes your choice of two entrees per table (turkey, ham, chicken, or roast beef) along with numerous country side dishes, such as mashed potatoes or sage dressing. Dessert consists of authentic shoofly pie, fruit pies, and vanilla date pudding. At about $12.00 per adult ($5.00 for kids), this is the best bargain Amish Acres has to offer. Dinner is served 11 A.M.–6 P.M. Phone (219) 773–4188.
Return home via I–94.

There's More

Antiques/Flea market. Thieves Market, 2309 East Edison Road, South Bend; (219) 233–9820. About forty dealers in antiques, collectibles. An especially good selection of Oriental carpets. Weekends only, 10 A.M.–6 P.M.

Shipshewana Flea Market, Shipshewana. (219) 768–4129. One of the most famous flea markets in the Midwest, with some 150 vendors. Unfortunately, open only Tuesdays and Wednesdays, May–October. On Wednesdays, everything that isn't sold goes up for auction, which is when you can really find some great furniture buys. (For more details, see Indiana Escape Three.)

Baseball. Catch a minor league game at Stanley Coveleski Baseball Stadium, 501 West South Street, home of the South Bend White Sox. April–August. (219) 284–9988.

Potato Creek State Park, 7 miles south on U.S. Highway 31; (219) 656–8186. Bike rentals and paved paths. Cross-country skiing rentals; well-groomed trails.

Notre Dame Golf Course, on campus, is open to the public. Phone (219) 239–6425.

100 Center Complex, 700 Lincoln Way West, Mishawaka (just southeast of South Bend). Thirty-five retail shops and restaurants housed in the 1853 Kamm's Brewery. You can also take a short trip down the St. Joseph River on the *Island Queen,* a paddleboat.

Special Events

May. Studebaker Festival. Car enthusiasts come from all over the country for a swap meet. Studebaker Museum.

July. Ethnic Festival. Food, art, crafts. Downtown South Bend.

June–August. Firefly Festival. St. Patrick's Park, off U.S. Highway 31, just north of South Bend. All summer, outdoor entertainment that ranges from Shakespeare to the Platters.

Other Recommended Restaurants and Lodgings

South Bend

East Bank Emporium, 121 South Niles; (219) 234–9000. The draw here is steaks and seafood, with some attention paid to such accompaniments as homemade salad dressings. Moderate.

Hacienda, 5880 Grape Road; (219) 277–1318. Very good margaritas, salsa, and burritos. There's another location in Scottsdale Mall, on the outskirts of town, but this location has the best atmosphere. Inexpensive.

Jamison Inn, 1404 Ivy Road; (219) 277–9682. Fifty rooms, twenty-four of which are suites. Victorian style. All rooms have refrigerators stocked with soda. Rates range from $65 to $92 per night.

Malabar, 1709 South Bend Avenue; (219) 271–0115. Small Indian restaurant. No more than ten tables, but terrific tandoori chicken and curries.

Queen Anne Inn, 420 West Washington; (219) 234–5959. Five

rooms, some with fireplaces, all with private bath. Victorian style. Full breakfast included with cost of room. Rates range from $65 to $85 per night.
Tippecanoe Place, 620 West Washington Street; (219) 234–9077. South Bend's best-known restaurant and the original home of Clement Studebaker. With its forty rooms and twenty fireplaces, the decor dazzles. Stick to Midwestern basics (such as prime rib at an incredible $13) and you'll get your money's worth.

For More Information

South Bend–Mishawaka Area Convention and Visitors Bureau, 401 East Colfax, South Bend, IN 46634. (219) 234–0051 or (219) 234–6590.

Elkhart and Crystal Valley

The unhurried pace of Amish country is an antidote to urban stress.

A Weekend in Amish Country

_____ 2 NIGHTS _____

Crafts • Quilts • Golf • Sightseeing • Antiques/Flea markets • Amish village

Many overworked urbanites pay thousands of dollars to go to faraway retreats in search of solitude, when all they have to do is turn off the interstate and explore Indiana's Amish country. There you can enjoy a slow-paced weekend, amid beautiful, rolling countryside.

The Crystal Valley area is home to about 20,000 Amish and Mennonites. Today their life-style remains virtually the same as it was a century ago. They still drive horse-drawn buggies (something to keep in mind as you approach a hill), milk their cows by hand, and shun adornment. But the simple life here is more than just a hiatus from traffic jams. It's an attitude that permeates the entire community. You can feel it from tours that include stops to "real" people's homes to accommodations that treat guests like family.

If, however, your time is short you may want a more condensed experience, which can be had at Amish Acres in Nappanee, located in the southwest corner of Elkhart County (see Indiana Escape 2).

A few caveats: This is one getaway that you may want to schedule in the middle of the week. That is the only way to see the famous Shipshewana Auction and Flea Market, which operates only on Tuesdays and Wednesdays, and the county virtually closes down on Sunday. Also, while you'll find people to be hospitable, they ask that visitors respect their beliefs by not taking their photographs.

Day 1

Morning

Take I–180/90 east to exit 92 into Elkhart, a prosperous city that makes more than half of the nation's band instruments, and almost as many mobile homes and pharmaceuticals.

There are several exceptionally good small museums here. The **Ruthmere Museum** (302 East Beardsley Avenue; 219–264–0330) is another reason for planning a midweek excursion. This lovely Beaux Arts mansion belonged to Albert Beardsley, one of the founders of Miles Laboratories. Built in 1908, the house combines old money with modern conveniences. Furnishings include china and Tiffany lamps from Presidents Hayes, Jackson, and Harding. Don't miss the classic cars in the garage. The museum is open Tuesday through Friday (guided tours only).

Lunch: **The Tea Room,** 500 South Main Street (in the Greencroft Building, just across from the Midwest Museum of Art). Locals rave about the homemade soups, sandwiches, and breads. Phone (219) 522–9496.

Afternoon

If you are a rail fan, you'll want to include the **National New York Central Railroad Museum** (721 South Main Street; 219–294–3001) on your itinerary. You'll see the ongoing restoration of locomotives and rail cars and the display that details the story of "Curly Top," a young Elkhart girl who achieved fame in the 1930s by waving to the passing Twentieth Century Limited every day. Celebrities on board responded by throwing autographed menus at her as the train rumbled by. The museum, which opened in 1989, is open from 10 A.M. to 3 P.M. Thursday–Sunday. Admission is free.

The **Midwest Museum of American Art,** (429 South Main Street; 219–293–6660) is also worth a stop. Located in a renovated bank building downtown, the museum gives you a good overview of American art styles (Norman Rockwell rates his own gallery). Allow an hour to tour. Admission is $1.50. Open Tuesday–Sunday.

Travel about 15 miles east of Elkhart on U.S. Highway 20, right into

Middlebury, in the heart of what is called the Crystal Valley, home to about 20,000 Amish and Mennonites. *Dinner and Lodging:* **Checkerberry Inn,** 62644 County Road 37, Goshen; 219–642–4445. This is another spot that makes it onto everybody's "best" lists for its exceptional facilities and European approach, from the food (duck breast in orange port wine sauce and frozen chocolate Kahlua mousse) to the Swiss-milled soap in the bath. You'll find a curious marriage of decor here: Amish hats hang on the walls above the sleek, contemporary beds. Some rooms have whirlpools and fireplaces. The inn sits on 100 wooded acres. Four-course dinners are in the $20–$30 range. Room rates range from $96 for a double to $300 for a two-bedroom suite. To reach Goshen, take Highway 13 south from Middlebury to Highway 4 west. For a more scenic route, take Highway 22 from Middlebury.

Day 2

Morning

Breakfast: Checkerberry Inn. Continental breakfast of muffins, fruits, juices, and coffee are included in the cost of the room.

After breakfast, head to the **Menno-Hof Visitors Center** to get oriented. The center, which resembles a farmhouse and barn, explains the history of the Plain People. You can even experience a model dungeon, where early converts were punished for their beliefs, or a tornado room (the floor actually moves), which illuminates disaster-relief efforts. It's right across from the Shipshewana Flea Market on Highway 5. Phone (219) 768–4117.

The **Shipshewana Flea Market and Auction** is held every Tuesday and Wednesday between May and October. It is one of the largest flea markets in the country, with almost 1,000 vendors.

Visitors who arrive by 8 A.M. on Wednesdays also can bid for great finds at an indoor antiques auction, where up to twelve auctioneers work simultaneously. While the flea market certainly can boast size and scope, many people grumble that the merchandise has slipped in recent years and there are more manufacturer's closeouts (such as cookware and tube socks) than antiques. They skip the flea market altogether and stick to the auction. On Fridays, at 9:30 A.M., the weekly horse auction is a lively event.

Across from the flea market, in the Shipshewana Center, you'll find some local fixtures, including Yoder's Department Store, Yoder's Hardware, and Yoder's Supermarket.

Lunch. **Buggy Wheel Restaurant.** Morton Street; (219) 768–4444. Pass the platters of fried chicken, please. This is just plain good cooking served by young Mennonite women. But you may want to skip that second helping of mashed potatoes to leave room for a slice of pie (there are more than twenty varieties to choose from) or fresh-baked cinnamon rolls. Make your lunch reservation early in the morning to guarantee you'll get in. But even if the lines are long, you can buy a bag of goodies from the **Bread Box Bake Shop** right next door to munch on while you wait.

Afternoon

Veterans of the flea market/auction generally consider it a full day's attraction. (Many recommend if you really want to see the Amish and Mennonite way of life, you scrupulously avoid flea market days when a steady stream of traffic all but overwhelms the horse-drawn buggies.)

Still, the same things that primarily draw people to the flea market and auction—good food, antiques, and fine furniture—are available at any time in Amish country. The **Old Bag Factory** in Goshen, 1100 Chicago Avenue, a renovated warehouse, is home to numerous arts and crafts shops. Standouts include Quilt Designs, where custom quilts are made (219–534–5111), Swartzendrubber, a fine woodshop and showroom where you can watch craftsmen at work (219–534–2502), and Carriage Barn Antiques, great for eighteenth- and nineteenth-century furniture (219–533–6353).

In Shipshewana there are two complexes worth noting. The **Crafter's Marketplace,** 210 North Van Buren Street, houses almost a dozen shops. The Craft Barn Furniture Shop (219–768–4725) is known for its oak furniture, which you can watch take shape in the wood-shop.

The **Davis Mercantile,** at the corner of Harrison and Main Street, is named after the founder of Shipshewana. The two-story building is joined to the Old Davis Hotel, for decades the center of commerce for the community. Of the fifteen shops, arts and crafts lovers should hit the Craft Patch (219–768–7012) and A Touch of Country (219–768–7222).

Not all purchases have to be a family heirloom in the making. At **Yoder's Popcorn Shoppe,** on County Road 200S, just four miles south of Shipshewana you can choose from many varieties of popcorn. Their kernels are shipped all over the country—including Soldier Field and Comiskey Park. (800–537–1194).

Dinner: **Patchwork Quilt Country Inn,** 11748 County Road 2, Middlebury; (219) 825–2417. The inn, which is actually a century-old farmhouse, is known for its award-winning buttermilk pecan chicken. It's also worth remembering for lodging (four-poster beds). The lobby is comfortably furnished, with a huge fireplace as its centerpiece. Rates: $45–$55 (shared bath).

Lodging: Checkerberry Inn.

Day 3

Morning

Breakfast: Checkerberry Inn. Homemade breads, fresh fruit and juices are at the heart of Checkerberry's good country breakfasts. After breakfast take one of the "backroads tours," which depart from the Patchwork Quilt Country Inn. The four-hour tours are structured according to your interests. For instance, the gourmet tour includes heartland foods, farm markets, and bakery while the arts and crafts tour includes quilt, crafts, and woodworking shops. Many of the families you'll visit will be friends and neighbors of the tour guide, adding a warmth that you don't get at many tourist attractions.

Lunch: When in Rome . . . and when people are in Amish Country, they eat hearty, hefty fare. **Das Dutchman Essenhaus** (literally "eating house") is a popular, albeit touristy, choice. Meals include roast beef or ham *and* fried chicken, dressing, and mashed potatoes ladled with gravy. All is served family-style. Amish baking skills really shine, with a pie menu that goes from apple to shoo-fly. 240 U.S. Highway 20, Middlebury. Phone (219) 825–9471. There are also a number of stores (bakery, craft, country, clothing) in the Essenhaus complex. It's a fun finale before heading back to the city.

There's More

Bonneyville Mill Park, Bristol. Visit the oldest continually operating gristmill in Indiana. Built in 1832, the mill still grinds corn, wheat, and rye. Milling takes place hourly between 10 A.M. and 5 P.M., May through October. (219) 534–3541. On the Little Elkhart River, 2½ miles east on Highway 120, then ½ mile south on Highway 131.

Ideal Beach Family Water Park, Elkhart. Water activities. 56-foot corkscrew slide, beach, playground, miniature golf. Open daily, 10 A.M.–7 P.M., Memorial Day to Labor Day. (219) 262–1769.

Eby's Pines, Bristol. Roller skating.

Bristol Opera House. Elkhart Civic Theatre performs year-round. Call for schedule (219) 848–4116.

Special Events

March. Maple Syrup Festival. Wakarusa. The ultimate pancake breakfast.

June. Elkhart Jazz Festival. A major regional showcase for the best jazz. Downtown Elkhart.

July. Elkhart County Fair. One of the largest county fairs in the country. Music, carnival, livestock, harness racing, food. Elkhart County Fairgrounds, Goshen.

August. Amish Acres Arts & Crafts Festival. Artists, entertainment, farmer's market, and buggy rides, Nappanee.

September. Michiana Mennonite Relief Sale. Hundreds of quilts go on sale. Crafts, homemade foods and furniture are also part of this lively event at the 4-H Fairgrounds in Goshen.

November. Crystal Valley Country Christmas. Country crafts, merchant open houses. A weekend showcase of Amish culture that takes place in Bristol, Middlebury, and Shipshewana.

Other Recommended Restaurants

Middlebury

Berkey's Country Haus, Highway 13; (219) 825–5413. Country dining; big breakfasts called "Farmer's Breakfasts."

Harley's Soda Shop and Antiques, 422 South Main; Phone (219) 825–2565. Maker of Vic's ice cream, a local favorite for decades.

For More Information

Elkhart County Convention and Visitors Bureau, 26500 Caravan, Elkhart, IN 46514. (219) 262–8161; (800) 262–8161.

Crystal Valley Tourist Association, P.O. Box 55, Middlebury, IN 46540.

Indianapolis

Capital Commons epitomizes spruced up and blooming downtown Indianapolis.

A Town for All Seasons

_____ 2 NIGHTS _____

Museums · Sightseeing · Speedway ·
Theater · Ballet · Amateur and professional sports

Indianapolis may sound like an odd destination for a weekend escape. Why head for an urban landscape when you already live in one? Because Indianapolis offers a lot of the perks of city life with none of the hassles. In about three hours you can put yourself squarely in a place that offers an incredible amount of variety at a very affordable price—and you'll never have to search for a parking place.

During the 1980s, when many other cities slid into decline, Indianapolis waged a self-improvement campaign. The centerpiece of this urban renewal is Union Station, a once-dilapidated railroad terminal that has been turned into an eating/shopping/entertainment complex. Elsewhere you'll see the civic pride Hoosiers take in preserving their old landmarks. One of the most eye-catching is the 284-foot-tall Indiana State Soldiers and Sailors Monument, which was built in 1902 but updated into a lovely downtown plaza. In the summer it is the perfect place for a picnic and people watching. In the winter the monument is draped in thousands of tiny lights, while carolers and brass ensembles usher in the holiday season.

One word of caution: If you plan to extend your weekend to include Monday, don't. Virtually every museum is closed. A far better strategy is to play hooky on Friday. And this may be stating the obvious, but Indianapolis during Memorial Day weekend is like New Orleans during Mardi Gras. Unless you like huge crowds and higher prices and have your hotel reservations a year in advance, don't bother.

Also note that the towns of Noblesville (home of Conner Prairie, see Indiana Escape Six) and Zionsville are worthy detours, which can be scheduled en route to Indianapolis or on the way home (or hit one each way). If logistics make that impossible, they are both close enough to Indianapolis to qualify as day trips.

Day 1

Take I–94 to I–65 to Indianapolis. Get an early start (or arrive the night before), so you can spend as much time as possible at the **Children's Museum,** 3000 North Meridian Street. Considered the Disney World of children's museums, these five floors of magic alone are worth the trip—even if you don't have kids. Once you've bartered for goods in a 1700s French fur-trading post or sat behind the wheel of a race car or gone spelunking in a limestone cave, it's doubtful you'll have time to see much of anything else. But try not to leave without checking out the model train and antique doll collections—both claim to be the largest in the country.

The hand-carved carousel, which dates back to the 1900s, is well worth the extra 50 cents, but be advised that waits can be long. The museum also has a terrific playscape gallery for pre-schoolers, as well as a "living laboratory" for adolescents, where they can work everything from TV cameras to motorcycles.

Lunch: The restaurant at the museum is surprisingly good. Even eating is seen as an opportunity to learn, as kids watch the bakers at work.

Insider's tip: The scope here is really closer to a Museum of Science and Industry than any of the Chicago children's museums, so some extra planning is necessary. Schedule in mini-breaks, so everyone's circuits don't get overloaded. On weekends arrive when the museum opens, otherwise the lines at the most popular exhibits are interminable. If you need a well-timed bribe, the gift shop has nifty toys (educational, of course) that you'll find nowhere else. Open Tuesday–Saturday, 10 A.M.–5 P.M.; Sunday, noon–5 P.M. Closed Mondays from week after Labor Day to week before Memorial Day. Admission: adults, $4.00; children and seniors, $3.00; under 2, free. Phone (317) 924–KIDS.

Dinner: There are several options in and around **Union Station,** 39 Jackson Place. If you are exhausted from the museum and want a family restaurant without settling for McFood, try **Damon's** in the station. The moderately priced menu leans heavily toward barbecue, and the onion loaf should not be missed—even if you're just ordering dessert. (317) 638–9565.

While you're at Union Station, walk off dinner by perusing the shops. If you're here without children, try **Rick's Cafe American** (also in the station) for a nightcap and some jazz.

Lodging: The **Holiday Inn** at Union Station provides the opportunity to stay in one of twenty-six authentic Pullman sleeper cars that have been transformed into period hotel rooms. The rooms are meticulously appointed and probably would be quite pleasing if you were traveling by rail. But it may be hard to accept a narrow, claustrophobic room when you know more spacious accommodations exist just across the hall in conventional hotel rooms—and for about $20 less per night. The inconveniences (for example, only one person can watch TV at a time) likely will outweigh the comforts for all but the most passionate railroad buffs. There is also an indoor pool, sauna, and whirlpool. 123 West Louisiana Street. Rates range from $91–$180 per night. Phone (317) 631–2221.

Day 2

Morning

Breakfast: The hotel coffee shop is **The Original Pancake House.** This is a great breakfast for anyone who is a devotee of the apple pancake or Dutch Baby.

On today's agenda is the **Indianapolis Museum of Art,** 1200 West 38th Street. This is really four different art pavilions in one: The Mary Fendrich Hulman Pavilion houses the Eiteljorg Collection of African Art, the Clowes Pavilion features medieval and Renaissance art, the

Krannert features eighteenth- and twentieth-century European and American painting, and the Lily boasts extensive decorative arts shown in period settings. Consider the 152 acres of lush grounds and botanical gardens as a bonus. Admission free. A fee is charged for special exhibits, however, and a donation is requested at the Lily Pavilion. Phone (317) 923–1331. Open Tuesday–Saturday, 10 A.M.–5 P.M.; Sunday, noon–5 P.M.

Lunch: **The Garden on the Green,** located on the museum grounds, is a perfect spot for sandwiches, soups, and salads. Brunch is also served on Sundays, but reservations are required. Phone (317) 926–2628.

Afternoon

After lunch, head back toward downtown, for a tour of the **James Whitcomb Riley Home,** 528 Lockerbie Street. Built in 1872 and located in the 6-block historic Lockerbie Square neighborhood (just north of New York Street), this house is generally regarded as one of the best Victorian preservations in the country. The Hoosier poet's pen remains on his desk and his hat on the bed, as if he were due back any minute. Open Tuesday–Saturday, 10 A.M.–4 P.M.; Sunday, noon–4 P.M. Closed holidays. $1.00 admission. Phone (317) 631–5885.

If you are a fan of old homes, then make it a point to take in the **Benjamin Harrison Home,** 1230 North Delaware Street (north of Highway 65). The residence of the twenty-third president has been lovingly restored, right down to much of the original furniture. Also worth noting are the collection of gowns belonging to Mrs. Harrison and her daughter. Open Monday–Saturday, 10:30 A.M.–3:30 P.M.; Sunday, 12:30–3:30 P.M. Closed most holidays. Admission: adults, $2.00; children, $1.00. (317) 631–1898.

As you walk back toward the downtown hotels, stop at the **City Market,** 222 East Market Street. It's an ideal spot to pick up some fresh produce or just a chocolate chip cookie.

Itinerary note: If you are leaving for Conner Prairie or Zionsville tomorrow, you may want to fit in the two following suggestions today. If not, save them for your third day.

If Indianapolis means a checkered flag, then no visit here would be complete without a stop at what many consider a shrine: **The Speedway,** 4790 West 16th Street, just west of downtown. You can get a driver's-eye view of the track by taking a bus tour around the 2½-mile oval. Adjacent to the track, the **Hall of Fame Museum** displays all kinds of cars (racing, antique, and classic) and enough motor memorabilia to last a lifetime. Open daily, 9 A.M.–5 P.M. Closed Christmas. Admission: $1.00. Phone (317) 241–2500.

If you think cars are merely a way to get from Point A to Point B, however, consider taking in the **Indianapolis Zoo,** 1200 West Washington Street; it's large enough to be stimulating but not so large that it's intimidating. The 64-acre "cageless" facility includes the state's largest aquarium, an enclosed dolphin and whale pavilion, and animals in their natural habitats. There's also a critter "encounter" area where kids can have a hands-on experience with their furry friends. Open daily, 9 A.M.–6 P.M., June 1–Labor Day; 9 A.M.–4 P.M. rest of the year. Admission: adults, $7.00; children, $4.00. (317) 638–8072.

Dinner: Stay close to the hotel and dine at **St. Elmo's,** 127 South Illinois Street; (317) 635–0636. This quintessential steakhouse has been a local tradition since 1902. Sprawling twenty-ounce sirloins plus thick double filet mignons are the big draws, but the juicy veal chop shouldn't be ignored, either. Dinner only. Expensive.

There are a number of options for after-dinner activities. Art lovers can feast in Indianapolis—and at bargain prices as well. If music is your passion, you should know that Indianapolis has a first-rate symphony that plays in the newly renovated **Circle Theater,** 45 Monument Circle. Not only is this venue considered acoustically superb, but even the best seat in the house will set you back no more than $20. The season runs from October to May, with the annual Yuletide concert drawing an audience from all over the state.

First stop for theater fans should be the **Indiana Repertory Theater,** 140 West Washington Street, the state's only Equity company. The six-play season goes from October to May. (317) 636–2669.

The **Indianapolis Opera,** though less than twenty years old, is highly regarded, mounting four operas a year at **Clowes Hall** on the campus of Butler University. 4600 Sunset Avenue. For ticket information, call (317) 283–9696.

Even dance—hard to come by in all but the largest cities—is well represented with the **Indianapolis Ballet Theater,** 500 North Capitol Street. The company stages several major ballets each year, also at Butler, which is recognized as one of the premier ballet schools in the country. The IBT spends about half of its thirty-seven-week season on national tour, so the best way to keep on top of the schedule (or any arts event) is to use the Fun Fone, a twenty-four-hour hot line for special events; (317) 237–5210.

Lodging: Holiday Inn at Union Station.

Day 3

Morning

Get an early start for **Conner Prairie** in Noblesville. Take I–465 north to exit 35, then go 6 miles north. You'll feel as if you've stepped into a time machine and set the dial for 1836 as you enter this living-history museum. Like Greenfield Village in Detroit, the meticulous attention to detail is what makes this one of the state's best attractions (see Michigan Escape Five).

The other on-the-road option is **Zionsville,** which is really a northern suburb of Indianapolis (take I–95 north to Zionsville exit). There is no shortage of fun shops along the brick-paved streets of the 125-year-old Victorian business district. Though only six blocks, you'll find the ambience (window boxes overflowing with flowers, candlelit windows) most pleasant. You can pick up a map for a self-guided walking tour at the Chamber of Commerce, 135 South Elm Street; (317) 873–3836.

Adventurous palate alert: The heart of downtown Zionsville may seem like an unlikely place for an exotic restaurant, but there is one there called **Adam's Rib,** at 40 South Main Street. The menu includes such delicacies as buffalo, giraffe, camel, alligator, and zebra. Of course, tamer selections are available, and all are expertly prepared. Moderate to expensive. Open Monday–Saturday for lunch and dinner. Phone (317) 873–3301.

There's More

Eiteljorg Museum of American Indian and Western Art, 500 West Washington Street at the entrance to White River State Park. Home to one of the nation's finest collections of American Western and Native American art and artifacts. If your time is limited, peruse the paintings from the Southwest, particularly the work by the Taos, New Mexico, artists. Open Tuesday–Saturday, 10 A.M.–5 P.M.; Sunday, noon–5 P.M. Admission: Adults, $2.00; children, $1.00. (317) 636–9378.

Madame Walker Urban Life Center, 617 Indiana Avenue; (317) 236–2099. Named after the country's first black woman millionaire, this fabulous 1927 art deco building was originally used as a stage for vaudeville, but fell into disrepair after World War II. In 1988 it received a $3.2-million facelift and now serves as an arts and cultural center for the black community, as well as home to the popular weekly "Jazz on the Avenue" concerts.

Professional sports. The Indiana Pacers tip off at Market Square Arena (300 East Market Street; 317–239–5151.) The Indianapolis Colts kick off at the Hoosier Dome (100 South Capitol Avenue; 317–297–7000).

Special Events

Memorial Day. Indianapolis 500. The granddaddy of all auto races. Make sure you get your tickets well in advance. If you can't get tickets to the world's second-largest sporting event, the first day of qualifications is considered to be the next best thing.

June. Talbot Street Art Fair. Arts and crafts in the historic district of Herron-Morton Place.

June. Midsummer Fest. Entertainment and dozens of food booths from local restaurants.

July. Indiana Black Expo. Showcases the achievements of African-Americans in culture, art, history, and business. The three-day event is the largest exhibit of its kind in the United States.

August. Indiana State Fair. Carnival fun, horse shows, entertainment. State fairgrounds.

Other Recommended Restaurants and Lodgings

Indianapolis

Beaulieu, in The Canterbury, 123 South Illinois Street; (317) 634–3000. Although the food at Beaulieu is pricey by Hoosier standards, it is reasonable for Chicagoans who have become accustomed to $20 entrees. Dinner ranges from angel hair pasta with smoked salmon to moist, garlic chicken. Try the freshly baked croissants and buttery Danish pastries for breakfast. Open daily. Expensive.

The Canterbury, 123 South Illinois Street; (317) 634–3000. This hotel has 102 individually decorated rooms with Chippendale reproductions, four-poster beds, and marble baths. Most charming is the parlor—a mahogany-paneled sitting room of the lobby—that has a carved wooden fireplace and a bookcase with the works of Shakespeare, Dickens, and Kipling. The Canterbury hits just the right balance between British sophistication and down-home Hoosier hospitality. Rates range from $105 to $500 per night.

Chanteclair, in the Holiday Inn–Airport, 2501 South High School Road; (317) 243–1040. Another special occasion place, with the accent on French cooking. The strolling violinist sets the stage for romance. Expensive.

Hilton at the Circle, Ohio and Meridian streets; (317) 635–2000. Deluxe accommodations just 1 block north of Monument Circle. Rates: $95–$110 per night.

Hyatt Regency, 1 South Capitol Avenue; (317) 632–1234. One of the largest hotels in Indianapolis. Health club; luxury level available. Concierge on duty. Rates: $130–$180 per night.

Louisiana Street Restaurant and Bar, in Holiday Inn Union Station; (317) 631–2221. The *Indianapolis Star* calls this the city's best-kept secret. Creole specialties, with a blackened swordfish that is superb. Expensive.

Shapiro's, 808 South Meridian; (317) 631–4041. An authentic delicatessen that has been in the family for four generations, where you can find such ethnic specialties as juicy brisket, cabbage borscht, and cheesecake. Also good for breakfast. Inexpensive to moderate.

Tea Room at L. S. Ayres, 1 West Washington Street; (317) 262–2658. This is the local equivalent of the Walnut Room at Marshall Field's. Signature dishes include Chicken Velvet Soup and ice cream pie. A good place for a break from shopping.

Westin Indianapolis, 50 South Capitol Avenue; (317) 262–8100. Everything you would want from a spanking new, large (572 units) hotel. Heated indoor pool, whirlpool, health club privileges. Adjacent to the Hoosier Dome and Convention Center. Luxury level available, which includes a continental breakfast. Rates: $95–$140 per night.

For More Information

Indianapolis Convention and Visitors Association, 200 South Capitol Avenue, Indianapolis, IN 46225. Phone (317) 323–4639 or (800) 323–INDY.

Brown County

Brown County is a mecca for spectacular fall color.

Autumn Adventure

_____ 2 NIGHTS _____

Fall foliage • Hiking • Antique shops •
Shopping • Galleries • Fishing • Horseback riding

Autumn is to Brown County what skiing is to Aspen and the Derby is to Kentucky. The blazing of the colors in these richly forested foothills of the Cumberlands has become such a big event that it is not uncommon to find October weekends booked more than a year in advance.

While the drive to south central Indiana is on the long side (a little

over four hours from the Loop) and there undoubtedly are closer lo-
cales for viewing fall foliage, Brown County has enough other selling
points to make it worth the trek.

For starters, it has enjoyed a reputation as a crafts mecca ever since
it became a retreat for impressionist painters in the early 1900s. That
same reputation endures today and it is one that the natives take very
seriously. When you consider that Nashville, Indiana, has a population
of only 700—but more than 250 shops—you can see that art is
Nashville's meal ticket.

The following itinerary confines shopping to just one day. If you really are an addict, however, rest assured that you can spend your entire weekend in downtown Nashville and not do it all. Also, be
forewarned that if you visit during a peak autumn weekend, you will
probably encounter a preponderance of tour groups. If you're looking
for Walden Pond, head to the state park.

Any visit to Brown County may easily be combined with the two
counties that border it on both sides. To the east is Bartholomew
County, home of Columbus, one of the showplaces of American architecture (see Indiana Escape Six).

To the west is Monroe County, anchored by Lake Monroe (the
state's largest lake) and Indiana University in Bloomington. You'll find
several good ethnic restaurants in Bloomington, antique malls, and an
opera house that rates rave reviews from *The New Yorker*. All are worthy of a side trip or just a stop as you are coming or going.

Day 1

Morning

About the quickest way to get to Indianapolis is to take I–94 to I–65
south. Then take Highway 46 west right into **Nashville.** It is most efficient to get an early start and stop along the way for breakfast in
Lafayette, Indiana, which has a number of chain restaurants not far off
the interstate.

The sheer volume of boutiques, antique shops, and galleries in
Nashville can overwhelm even the most hard-core shopper. Get oriented at the **Brown County Convention and Visitors Bureau,** on
the corner of Main Street and Van Buren. If you haven't picked up a
free copy of the *Brown County Almanack* at your hotel, get one here.
It will be an invaluable source, particularly if you're searching for
something specific, such as cornshuck wreaths or stained glass.

Lunch: Gather up all your brochures, so you can read them over
lunch at the **Hob Nob,** right across the street from the visitors bureau.
This former apothecary shop is loaded with charm, from the wooden
booths to the soda fountain. Lighter fare includes quiche and home-

made soups and sandwiches, so you can leave room for the wickedly good sodas and sundaes. Phone (812) 988–4114.

Afternoon

Right above the Hob Nob is the **Brown County Craft Gallery,** a cooperative that showcases crafts exclusively made by local artists. If your time is limited and your concern is design integrity rather than just picking up a few knicknacks, the gallery's knowledgeable staff will help you plan the rest of your artistic itinerary.

If you do start here, then continue traveling north on Van Buren. There are about two dozen shops, which cover the craft spectrum from Shaker to Southwest. Taking even the smallest detour off the main drag can yield some delights, such as hand-crafted dulcimers at **Mountain Made Music** on West Main Street.

Going south on Van Buren, there are several clusters of shops (Calvin Place, Artists Colony) that are just made for exploring. Once again, get off the beaten track. If you go west on Franklin, you'll hit **Reflections,** a historic building that features ten rooms filled with prints, floral designs, and accessories. Right across the street is **Honey-suckle Place,** where you can check out Ditte Valbourg's lovely tapestries. Continue south a block and you'll come upon The Court-yard and the Barnyard Shops.

Dinner: **Brown County Inn,** Highways 46 and 135. This family restaurant is a convenient spot to end your shopping spree, since it is located at the end of Van Buren Street. The inn features fried chicken, prime rib, and fried catfish; moderate prices (most entrees fall in the $10–$12 range); and plentiful portions (soup and salad bar are included). The hash browns and the fruit cobblers are standouts.

From June through October, Brown County Inn holds a backyard barbecue every Saturday from 4 to 7 P.M. The buffet, which includes everything right down to the watermelon, is about $11.00 for adults ($5.00 for kids). With a playground nearby, mom and dad can linger over coffee and still keep an eye on the little ones. Phone (812) 988–2291.

Lodging: **Brown County Inn.** The furnishings here have clearly seen better days, and the ambience is closer to a Travel Lodge than a rustic inn. With ninety-nine rooms, the hotel does a big convention business and offers some amenities (cable TV, indoor pool, tennis). Rates range from $100 to $150 per night. Highways 46 and 135. Phone (812) 988–2291.

Day 2

Morning

Breakfast: A full and fortifying breakfast at **The Seasons Lodge**

(Highway 46; 812–988–2284). The specialty of the house is hot fried biscuits and apple butter. Try to get a seat near the window, where the bluffs provide the best floor show in town.

Presuming you've gotten all the shopping out of your system, make this your outdoorsy day. City dwellers will find everything from hayrides to hiking readily available at **Brown County State Park,** the largest in Indiana. It's located on Highway 46, 16 miles west of I–65. You can easily spend a day amid the lush 16,000 acres, including Weed Patch Hill, one of the state's highest elevations. There's also fishing, swimming (Olympic-sized outdoor pool), a nature center that provides hands-on experiences and programs on wildlife, and eight well-marked trails where you may catch a glimpse of white-tailed deer. The 2-mile trek starts at the lodge and includes the North Lookout Tower and is a good route for the average hiker. More advanced hikers may prefer the more rugged terrain that loops around the Ogle Hollow Nature Preserve. Be sure to pick up a trail map at the lodge.

Lunch: **Abe Martin Lodge,** Brown County State Park. Built in 1932 of hand-hewn native stone and oak, the dining room offers soups, salads, and sandwiches at very affordable prices. Phone (812) 988–7316.

Afternoon

Outside of Nashville, visit the **home and studio of T. C. Steele,** about 2 miles south of Belmont, off Highway 46. Considered one of Indiana's most esteemed artists, Steele's home and studio, all set amid 200-plus acres of beautiful gardens, can be toured. Open Monday–Saturday, 9 A.M.–5 P.M.; Sunday, 1–5 P.M. Free. (812) 988–2785.

If you are not planning a trip back to central Indiana soon, save the afternoon—or the whole second day—for a visit to Columbus. The architectural tour, which leaves by minibus from the Columbus Visitors Center at Fifth and Franklin streets, is conducted by knowledgeable guides. Or if you prefer, pick up a map and wander at your own pace (see Indiana Escape Six).

Dinner: **Story Inn,** Highway 135; (812) 988–2273. The best place to satisfy the sophisticated palate, this turn-of-the-century general store has carved out a reputation throughout Indiana. Menus change monthly and the kitchen does it all, from fettucine to rack of lamb. Service would be called leisurely by some, slow by others. Open year-round except Mondays. Reservations are a must for dinner; walk-ins accepted for breakfast and lunch. Moderate to expensive. It is also considered a first-rate place to stay (see Other Recommended Restaurants and Lodgings). Phone (812) 988–2273.

The emphasis on the visual arts has spilled over to the performing arts as well, which means that there are more entertainment options than you usually find in a town this size.

The **Brown County Playhouse,** operated by the theater department at Indiana University, has been going strong, from June through October, for thirty years. The repertoire is bound to have something by Neil Simon, and at about $10.00 a ticket ($5.00 for children), it represents one of the area's best buys. Call (812) 988–2123.

If your tastes run more toward country than cabaret, check out the **Little Nashville Opry,** located off Highway 46, which attracts big names at small-town prices ($12–$16). Saturday nights from May through November. Call (812) 988–2235.

Lodging: Brown County Inn.

There's More

Tours. If you are staying at one of the big hotels (Brown County Inn, Seasons Lodge), you can take a tram, called the Nashville Express, to Richard's Ice Cream, right in the center of town. It makes a 2-mile loop and runs from June through October, 10 A.M.–5 P.M.

More extensive sightseeing is offered by Brown County Tours. One- and two-hour options are available. (812) 988–1855.

Antiques. While Brown County itself is one big antiques fair, there are some malls devoted exclusively to antiques. One of the largest is Alberts' Mall, with fourteen rooms of antiques from 1800–1920. It's located 1 mile from Nashville on Highway 46W. (812) 988–2397. Others include Brown County Antique Mall I (located downtown) and II (3 miles east of town). If that's not enough, there are more antique malls in nearby Columbus, Morgantown, and Bloomington.

Golf. Eighteen-hole course located adjacent to Brown County State Park north entrance on Highway 46, just 2 miles east of Nashville. (812) 988–7888.

Duffers should also know that down the road in Columbus is Otter Creek Golf Course, which has been consistently ranked as one of the top twenty-five public courses in the country by *Golf Digest* magazine. 11522 East 50 N. Phone (812) 579–5227.

Ogle Lake. Fishing, mostly bass and bluegill. State license is required; one can be obtained at the Brown County State Park office.

Schooner Valley Stables, Inc. Horseback riding. Moonlight and overnight riding can also be arranged. Phone (812) 988–2859.

Ski World. Seven slopes, a bunny slope for beginners, chair lifts, rope tows, lodge, and dining facilities. Open mid-December to early March, weather permitting. (812) 988–6638.

Special Events

April. Spring Blossom Festival. Arts, crafts, food, entertainment.

June. Log Cabin Tour. Tour a half dozen of the area's log cabins.
November. Christmas in Brown County. Special open houses at all shops and galleries.

Other Recommended Restaurants and Lodgings

Three of Brown County's best-known restaurants—The Ordinary, The Nashville House, and The Seasons—are all under the same ownership. If you're looking for cuisine that's more sophisticated, seek out the bed and breakfasts mentioned here and in Columbus (Indiana Escape Six).

Nashville

Abe Martin Lodge, located in Brown County State Park. Like most state park inns, prices are moderate (rates start at $60). Call (812) 988–7316.

The Allison House Inn, 90 South Jefferson Street; (812) 988–0814. A restored Victorian home, located within walking distance from downtown. Five bedrooms, all with private baths. Breakfast included (the caramel nut rolls are especially tasty). Rates: $75 per night.

Chestnut Hill, Hoover Road, R.R. 4, Box 295, Nashville; (812) 988–4995. A historic log cabin situated on eighty-five acres, about 8 miles east of downtown. Three rooms (one with private bath). Decorated with antiques. Warm yourself in front of the Franklin stove in the sitting room or climb up the ladder to the loft, which is stocked with books. Dig into a full breakfast either in the country kitchen or on the front porch. Rates: $71 per night.

The Daily Grind, in Calvin Place, near Van Buren and Franklin; (812) 988–4808. The best cup of coffee in town, regardless of which of the twenty varieties you choose. This place feels like the coffeehouses of the sixties right down to the live folk and bluegrass music, which is featured on the weekends.

Hotel Nashville, Highway 135 and Mound Street; (812) 988–0740. In the heart of downtown. Year-round pool, sauna, and spa. Some suites available. Rates: $52–$95 per night.

The Nashville House, corner of Main and Van Buren; (812) 988–4554. The restaurant is closed on Tuesdays, except in October, when it is open daily.

The Ordinary, on Van Buren a block north of Franklin; (812) 988–6166. Breakfast served anytime. Note that the restaurant is closed on Mondays, except in October, when it is open daily.

Seasons Lodge, Highway 46, ¼ mile east of State Road; (812)

988–2284. With 80 rooms, this lodge offers such extras as a pool and gameroom, and some of the rooms have fireplaces. Known for its rustic surroundings. Rates: $65–$105 per night.

Story Inn, Highway 135 South; (812) 988–2273. Located on the edge of Brown County State Park, the Story Inn is best known for its restaurant. Built in 1850 as a general store, it also has accommodations, including four suites, three double rooms, and six cottages. (No children under twelve are allowed in the Main House.) Breakfast (try the banana pancakes) is included. Rates: $65–$85 per night.

For More Information

Brown County Convention and Visitors Bureau, corner of Main and Van Buren streets, P.O. Box 840, Nashville, IN 47448. (800) 753–3255 or 988–7303.

Columbus

The Irwin Union Bank and Trust, a landmark on the Columbus
architectural tour

Showplace of American Architecture

_____ 2 NIGHTS _____

Architecture · Antiques · Sightseeing · Hiking · Fishing · Historic village

Columbus is one town that can lay claim to that overworked adjec-
tive *unique*. It ranks fourth—behind New York, Chicago, and Los An-

geles—for buildings designed by famous architects. Not bad for a town of 35,000 people in central Indiana.

How did Columbus snare such stars as Harry Weese, I. M. Pei, and Cesar Pelli? The answer goes back to Joseph Irwin Miller, chairman of Cummins Engine Company, one of the town's biggest employers. Miller commissioned Eliel Saarinen, a well-known architect, to design the First Christian Church. In 1942 the striking brick-and-limestone structure tower was completed, and the town's reputation as "the Athens of the Prairie" was born.

Twelve years later Miller again sought out a Saarinen. This time it was Eliel's son, Eero, who was Miller's classmate at Yale, and the project was the Irwin Union Bank. Miller was so delighted with the glassy, lushly landscaped structure that he set up a foundation to attract top-notch talent to Columbus. Today more than forty buildings are a testimony to his vision.

Day 1

Morning

Take I–94 east to I–65 south. Then get on Highway 46 and head east into Columbus, 45 miles south of Indianapolis. The traveling time—four hours—is almost identical as that to Nashville (Indiana Escape Five). In fact, many people tack on an extra day and combine the two.

Since most visitors are too tired to "do" the architecture tour the day of arrival, you may find it more efficient to plan a side trip for the first day and save the Columbus sightseeing for the second day.

A stop at **Conner Prairie,** a living history museum in Noblesville—about 10 miles north of Indianapolis—fills the bill quite nicely. Turn off I–65 at Lebanon and take Highway 32 about 20 miles east to 13400 Allisonville Road, Noblesville.

Lunch: Start your visit at the museum center, where you'll find **Governor Noble's Eating Place,** which offers traditional cooking. There's a bakery adjacent to the restaurant, if you want to pick up a bag of goodies to nosh on during the afternoon.

Afternoon

After lunch you can peruse the galleries and gift shop at the Museum Center before touring the historic buildings. Here, first-generation Indiana settlers come to life in the schoolhouse, blacksmith shops, and gardens. Costumed guides and lots of hands-on activities make this more a personal encounter than a history lesson.

Conner Prairie also holds many special events, from weddings to performances by the Indianapolis Symphony Orchestra. The Candlelight Christmas Tours, held at 5:30 P.M. during most of December, are especially popular. Call for a schedule. Admission: adults, $7.00; kids, $4.00. (317) 776–6000.

For an entirely different kind of experience, you can hit **Manufacturers Marketplace** on I–65 (take exit 76B), about a half hour north of Columbus. Compared to similar outlet malls at Michigan City and Kenosha, the prices here are slightly cheaper, probably because the clientele comes primarily from Louisville and Indianapolis instead of Chicago.

Get back on I–65 to Columbus.

Dinner: **Left Bank,** 418 Fourth Street; (812) 379–2376. Located in the 1880 home of "The Columbus Republic," this comfortable restaurant has a more sophisticated kitchen than most. It also delivers room service to the Columbus Inn.

Lodging: **The Columbus Inn,** 445 Fifth Street; (812) 378–4289. This is one of the most acclaimed B&Bs in the country and the only one to have been awarded four diamonds by the AAA. In keeping with the town's architectural theme, Columbus Inn is appropriately enough the old city hall, but you'd never guess. The guest rooms are spacious and scrupulously clean, decorated in reproduction American Empire. All rooms (five suites, twenty doubles, nine singles) have private baths. Afternoon tea will give you a wonderful feeling of welcome.

Unlike with many other elegant inns, children are welcome, and even babysitting can be arranged with the front desk. Rates from $80 to $225 per night (breakfast included).

Day 2

Morning

Breakfast: Breakfast buffet at the Columbus Inn includes everything from juices to pancakes to sunflower seed bread (the recipe was printed in *Gourmet*).

Begin your architectural tour at the **Columbus Visitors Center,** located in a nineteenth-century home at 506 Fifth Street (812–372–1954). Here's where you can pick up maps and cassette tapes (which supply a running commentary on buildings and instructions on how to follow the tour route) for self-guided tours. Directional signs are also posted on all streets.

Thirty-five of the area's guidebook buildings are in Columbus; six others are within a 12-mile radius of the city limits. According to *Chicago Tribune* architecture critic Paul Gapp, "structures range from the brilliant to the commonplace and . . . at least a couple are absolute bombs." In addition to the Irwin Union Bank, Gapp cites the following buildings as especially noteworthy:

The First Christian Church, designed by Eliel Saarinen and where the whole effort began, is on the corner of Fifth and Lafayette. (You won't have any trouble finding it; the 166-foot-tall chimes tower can be seen from miles around.) Across the street is the **Cleo Rogers Memorial Library,** designed by I. M. Pei. On the same block is **Lincoln Elementary School** by Gunnar Birkerts. Said Gapp of the school: "It completes the ensemble of structures with satisfying harmony. Nowhere else in Columbus, perhaps, do buildings visually interact so well."

Rounding out the list is the **North Christian Church,** a few miles away at 850 Tipton Lane. It is Eero Saarinen's last work before his death and arguably Columbus's most famous building. Chicagoans should note that while most of the architects are represented by one or two designs, Chicago architect Harry Weese is credited with thirteen of the forty-one buildings listed in the guidebook.

If you skip the outlying buildings, the driving time takes between two and four hours, depending on how long you linger at each stop.

If you'd rather sit back and leave the driving to someone else, however, try the minibus tour. Reservations may be made in advance for the tour, which leaves from the visitors center daily from April through October. Arrangements can be made at the visitors center.

When you return you may also want to spend some additional time at the visitors center, which also houses a branch of the Indianapolis Museum of Art.

Lunch: A Columbus tradition, **Zaharako's Confectionery** has been located at the same address (329 Washington Street) since 1900. This amazing ice cream parlor features a Mexican onyx soda fountain (courtesy of the St. Louis World Exposition in 1905), Tiffany lamps, a working pipe organ, and delicious sandwiches and fountain creations. (812) 379–9329.

Afternoon

Across the street from Zaharako's is the **Commons,** designed by Cesar Pelli. This mall includes the usual stores, as well as an indoor playground that will be tough to tear the kids away from. The other big draw is the thirty-foot-tall, seven-ton kinetic sculpture by Jean Tinguely. Appropriately called "Chaos," the sculpture has a strangely hypnotic effect.

Antique lovers will want to check out the **Columbus Antique Mall** and its 260-plus dealers at 417 Washington Street.

Dinner: **Peter's Bay,** right in the Commons (812–372–2270). Opened at the end of 1990 by Marty Dittman, who was raised on a fishing boat. Fish is flown in daily from his family's boat near Boston. Moderate to expensive.
Lodging: The Columbus Inn.

Day 3

Morning

Breakfast: The Columbus Inn.
Make this your outdoorsy day. While architecture may get center stage in Columbus, the recreational opportunities represent one of the Midwest's best-kept secrets.

Depending on the season, the 16,000 acres at **Brown County State Park** offer hiking, boating, swimming, horse trails (see Indiana Escape Five). And if you're a serious angler, **Lake Monroe,** Indiana's largest body of water, is such a mother lode for bass and bluegills that it was listed as one of the top twenty-five locations for a fishing vacation in the angler's guidebook, *Fishing Hotspots.*

Boaters should note that the lake has two different characters, divided by Highway 446. Head to the western side—a.k.a. "the fast side"—for boating and waterskiing. The east side is more tranquil, with boat speed limits held to a minimum. Lake Lemon, which borders Brown and Monroe counties, is smaller than Lake Monroe, but with the same splendid scenery and facilities. For information, contact the visitors center at (800) 678–9828.

Lunch: Many of the area restaurants will pack you a picnic lunch, perfect for enjoying the area's beautiful vistas.

Afternoon

Wend your way home via I–65. If you haven't browsed Nashville's 250 galleries and shops, this is the time to break out those credit cards. Depending on your budget, patience, feet (or all of the above).

There's More

Bicycling. There are plenty of places to pedal in both Brown and Monroe counties, but if you are into cycling in a big way, Bloomington should be on your itinerary. *Bicycle Magazine* ranked it the seventh best city in the United States. The "Little 500" (remember the film *Breaking Away?*), held every April, and the "Hilly Hundred" are two of the premier events on the cyclist's calendar.

Camping. Fourteen public and private campgrounds are available throughout the Lake Monroe area. For information contact the Convention and Visitors Bureau, 441 Gourley Pike, Bloomington (812–334–8900). See also Brown County State Park.

Otter Creek Golf Course, the only Robert Trent Jones course designed in the state, has been ranked as one of the top twenty-five courses in the country by *Golf Digest.* For information call (812) 579–5227.

Boating. Blue's Canoe Livery will arrange everything you need for a canoe trip on Lake Monroe. Phone (812) 576–9851. Boat rental is also available at Lake Monroe recreational area.

Fishing. There are a number of charter services that will take you out on Lake Monroe.

Special Events

May. Fair on the Square. Arts and crafts, entertainment, and food. Downtown Columbus.

June. Popfest. The Indianapolis Symphony Orchestra and Pro Musica Orchestra play on the public library plaza. Attracts up to 10,000 visitors.

October. Ethnic Expo. On the second weekend of October, a three-day festival of food, cultural exhibits, entertainment, and a kite flying contest, all of which celebrate the city's cultural diversity.

October. Historic Homes Tour. Families living in historically significant homes open their doors to the public. Sponsored by Bartholomew County Historical Society and held every other year (on the odd-numbered year). Call (812) 372–3541.

Thanksgiving through early January. Holiday Lights Festival. Public displays transform Columbus into a winter wonderland.

Other Recommended Restaurants and Lodgings

Columbus

Columbus Bar, 322 Fourth Street; (812) 376–7046. Known locally as "The C.B.," this tavern is highly recommended for its tenderloin sandwiches and its onion rings.

Columbus Holiday Inn, 2480 Jonathon Moore Pike; (812) 372–1541. Indoor pool, sauna, exercise equipment; newly refurbished. Rates range from $50 to $75.

Ramada Inn, 2485 Jonathon Moore Pike; (812) 376–3051. Pool, free continental breakfast, tennis. Rates range from $45 to $60; some suites also available.

Weinantz Food & Spirits, 3450 Jonathon Moore Pike; (812) 379–2323. This is located as you get off I–65. Locals praise the "good, plain cooking."

For More Information

Columbus Visitors Center, 506 Fifth Street, Columbus, IN 47201. (812) 372–1954.

Michigan Escapes

MICHIGAN

Southwest Michigan

Untamed beaches at Warren Dunes attract sunseekers and hang gliders alike.

Harbor Country

_____ 2 NIGHTS _____

Antiques · Bicycling · Sailing · Orchards ·
Hang gliding · Swimming · Winery tours · Hiking · Camping

Harbor Country—the chamber of commerce moniker—extends from
the Indiana border on the south through New Buffalo, Union Pier,
Lakeside, and Bridgman. It's been a vacation haven for Chicagoans for
more than a century, but it was only during the 1980s that the area got
a giant dose of glamour, thanks to an influx of such celebrities as movie
mavens Gene Siskel and Roger Ebert and novelist Andrew Greeley.

Today pricey condos line the largest full-service marina on Lake
Michigan, and there are long lines at restaurants on the weekends.
Even so, Harbor Country is blessed with sand, surf, and breathtaking

sunsets. Everything moves just a little bit slower (except your watch; don't forget that Michigan is an hour ahead of Chicago).

Day 1

Evening

You'll want to make the quick trip right from work, taking I–94 to the Union Pier exit.

Dinner: **Panozzo's Cafe,** 15300 Red Arrow Highway, Lakeside; (616) 469–2370. If you time it just right, you'll arrive on a Friday night between six and nine for the pasta buffet, with its endlessly creative sauces (gorgonzola, zucchini with fresh rosemary). Owner Patty Panozzo has carved out quite a reputation for using locally grown produce and elevating it to culinary heights. Moderate.

Lodging: **Pine Garth Inn,** 16790 Lakeshore Road, Union Pier; (616) 469–1642. (Take Red Arrow Highway south). All rooms but one have a captivating view of the lake. Each room is individually decorated, so even repeat visits have a different feel. Several rooms on the main floor have lookout decks, just made for stargazing. Or browse the shelves in the library and pick out an old movie, which you can take up to your room and pop into the VCR (hidden in the armoire). Rates range from $105 to $130 per night.

Day 2

Morning

Breakfast: Pine Garth's restaurant.

Visit **Warren Dunes,** Michigan's busiest state park. Each year thousands of visitors enjoy the more than 2 miles of beach with dunes so high that the area has become a hotbed of hang gliding. The gentle breezes that blow off the lake combined with the soft "landing pad" below attracts dozens of colorful gliders, especially in the fall and spring. Adventurous types can sign up for a one-day lesson with the Southwestern Michigan School of Hang Gliding (219–778–4974).

Not that you have to be airborne to have a good time. The hiking and skiing trails, along with excellent picnic and campsite facilities, make Warren Dunes a popular spot all year. For more information contact the Southwestern Michigan Tourist Council (616–925–6301).

Lunch: **Golda's,** Red Arrow Highway near the entrance of Warren Dunes; (616) 426–4114. A Chicago hot dog with all the trimmings is the specialty of the house. It goes particularly well with a triple-thick chocolate malt (made with Ben & Jerry's ice cream).

Afternoon

Since many shops don't open until eleven, the afternoon is prime time for browsing. The area has about a dozen boutiques and galleries, with many clustered along Red Arrow Highway. **Lakeside Gallery,** 15486 Red Arrow Highway, is the most well known. This is a serious gallery that attracts serious artists (you'll frequently see announcements in the *Tribune's* Sunday calendar). There's also a rustic hotel (translation: no phones, TVs, or air-conditioning). It originally was set up to house visiting artists but now even takes people who haven't held a paintbrush since kindergarten. Phone (616) 469–3022.

Equally well known in the collectibles department is **Rabbit Run Antiques,** 15460 Red Arrow Highway, which has a terrific selection of English and Irish pine furniture. There are also quilts, rugs, and country folk arts.

A little farther south are **Royal Veil Antiques** for fine collectibles and **Filoni Vestimenti,** which sells fashionable clothing and accessories. Both are at 15300 Red Arrow Highway (next door to Panozzo's).

Off of Red Arrow is **Rainbow's End Antiques** (take Lakeside Road and go south 6 miles). This farm-turned-antiques-haven has everything from delicate glassware to massive furniture. For jewelry, especially, earrings, don't miss the **Silver Crane Gallery,** right in the center of Lakeside on Lakeside Road. The owners operate their own workshop in Taxco, Mexico, and the gallery offers excellent buys. (616) 469–4000.

If there's still room on the credit card, then go still farther south into New Buffalo. There the main drag is Whittaker. Check out **Le Grand Trunk** (447 Whittaker) for upscale clothing, **Compassions** (207 Whittaker) for hand-crafted jewelry (one of the owners is an artist), and the **Art Barn** (419 South Whittaker) for art and home accessories. **Country Mates,** which specializes in Christmas items, is on the cross street at 120 West Buffalo.

Dinner: **Miller's Country House,** 16409 Red Arrow Highway, 3 miles north of New Buffalo; (616) 469–5950. Char-grilled specialties such as Norwegian salmon, along with an airy, garden ambience, are what make Miller's such a popular spot with Chicagoans. The prices are as cosmopolitan as the clientele ($12–$18 for complete dinners, which include terrific French bread). The grill room is more clubby and casual, with a menu to match. (On Saturday nights during peak season, it's one menu only.)

Lodging: Pine Garth Inn.

Day 3

Morning

Breakfast: Don't leave without a breakfast at Panozzo's. When will you get an opportunity to try such concoctions as cocoa almond waffles or carrot and walnut pancakes?

Head away from the coast by traveling east on Highway 12. About 7 miles away is Three Oaks, where you'll find the **Three Oaks Bicycle Museum and Information Center** right downtown at 110 Elm Street (616–756–3361). Not only does this quirky museum include all kinds of relics and memorabilia, but it also offers very reasonable rates ($10 per day) for its well-maintained bikes. It also has toddler seats, helmets, and any other accessories you might need. In addition, you can get a map of bike routes in the area; it is designed for people who are just weekend riders as well as serious cyclists.

In fact, Three Oaks tourism is almost entirely built on the humble bike—especially during the third week of September, when some 7,000 cyclists flock to town for the **Apple Cider Century,** a one-hundred-mile bicycle tour through the colorful backroads of Berrien County.

Also on Elm Street (which intersects with U.S. Highway 12), you'll find the only meat market that qualifies as a tourist attraction. **Drier's Butcher Shop** (14 South Elm Street; 616–756–3101) sells hot dogs, sausages, and cheeses amid antiques, art, and homespun philosophy. Load up for the way home.

All that cheese and sausage will go especially well with the next stop. Go back to U.S. Highway 12 to Bridgman. Go north to Lake Street (which becomes Shawnee Road), and then go east and follow the signs to **Tabor Hill Winery and Vineyard**.

Lunch: At Tabor Hill, you can either picnic on the grounds or eat at the restaurant, which has such creative fare as chicken breast breaded in crushed pecans or simple grilled foods, including soft-shell crab. Prices range from $7.00 to $10.00.

Afternoon

After lunch you'll be ready to join the tour of the winery. Tabor Hill began when two Chicago salesmen brought a selection of hybrid grape vines back from France in the late sixties. They chose Southwest Michigan because they thought the gentle breezes off the lake would closely duplicate the conditions of the French provinces. Their hunch was right. The transplanted vines grew into a successful venture that produces about 40,000 gallons a year, making it the second busiest winery in the state, behind St. Julian in Paw Paw (which also operates a tasting center in Union Pier).

The half-hour tour begins where workers bottle the wine and then heads out into the vineyard. Next is a descent into the wine cellar for a look at the hand-carved oak casks (which depict scenes from Tabor Hill's history). The tour winds up in everyone's favorite place—the tasting room—for samples of some whites, reds, and blends. If you are visiting in mid-August, find out when the harvest festival will be held. This spirited event features food, entertainment, and even a competitive grape stomp. The winery is open daily June through mid-September; otherwise weekends only. Phone (616) 422–1161.

If you have time on your way home, even a brief stop is worthwhile at **Fernwood,** a nature facility and botanical garden (13988 Range Line Road, between Berrien Springs and Buchanan). This little six-acre gem includes a lilac garden, a boxwood garden, a perennial garden, a fern trail, and a rock garden. The new visitors center has a sunny plant room, a gift shop, and a tea room. Phone (616) 695–6491.

There's More

Cook's Energy Information Center, Red Arrow Highway, 3 miles north of New Buffalo; (616) 465–6101. Worth remembering on a rainy day, the Cook Nuclear Plant is one of the largest in the country. The center features three video presentations, including a robot-led trip through time. Open daily during season; check for off season hours.

Lemon Creek Fruit Farms, Vineyards, and Winery, 533 Lemon Creek, east of Baroda. (From I–94, take Bridgman exit.) What used to be strictly a produce operation has been turning out credible medium-priced wines since the early 1980s. Lemon Creek supplies Tabor Hill, St. Julian, and other local wineries with grapes as well. Much less showmanship than other winery tours, which some folks will find appealing. It's a seasonal operation, so check for hours by calling (616) 471–1321.

Michiana Antiques Mall, 2423 South 11th Street, Niles; (616) 684–7001. Some of the first-rate antique stores have been mentioned, but the Michiana Antiques Mall is worth remembering for its one hundred dealers and one-stop shopping.

Berrien Springs Courthouse, on U.S. Highway 31 (Cass) at Union Street, 3 blocks north of downtown Berrien Springs. The 1839 Greek Revival courthouse is the oldest county government building in Michigan. It holds a worthy collection of artifacts from Native American to Civil War memorabilia to information on how the area became a mecca for Seventh-Day Adventists. The complex includes a sheriff's office and a log home. Admission is free. Phone (616) 471–1202.

Tree-Mendus Fruit, East Eureka Road, 5 miles northeast of Berrien Springs. In a land of orchards and produce markets, this is the granddaddy of them all. You can have a delightful one-hour orchard tour, watch an apple cider press in action, or do nothing more taxing than buy jams and jellies. There are also 560 acres of U-pick orchards, a nature park with hiking trails, and even a chapel in the woods in case you feel like getting married. Phone (616) 782–7101.

Special Events

June. Three Oaks Flag Day. Billed as the largest Flag Day celebration in the country. Includes an old-fashioned tent circus. Downtown Three Oaks.

July. International Cherry Pit-Spitting Contest. Doesn't the title tell you everything you want to know? Tree-Mendus Fruit Orchards, Berrien Springs.

August. Ship and Shore Festival. Entertainment, food, art. Downtown New Buffalo.

August. Berrien County Youth Fair. The prize-winning animals owned by local 4-H youngsters are always fun to see. Carnival rides. Berrien Springs.

Other Recommended Restaurants and Lodgings

Union Pier

The Inn at Union Pier, 9708 Berrien Street (just off Lakeshore Drive); (616) 469–4700. Ranking with Pine Garth as one of the area's best-known inns, it is located just 200 steps from the beach. Swedish ceramic fireplaces (called Kakelugn) grace the five second floor rooms of the main house and the six rooms in the pierhouse, which makes this an especially worthy destination in fall and winter. Enjoy hearty, homemade breakfast in the morning, Michigan wines and popcorn in the evening. Rates: $85–$110 per night (less midweek).

Lakeside

The Pebble House, 15093 Lake Shore Road; (616) 469–1416. This seven-room inn is known for its pared-down Arts & Crafts style. In fact, special weekends that celebrate this early twentieth-century design movement are held here. Adjacent tennis courts. The beach is across the street. Full breakfast buffet includes meats and cheeses. Rates: $90–$130 per night.

New Buffalo

Burhops Crabhouse, 244 North Whittaker Street; (616) 469–4001. The new branch of the popular Chicago seafood restaurant. Known for its fresh fish, prepared just about any way you like it. Live entertainment. Moderate to expensive.

Comfort Inn, exit 1 at I–94; (616) 469–4440. This is a spot to remember if you're traveling with kids, since many B&Bs are for adults only. Even though Comfort Inn has a reputation as a national chain, this property is more upscale and even offers king-sized suites that include a Jacuzzi, refrigerator, and wet bar. Pool/sundeck. Continental breakfast included. Rates: $50–$90.

Redamak's, 616 East Buffalo; (616) 469–4522. Redamak's and New Buffalo are synonymous. Anyone who has waited in the long lines here knows that this hamburger haven needs little introduction. The burgers are delicious, the fries are crispy, and it's all a terrific buy, especially if you're there during the week when "the workingman's special" kicks in (burger and fries for a mere $2.00). Stick to the basics and you won't be disappointed. In balmy weather, try for a table on the patio.

Bridgman

Hyerdall's, 9673 Red Arrow Highway; (616) 465–5546. A very popular restaurant that turns out basic American fare, such as meat loaf or chicken with mashed potatoes and gravy, polished off with apple pie. The bread basket—abundant with rolls and muffins—could qualify as a meal in itself.

For More Information

Harbor Country Chamber of Commerce, 3 West Buffalo, New Buffalo, MI 49117. (616) 469–5409.

South Haven

South Haven's proximity, marina, and beaches make it a baby-boomer favorite.

From Bikes to Blueberries

_____ 3 NIGHTS _____

Antiques · Biking · Fishing · Watersports · Museums

As recently as a decade ago, the only thing South Haven had to offer was nostalgia.

From the 1920s until the late 1960s, South Haven was a popular vacation spot. But a variety of factors conspired to turn South Haven into a ghost town. Young baby boomers didn't want to go where their parents went—and they certainly didn't want to go where the activities centered around eating, card playing, and seeing third-rate comedians. They wanted tennis courts, golf courses, and aerobics classes. With the advent of cheap air fares they could have any of these—and at prices that weren't much different than a South Haven weekend. When those stinky little fish called alewives washed up on Lake Michigan's shores during the 1970s, the beaches were off limits and so was South Haven. Hotels were boarded up and lawns became choked with weeds.

Fast-forward to the late 1980s. The energy crisis and the time crunch have put South Haven back into the tourism business. The same baby boomers are bringing their own children to its pristine beaches, casual ambience, and easy commute (about two hours from the Loop).

The South Haven of the nineties is different because most hotels and resorts have been replaced by condominiums (watch the Sunday paper for rental information). The list of good accommodations is short, but if you are shut out, check out the larger neighboring communities of Saugatuck and Holland.

Day 1

Morning

Head east on I–94 to St. Joseph. Founded as a shipping port in the 1830s, St. Joe (as nearly everyone calls it) has a genteel air. The downtown with its early twentieth-century architecture features such landmarks as the People's State Bank and the once-grand Whitcomb Hotel (now a retirement home). True history buffs will want to pick up a visitor's guide and follow the entire walking tour.

If you want something a little more hands-on, try the **Curious Kids Museum,** 415 Lake Boulevard (between Broad and Elm streets). While it doesn't have the five floors of spectacle you'll find at the Children's Museum in Indianapolis, there is plenty here to warrant a stop, especially if your kids like—and you can stand—messy (bubbles and face painting) and noisy (musical instruments) activities. The gift shop is a nifty opportunity to pick up some educational toys. Open Wednesday–Saturday, 10 A.M.–5 P.M.; Sunday, noon–5 P.M. Admission: adults, $2.50; children, $1.50. Call (616) 983–CKID.

Lunch: **Wilbur's Ice Cream and Sandwich Shop,** 609 Broad Street; (616) 983–5065. Wilbur's is not some nostalgic recreation, but the real thing, circa 1903. Perhaps the sandwiches are light (tuna, egg salad) because the sodas are so gargantuan. (The ice cream is made right on the premises.)

Or you can always grab a cone and stroll through **Lake Bluff Park.** You get a splendid view of Lake Michigan as well as a crash course in the city's past. The park is dotted with monuments, including a bronze firefighter carrying a child, which commemorates twelve city firemen who perished in an opera house fire at the turn of the century.

Afternoon

Just a few blocks away, at 707 Lake Boulevard, is the **Krasl Art Center.** The Krasl is another well-run, accessible museum. The exhibits are constantly changing, from fine arts to folk arts. The **Holly Market,** the center's Christmas crafts fair, attracts a huge following. Free. Call for a schedule: (616) 983–0271. Open Monday–Thursday and Saturday, 10 A.M.–4 P.M.; Friday, 10 A.M.–4 P.M.; Sunday, 1–4 P.M.

Get back on I–94 toward South Haven, but if you're a furniture lover, schedule a slight detour (about ⅛ mile off the expressway) and stop at **Bay Antiques,** 5907 Mountain Road, just outside Coloma. (Take the Coloma exit and turn left on Mountain Road.) You can find some fine pieces, as well as architectural artifacts, such as friezes and leaded glass. Call (616) 468–3221. From there, it's only another fifteen minutes to South Haven.

Dinner: **Sea Wolf,** Blue Star Highway, 3 miles north of downtown South Haven. Considered one of the best restaurants in southwest Michigan. Choose from whitefish prepared eight different ways. Blueberry pie and other desserts provide a taste of the region's produce. Complete dinners include chopped liver and matzo ball soup, reflecting the restaurant's earlier lineage as the well-known Weinstein's Resort. Prices start at about $13. Open for dinner only, May–October. Phone (616) 637–2007.

Lodging: **Yelton Manor,** 140 North Shore Drive; (616) 637–5220. This lovely Victorian inn has a great location (right across from the beach) as well as charming rooms (some with Jacuzzis) and gracious hospitality. A full breakfast and hors d'oeuvres are included with the cost of a room. If you stay between Thanksgiving and mid-January, you'll find a Christmas tree in every room. Rated by Amoco as one of the top twelve B&Bs in the country. Rates range from $90 to $170 per night.

Day 2

Morning

Breakfast: Yelton Manor. A multicourse affair, from fresh fruit to eggs and American fries to warm-from-the-oven coffee cake.

People come to South Haven for relaxation. At **North Beach,** 5 miles of sand and gentle waves (Lake Michigan averages five degrees warmer on the Michigan side than on the Illinois side) make it easy to mellow out. Type-A personalities, however, can always get into a lively game of volleyball or participate in a variety of watersports. **North Shore Aquasports** (114 Dyckman Avenue; 616–637–6208), just a few blocks from the beach, rents sailboards and has certified instructors in windsurfing.

Lunch: **Jensen's Fishery,** just over the drawbridge on Dyckman, is such a no-frills operation that you don't even have to change out of your swimsuit. It is a fish market with a handful of tables, and the service is strictly paper plates. Shrimp any way you want it—grilled, fried, smoked—is the claim to fame here, but perch runs a close second. (616) 637–2008.

Afternoon

Lake Michigan Maritime Museum, right next door to Jensen's, provides a good overview on the link between shipping and the Great Lakes. Boats are displayed outside as well. Admission: $1.50. Call for hours, (616) 637–8078.

Adjacent to the museum is **Old Harbor Village,** a retail complex that is part of the South Haven renaissance. While the shopping is lackluster, the cobblestones make you feel as if you're really on vacation.

From Old Harbor Village, you're just a few blocks from Phoenix, the main drag. There's a sprinkling of interesting antique and gift shops, most notably the **Arkins Book Store** (where you can find lots of books on the shore) and **Blueberry Store,** which sells everything from soup to soap in South Haven's favorite flavor and scent.

Dinner: While you're here, you might as well put your name on the list at **Clementine's Saloon** (418 Phoenix; 616–637–4755). Tourists and natives alike are drawn to the moderate prices and large portions, so count on long lines between Memorial Day and Labor Day. During the summer the grilled chicken salad is a good bet, but when the mercury drops, go for the homemade soups. Specialty of the house is the golden onion rings, which are served on a wooden peg and are stacked vertically.

After dinner walk across the street and rediscover the charm of going to a small-town movie theater (as opposed to the concrete bunker at the mall). **The Michigan** shows first-run movies, and you'll pay a few bucks less and get real butter on your popcorn to boot.

After the movies, end up the evening with an ice cream cone. You have a couple options. **Sherman's Dairy Bar** (on the corner of Phoenix and I-196; 616–637–8251) is the place for a late-night run (open until 11 P.M. daily during the summer). But if you don't want to drive (the store is next to the actual dairy on the outskirts of town), you can satisfy your sweet tooth at **Captain Nemo's,** a nondescript coffee shop at the end of Phoenix.

But if an ice cream drink is more what you had in mind, then board the *Idler,* an 1897 riverboat docked at Old Harbor Village (616–637–8435). Built by a wealthy merchant as a pleasure craft, it hasn't changed its function a bit almost a century later. There's also a below-deck dining room featuring Cajun cuisine.

Lodging: Yelton Manor.

Day 3

Morning

Breakfast: Yelton Manor. If you tried the egg casserole yesterday, go for the stuffed French toast today.

Pick up a picnic lunch at **North Shore Deli** (it shares the same building with North Shore Aquasports) and the **Kal-Haven Trail,** which many people consider to be one of the best bike paths in western Michigan. The former Penn Central Railroad bed offers 34 miles of smooth, level riding, making it accessible to even young cyclists. In addition, the landscape changes from wetlands to wildlife and is spectacular for viewing fall foliage. The trail passes by the small towns of Lacota, Grand Junction, Bloomingdale, Gobles, Kendall, and Alamo before ending in Kalamazoo. It's also a favorite of hikers and snowmobilers. Be forewarned: If you decide to ride to Kalamazoo, there's little in the way of accommodations beyond the Kal-Haven Bed and Breakfast in Gobles (23491 Paulson Road; 616–628–4932).

The start of the trail is on Blue Star Highway, ½ mile north of Phoenix Road. Trail fee: $2.00 per person per day; $5.00 per family. For an illustrated map, call (616) 637–2788.

Afternoon

If you've totally exhausted yourself, head back to the beach. If not, muster up the energy to visit the **Bangor Train Factory,** 10 miles west of South Haven. You'll know you're in the right place when you see the old depot, home of the only manufacturer in the United States to make Number 1 Grade Trains. Models are set up and running, and a visit is bound to be a highlight of the trip for children of all ages. Tours are free, but call for hours: (616) 427–7927.

About ½ block from the train factory is the **Bangor Antique Mall,** 215 West Monroe (616–427–8557). It's worth your time with thirty dealers. You'll also find some bargains at **Palmer's Antiques,** 139 West Monroe (616–427–8663).

Dinner: **Three Pelicans,** at the south end of North Shore Drive, overlooks the Black River. Try the Dijon-glazed salmon ($13), although there are many entrees in single digits. The restaurant puts on a fine Sunday morning buffet ($7.95 for adults, $4.95 for children). It's worth waiting to get a table by the window. (You can always pass the time by perusing all the photos of celebrities.) Open year-round.

Walk off dinner on South Haven's **South Pier,** which is now adorned with twinkling lights. It's a romantic stroll down to the lighthouse at the end of the pier, but do pay attention to the weather. The waves have been known to sweep visitors off the pier.

Still have that spring in your step? Check out **Max's,** 1701 North Shore Drive, about a mile down from Yelton Manor on North Shore Drive, for late-night dancing.

Lodging: Yelton Manor.

Day 4

Morning

Breakfast: You can't leave South Haven without having breakfast at the **North Beach Inn** (51 North Shore Drive; 616–637–8943). The pancakes and waffles are bursting with blueberries, and motherly waitresses make sure your coffee cup is never empty. The lines at the North Beach can be long, but they move quickly. This Victorian home is also a B&B. People have been known to check in here strictly to ensure that they get a terrific breakfast.

Head to the **South Haven Antique Mall,** 424 Quaker Street (1 block north of Phoenix), which has about twenty dealers, and **Anchor Antiques,** 209 Center Street (just across the street). You'll find very good prices and high-quality merchandise.

If that breakfast whetted your appetite for blueberries, you're in luck. The last stop before you go home is **DeGrandchamps Blueberry Plantation,** 3 miles south of South Haven on Blue Star Highway (616–637–3915). Picking your own isn't much cheaper than buying produce, but it's a lot more fun. With 100 acres, DeGrandchamps is the largest in the region. You can also watch the processing and packing operations.

There's More

Arcade/amusements. Fideland Fun Park, Blue Star Highway (3 miles east of South Haven). Go-carts, batting cage, driving range, miniature golf. (616) 637–3123.

Golf. Glen Shores Country Club (616–227–3226) and South Haven Golf Club (616–637–3896), both on Blue Star Highway, just north of South Haven.

Captain Nichols. Fishing, primarily perch. Can arrange any type of charter. Phone (616) 637–2507.

Van Buren State Park, Blue Star Highway, 3 miles south of South Haven. Camping, hiking.

Special Events

May. Mini-Indy. Bed races, remote control toys, and go-karts travel a course through downtown South Haven.
June. South Haven Fine Arts Fair.
July. Blueberry Festival. Crafts, entertainment, and a blueberry pie eating contest. Downtown South Haven.
September. Venetian Night and All Crafts Fair. Decorated, lighted boat parade and some 250 crafts booths. Downtown St. Joseph.

Other Recommended Restaurants and Lodgings

South Haven

A Country Place, North Shore Drive, about 1½ miles from downtown; (616) 637–5523. A very sweet place, just as the name implies. "Innkeepers are so delightful that they actually make the weekend," said one visitor. Greek revival farmhouse paired with country decor. A full breakfast, taken on the deck in the summer and around the fire in the winter, is a highlight. About one block from the beach. Rates: $50–$60 per night.

Golden Brown Bakery, 421 Phoenix; (616) 637–3418. Right downtown; a good place to pick up rolls and juice for a breakfast outing. English muffin bread makes for great beginnings.

Old Harbor Inn, 515 Williams; (616) 637–8480. Located at the drawbridge, this is a good selection for those who want more hotel and less inn. None of the thirty-seven rooms has the same decor. Most rooms have balconies that overlook the river. Some have Jacuzzis and fireplaces. Peak season rates range from $75 to $175 per night.

Sleepy Hollow Resort, North Shore Drive; (616) 637–1127. A very popular choice with families because of the children's programs and pool (as well as private Lake Michigan beach). Lodging options include hotel, cottages, and apartments. Open May 1–October 10. Room rates average $90 a night.

For More Information

Lake Shore Convention and Visitors Bureau, P.O. Box 890, South Haven, MI 49090. (616) 637–5252.

Saugatuck

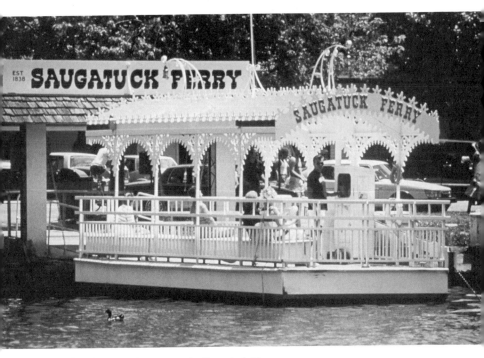

A chain ferry brings visitors across the Saugatuck River.

The Artists' Colony

_____ 2 NIGHTS _____

Ferry rides • Galleries • Boating • Shopping • Fishing • Golf

Saugatuck's name has been linked with painters and sculptors since 1910, when the Art Institute of Chicago opened an artists' camp there. Creative types were drawn by the same balmy breezes, untamed marshes, and slightly bohemian atmosphere that attract tourists today.

To truly savor the area's unspoiled beauty, consider off-season. Like Lake Geneva and Door County, the crowds queuing up at restaurants can make you think you never left the city. Off-season does not mean dead of winter, however. Late August can be early enough.

One word of caution: Saugatuck can be a very tough place to find lodging, so book reservations well in advance. Also, more accommodations are available in Holland, just fifteen minutes away. Because there is so much to do in both towns, they are listed here as separate destinations, but you can easily combine the two for one terrific weekend.

Day 1

Morning

Take I–94 east to I–196 north into Saugatuck. (If the trip is leisurely and you'd like to make some stops along the way, see Indiana Escape One and Michigan Escapes One and Two).

Lunch: Stop for lunch at the **Loaf & Mug,** 236 Culver Street. Walk right through the dining room to the backyard terrace, where the umbrella tables and wrought-iron furniture are the perfect complement to the fresh salads, just-baked muffins, and tall, cool glasses of lemonade and iced tea. The house specialty is a hollowed-out round loaf that serves as a "bowl" for the soup du jour (which is actually closer to stew du jour). Casual and inexpensive. Phone (616) 857–2974.

Afternoon

Because Saugatuck has some fifty shops, your eyes can easily glaze over. A better strategy is to divide your shopping over two days.

The main street is Butler, where virtually every craft is represented. There are also numerous antique shops. Don't expect to find any real bargains because of the large Chicago clientele, but the looking is great fun.

An especially interesting complex is the **Old Post Office Shops** (238 Butler Street), about a half dozen little boutiques, including one of the most fantastic stationery stores, which carries everything from beautiful gift wraps to hand-illustrated Florentine paper.

Also stop in at **Saugatuck Drug,** 201 Butler Street (616–857–2300). This is really a department store masquerading as a drugstore. It has everything from beach towels to video rentals—even an old-fashioned ice cream fountain and a video arcade, tucked in the back. If it's a rainy day and you have kids, this is your best bet.

Other stand-outs include **das bauhaus** (546 Butler Street; 616–857–2495), a mecca for art deco jewelry; open only on weekends.

Cain Gallery (322 Butler Street; 616–857–4353) is another spot to find wonderful jewelry as well as sculpture and art glass. This is the summer home of a gallery of the same name in Oak Park (at 111 North Marion), and items are always being shuttled between the two—good to remember if you see something you love on vacation and can kick yourself later for not buying it.

At **Joyce Petter Gallery** (134 Butler Street; 616–857–7861) you can always see top-notch work, from about fifty American artists. Don't miss the courtyard and rear garden for ceramics and sculpture.

Dinner: **Chequers,** 220 Culver Street, is a comfortable English-style pub with a convivial atmosphere. Fish and chips, shepherd's pie, and mixed grill are hearty and fairly inexpensive. An ample selection of beers and ales. Come early, or be prepared to wait. Phone (616) 857–1868.

Savvy tourists gather on **Oval Beach** at dusk to see the sun put on its splendid show as it disappears into Lake Michigan. Of course, you don't have to be sedentary. Climb **Mt. Baldhead,** the 250-foot dune near Oval Beach, for a cardiovascular workout, to say nothing of a great vantage point.

Lodging: The variety of accommodations in Saugatuck varies from the most elegant inns to no-frills motels. Here are two options; one for a romantic weekend; the other for a family outing.

The Wickwood Inn, 510 Butler Street, offers terrific creature comforts and a location to match (on the edge of the business district, but one sand dune away from the beach). Country-English furniture will make you feel as if you are in the Cotswolds, not southwestern Michigan. While many resort hostelries operate in a half-hearted manner during the winter months, the Wickwood turns Christmas into a two-month-long affair. From mid-November until mid-January, there's a tree in every bedroom. But don't count on waking up in one of the four-poster canopy beds on Christmas Day. It's closed. Rates range from $80 to $115. Phone (616) 857–1097.

When the kids are in tow, consider the **Beachway** (106 Perryman; 616–857–3331), which is the closest resort to the public beach. The casual, friendly atmosphere is very suitable for families. While the decor is more bargain basement than Laura Ashley, the rooms have the comfortable feel of your own summer rental. Inflatable toys and air mattresses float in the pool—thus saving the expense when you discover that you've left yours at home. Rates range from $50 to $100 (suites).

Day 2

Morning

Breakfast: Continental breakfast at the Wickwood. Or start the day at **Pumpernickel's,** 210 Butler Street (616–857–1196), right in the heart of downtown. Daily egg specials are served with homemade breads. Don't miss the splendid sticky buns.

Check out **Saugatuck Dunes State Park,** located 3½ miles north of Saugatuck. Its remote location makes it one of the best-kept secrets in western Michigan, and it's especially tranquil in the morning. The 1,100 acres include more than 2 miles of Lake Michigan beach and 14 miles of hiking trails, where you can find wonderful dune-top views of the lake. It's an outstanding place for a picnic lunch, which either the Mug and Loaf or Pumpernickel's can arrange.

Afternoon

This would be an opportune time to take a dune ride aboard a sixteen-seat open-air vehicle. **Saugatuck Dune Rides,** ½ mile west of I–196; (616) 857–2253. Adults, $7.50; kids, $4.50.

After the half-hour ride, head into Douglas, just a few miles from Saugatuck. Douglas does not have the business district of its more famous neighbor, but it does have the SS ***Keewatin*** ship museum. The 336-foot vessel is permanently moored here and a fine example of a luxury passenger boat from back in the days when steamships regularly crossed Lake Michigan. The Edwardian dining room and ornate mahogany make you yearn for a more elegant era. Open Memorial Day–Labor Day. Adults, $3.00; kids, $1.50.

While you're longing for the open seas, head back to Saugatuck for a ninety-minute cruise on the ***Queen of Saugatuck.*** The eighty-two-passenger sternwheeler travels down the Kalamazoo River to Lake Michigan as the captain furnishes fact and folklore. In July and August, weather permitting, cruises depart every two hours Monday through Saturday 10 A.M. until 5 P.M., with a sunset sojourn pushing off at 7:30 P.M. On Sundays, the first cruise sails at 1 P.M. The schedule is more abbreviated in May, June, September, and October. The pier is at 716 Water Street. Phone (616) 857–4261. Rates are $6.00 for adults, $3.00 for children.

Dinner: **Clearbrook Golf Course,** 65th Street at 135th Avenue, just a few minutes from the center of town. Many residents consider this Saugatuck's best restaurant. Specialties include rack of lamb, beef tenderloin, and fresh walleye. Insider's tip: Tuck this place away for lunch, too. Between 11 A.M. and 3 P.M., you can enjoy grilled food on the patio that overlooks the first tee. There's also a fine Sunday brunch. Moderate to expensive. Reservations recommended. Phone (616) 857–1766.

Unlike many resort towns that roll up the sidewalks at dusk, Saugatuck has a bustling nightlife. **Coral Gables,** 220 Water Street, boasts four bars and is a late-night magnet. The **Crow Bar** gets a younger (and louder) crowd, while the **Rathskeller** gets the over-thirty set.

If the bar scene isn't for you, peruse the marquee at **Red Barn**

Playhouse (3657 63rd Street), where you can see surprisingly polished musicals, despite the fact that stagehands hand out lemonade at intermission. Season is from Memorial Day through October. Call for schedule: (616) 857–2105.

Day 3

Morning

Breakfast: Continental breakfast at Wickwood Inn. Or try the **Auction House** in downtown Douglas (616–857–4292), which offers bountiful breakfasts at ridiculous prices (for instance, pancakes loaded with fresh strawberries for less than $3.00). People come from all over for the biscuits and gravy, but with everyone so cholesterol conscious, the chef also offers egg substitutes.

After breakfast, stop at any of the Saugatuck boutiques you couldn't fit in the first day before heading out of town.

Travel south on I-196 and take Highway 89 east to Fennville, about 6 miles southeast of Saugatuck. A stop in Fennville—either coming or going—is a must. To be in the vicinity and not stop at **Crane's Orchards and Pie Pantry Restaurant**, 6054 124th Avenue, would be to miss out on one of the best orchards in Michigan. (616) 561–2297.

It is well worth your time, whether you're there to cool off with an apple cider popsicle on a July afternoon, to take the bite off an October morning with a cup of hot cider (watch it being pressed), or to pick a bushel of apples to bring home. Try to arrange your departure so you are here for lunch. The food is basic good cooking—homemade soups, chili, and roast beef and turkey sandwiches on freshly baked bread, all washed down with Crane's trademark cider, which arrives in a pitcher. Save room for apple and cherry crisps and pies, but if you can't loosen your belt another notch, you can always buy one to take home.

There's More

Saugatuck Antique and Auction Center, Blue Star Highway at 64th Street. Auctions are held Thursdays only at 6 P.M. There are bargains to be had here (quilts, oak furniture), and the bidding can get fast and furious. Summer season only.

Ballooning. One of the fastest-growing sports in western Michigan, balloon rides can be arranged by the hour or the day. For rates and information call (616) 335–3363.

Boating. Tower Marine (616–857–2151), Sergeant Marine

(616–857–2873), and West Shore Marine (616–857–2181) all have boats to rent. Call them for specific information.

Fishing. Sport fishing (chinook and coho salmon, lake, brook, and steelhead trout) is very big in these parts. The season starts in early April and winds up around November 20. A number of charters provide everything you need, right down to the box lunch. (They'll even clean and package your catch.) Here are a few: "Can't Miss" Charters (616–561–2252) and "Best Chance" Charters (616–857–4762). Pete's Charter Service (616–857–2942) offers "design your own" cruises and excursions to the nearby ports of South Haven and Holland. It's as much for camera buffs as for anglers.

Golf. West Shore Golf Club, Douglas. The second oldest golf course (1917) in the state of Michigan. Phone (616) 857–2500.

Hunting. Allegan State Game Area, 4590 118th Avenue. About 45,000 acres of marsh and fields between Fennville and Allegan. Canada geese migrate here each fall, making it one of Michigan's largest and most popular hunting areas. In addition to waterfowl, hunters recommend it for deer, turkey, and small game. For information call (616) 673–2430.

Skiing. The tourism folks are doing their best to market the area as more than just a summer resort town. Saugatuck State Park has well-groomed marked trails, as does the Allegan State Game Area.

Special Events

July. Harbor Days/Venetian Night. Decorated boats, entertainment. Saugatuck.

October. Gallery Stroll Weekend. Galleries and craft shows host special exhibits, complete with hors d'oeuvres and wine. Saugatuck.

October. Halloween Harvest. Craft bazaar, pie eating, country music, and Saturday-night parade. Fennville.

Mid-October. Fennville Goose Festival. A celebration of the goose migration at Allegan State Game Area. Arts and crafts, Dixieland band, goose-calling contest, cook-your-goose cooking demonstration.

Other Recommended Restaurants and Lodgings

Douglas

Cafe Sir Douglas, 333 Blue Star Highway; (616) 857–1401. Eclectic fare, pâtés to Emma's meat loaf. Complete dinners from $8.00 to $14.00. An exhaustive wine list.

Kirby House, 294 Center Street; (616) 857–2904. Oak woodwork, four fireplaces, antiques with 1990s conveniences (hot tub). About a twenty-minute walk from downtown Saugatuck. Rates include a full buffet breakfast (quiche, meats, cheeses, cereal, fruit). Rates: $65–$100; some private baths.

Fennville

Crane House, 6051 124th Avenue; (616) 561–6931. The 1872 family homestead of the Cranes, who operate the orchards and restaurant across the street. Most of the antiques come from the owners' collection, and the quilts that grace the feather beds in the five rooms add to its appeal. Rates: $60–$80.

Kingsley House, 626 West Main Street; (616) 561–6425. Guest rooms are named after varieties of apples. During the winter you can cross-country ski in the orchards behind the house. A winding oak staircase leads to five rooms decorated with Victorian antiques. Family-style breakfast. Rates: $50–$65.

Su Casa Restaurant, 306 Main Street; (616) 561–5118. Good Mexican food on the backroads of Michigan? Believe it. This is the real thing, complete with fried plantains, freshly chopped chilies, and chorizo.

Saugatuck

Fairchild House, 606 Butler Street; (616) 857–5985. As well known for its champagne breakfasts (don't miss the eggs crab Benedict and the raspberry nut bread) as its gracious accommodations, which include European feather beds, down comforters, and even bathrobes. Rates: $85 per night.

Kemah Guest House, 633 Pleasant Street; (616) 857–2919. The Kemah is known for its lovely interiors, including stained-glass windows. Lots of details—newspaper in the morning, mints at night, and thick, thirsty towels—make this an especially nice choice. Breakfast is on the simple side (fruit, baked goods, coffee), but it tastes especially good when sitting on white wicker on the sun porch. Walking distance from downtown shops. No private baths. Rates: $45–$95.

For More Information

Fennville Area Chamber of Commerce, P.O. Box 84, Fennville, MI 49408. (616) 561–2036.

Saugatuck/Douglas Convention and Visitors Bureau, P.O. Box 28, Saugatuck, MI 49453. (616) 857–5801.

Holland and Grand Haven

A 1780s operating windmill brought to Holland, Michigan, from the Netherlands

A Touch of Dutch

_____ 2 NIGHTS _____

Boating · Shopping · Fishing · Museums · Galleries · Wooden-shoe factory

It's time to hit the road and head to Holland, a mere fifteen-minute drive from Saugatuck. Nestled in tulip country, the village is replete with Dutch nostalgia, including wooden-shoe dancers and flower pastures dotted with old windmills spinning in the breeze. The countryside is particularly spectacular in May, when acres of tulips proudly display their magnificent charm.

The townsfolk are still largely of Dutch ancestry—all you have to do is open the phone book and see the pages of "vans" and "vons." Indeed, some families have roots in the area that go back to the 1840s, when tens of thousands of Dutch separatists fled the Netherlands for the United States. What many visitors don't realize, however, is that

Holland boasts the largest concentration of Hispanics in the state as well.

Visitors like Holland for its combination of attractions and leisure activities. The pace here progresses at a comfortable speed, slow enough to jump aboard but quick enough to take you to another world.

About 20 miles up the road is Grand Haven, a city that has done an excellent job of coaxing the fun out of its lakefront without killing it with overdevelopment. The focal point is a magnificent new board-walk that stretches for almost 3 miles. While Grand Haven is the end of this swing around Lake Michigan, it can be the jumping off point for exploring the northern reaches (Muskegon, Ludington, and be-yond) when you have more time.

Day 1

Morning

Take I–94 to I–196 and into Holland. For stops along the way, see Indiana Escape One and Michigan Escapes One, Two, and Three)

If you visit Holland in May, you'll know you're in the right place by the millions of colorful tulips (and about an equal number of tourists). The whole town rolls out the red carpet, from the street scrubbers (there's even an inspector, called the *burgemeester*) to the costumed dancers who clip-clop down those same streets in their wooden shoes. There are flaky pastries and a parade of bands—all the ele-ments for the quintessential ethnic festival.

But Holland is in full flower even after the Tulip Festival is over. There's plenty of Dutch charm to go around all year long—especially at **Dutch Village,** your first stop, which re-creates a Netherlands town from a century ago. But after the 2½-hour ride from Chicago, the first order of business is lunch.

Lunch: **Queens Inn** (U.S. Highway 31 at James Street) claims to be the only restaurant in Holland to serve authentic Dutch fare. Try Pigs in a Blanket, served only at lunch, which comes with pea soup and Dutch apple pie. Prices are about $6.00 for lunch and about $10.00 for dinner. Reservations are recommended for weekend dining. Phone (616) 393–0310.

Afternoon

You'll find Dutch Village to be that slightly hokey type of family at-traction. A genuine re-creation of an old-fashioned street fair delights folks with a carousel; two enormous, elaborately carved street organs;

and an ornate *Zweefmolen* swing. You'll encounter the wooden-shoed "klompen" dancers, whose foot-stomping style is accompanied by the Gauen Engle street organ for five performances daily (10:30 A.M., noon, 2:00 P.M., 4:00 P.M., and 6:00 P.M.), which may inspire you to buy a pair of hand-carved clogs at one of the gift shops nearby.

There are lots of activities to keep the younger set amused. They can feed live animals in the kid-sized barn near an old-fashioned Dutch farmhouse and a pond that bobs with ducks.

From kitsch to class, Holland's gift stores offer a souvenir to suit every taste. The high-end market has everything from carved porcelain figures and costumed dolls to Delftware, lead crystal, and Dutch lace. On the lower end, you'll find the usual trinkets and T-shirts. Some of the shops extend their hours from 9 A.M. to 7 P.M. daily, from May 1 to Labor Day. Hours fall back to 9 A.M. to 5 P.M. during the rest of the year. Admission is $3.00 for adults and $2.50 for children 3–11. For more information call (616) 396–1475.

Dinner: **Sandpiper,** 2225 South Shore Drive, Nouvelle cuisine that includes smoked rabbit ravioli, prosciutto, and sun-dried tomatoes in balsamic vinaigrette. Overlooking the lake, its atmosphere is sophisticated but affordable. Named the best restaurant in Southwest Michigan by *Grand Rapids* magazine. Phone (616) 335–5866. Moderate to expensive.

Lodging: **The Old Holland Inn,** 133 West 11th Street. Antiques are displayed throughout the guest rooms and common areas of this nationally registered Victorian home constructed by Dutch woodcarvers at the turn of the century. The inn offers five private rooms, all but one sharing a bath. Rates (including a continental breakfast) range from $45 to $75 per night. (616–396–6601).

The **Hope Summer Repertory Theater** (DeWitt Cultural Center, 141 East 12th Street) is a delightful way to spend a summer evening. The repertoire ranges from Shakespeare to Simon, and it is extremely popular. If you know that you want to make theater a part of your weekend, be sure to call ahead for tickets (616–394–7890).

Day 2

Morning

Breakfast: **The Old Holland Inn.** In the summer, guests take a breakfast of fruit, muffins, and breads out on the deck.

You can tiptoe through the **Veldheer Tulip Gardens** (12755 Quincy Street, a couple miles northeast of U.S. Highway 31), where a glorious spectacle of sights and scents of some one hundred varieties of tulips and other bulbous blossoms are displayed. It's best to come during April and May, for a truly splendid sight. During the off-season, other flowers take over. You can also buy bulbs and flowering plants. Admission, charged only during April and May, is $2.00 for adults and $1.00 for children ages 5–16. The gardens open at 8 A.M. daily and close at around dusk. Phone (616) 399–1900.

Right next to the tulip gardens is **DeKlomp Wooden Shoe and Delftware Factory,** where you can see the trademark blue-and-white china, as well as wooden shoes, being made.

Windmill Island Municipal Park, just northeast of downtown, provides an even more in-depth experience. It's a unique municipal park that sits on a thirty-six-acre island. A replica of a Dutch village, the island boasts a working drawbridge and tulip gardens. Its 200-year-old operating windmill, which was shipped here in 1964, is the last windmill the Dutch government allowed to leave the Netherlands. Called DeZwaan, the mill cranks out a fine graham flour, which can be purchased at the park's concession stands.

The post house is a re-creation of a fourteenth-century Netherlands wayside inn furnished with an interesting collection of Dutch furniture. The half-hour documentary will bore all but the most die-hard nationalists, but the klompen dancing is mildly entertaining. The park, located at Seventh and Lincoln streets, is open from May to Labor Day, Monday to Saturday, 9 A.M. to 6 P.M., Sunday, 11:30–6:00 P.M. Limited hours from Labor Day to October 31. Tickets are $3.50 for adults, $1.75 for children. Call (616) 396–5433. Included in the price of admission is a tour of the wooden shoe factory, located nearby at U.S. Highway 31 and 16th Street.

If you've had enough Dutch culture and want to steep yourself in good old American shopping, swing over to downtown Holland. Its business district boasts a number of upscale retailers. The **Toy Shop,** 12 East Eighth Street, is like stumbling upon a small-town FAO Schwartz. Bookish types will love thumbing through the old and rare volumes at **J. E. Sheldon Fine Books,** 1 East Eighth Street.

In addition to the small boutiques, outlet fever has swept Holland, too. **Manufacturer's Marketplace,** on James Street just east of U.S. Highway 31 (616–396–1808) features fifty factory-direct stores in a re-created old Dutch village.

Dinner: **Til Midnight,** 208 College Avenue. A great choice for either lunch or dinner. Known for its sophisticated pastas. Don't miss the scallop and shrimp linguini with prosciutto, shrimp, sun-dried tomatoes, and a touch of saffron. Sandwiches start at about $6.00; full dinners go up to about $14.00. Finish up with the Midnight Cake, a rich, dense chocolate confection that is as close to pudding as cake. As the name implies, Til Midnight is also one of the few late-night spots around. Phone (616) 392–6883.

Since Grand Haven is just a half hour away, leave after dinner so you can get in a full day of activity. Take U.S. Highway 31 straight north into downtown.

Lodging: **Harbor House Inn,** corner of Harbor and Clinton, Grand Haven; (616) 846–0610. Sit out and enjoy continental breakfast or just breathe in the evening air from the wraparound porch. Great location overlooking the boardwalk and the harbor, but if it's tranquility you're after, you may want to stay a little more off the beaten track. Rates range from $95 to $115 per night.

Day 3

Morning

Breakfast: **Dee Lite,** 24 Washington Avenue (616–842–9839), on the boardwalk downtown, has French toast, omelets, and other hearty fare. The house specialty is the Farmer's Breakfast.

After breakfast explore the **boardwalk,** which extends for 2½ miles from Chinook Pier to the Grand Haven pier. Here you can find an eclectic range of attractions. First, get your bearings by perusing the brass sidewalk map, which highlights the waterways that feed into the Grand River, all fabricated in brass. (In a display of civic pride, employees of the Grand Haven Brass Foundry donated time to the project.)

Of course, if you really want to get oriented, hop the **harbor trolley,** which takes visitors on short guided tours of the area daily from 11 A.M. to 10 P.M. and is one of the best bargains in town ($1.00 for adults, 50 cents for children). The red trolley leaves every thirty minutes and tours Grand Haven; the blue one leaves every forty minutes and tours nearby Spring Lake and Ferrysburg.

Washington Street, the main boulevard, is lined with chic boutiques, such as **Country House** (110 North Third Street) and **Grand River Dry Goods** (100 North Third Street), for women and men, respectively. Top galleries include **Ad Lib** (218 Washington Street), which stocks fine linens, crystal, and other gifts; **Carlyn Gallery** (134 Washington), specializing in Southwest art; and the **Gallery Upstairs,** a cooperative of the area's best artisans, where you'll find reasonable prices, partly because the artists donate one day a month to run the gallery.

Turn into **Harborfront Place,** formerly the Story & Clark Piano Company, which has upscale shops, restaurants, and condominiums.

Lunch: Pass on the usual food-court offerings and try the **Basket Emporium,** at 222 Washington. It's a cookware and gourmet food shop with its own cafe tucked in the back, where you can enjoy salads and sandwiches in a courtyard setting.

Afternoon

Now, for a little enlightenment. The **Tri-Cities Historical Museum,** 1 North Harbor (616–842–0700) has something for everyone, whether your interests run from railroads (it's housed in an old train depot) to Victoriana. Open May–October. Hours vary, so call for information. Admission is 50 cents.

There's also some shopping with personality in Nunica, located 4 miles east of Grand Haven. People all over western Michigan make a special trip to **Moser's Dried Flower Barn,** 14065 Cleveland (616–842–0641), especially during the holiday season. Dutch native Reini Moser decks the halls with boughs of holly, as well as fir, juniper, and cedar. Open January 1–March 21, Tuesday–Saturday, 10 A.M.–5 P.M.; balance of year, seven days a week, 9 A.M.–5 P.M.

Dinner: **Arboreal Inn,** 18191 174th Avenue; (616) 842–3800. A classic country inn tucked into a woodland setting. The mushroom bisque is ultra-silky, the seafood is always fresh, and the wine list is exhaustive (with more than 175 varieties to choose from). Recognized as one of the best dining experiences this side of Lake Michigan. Expensive.

The **Musical Fountain,** located on the boardwalk at the foot of Washington, is Grand Haven's pride and joy. While it's hopelessly corny, it seems to be a must for tourists. For about a half hour, computer-generated music is matched with computer-synchronized fountain light. Tuesday nights feature rock music; Sundays feature gospel and hymns accompanied by the rising of a large cross. Suffice it to say that it borders on the campy.

Return to Chicago.

There's More

Amusements. Craig's Cruiser's, U.S. Highway 31 at Pontaluna Road; (616) 798–4936. Go-karts, batting cages, game room.

Antiques. Tulip City Antique Mall, 1145 South Washington, Holland. About fifty-five dealers with a better-than-average range of collectibles, furniture, books, and jewelry.

Bicycling. In Holland you can enjoy a most picturesque drive on the Park Township bike path, which is parallel with Ottawa Beach Road and Lake Shore Drive. It ends in Holland State Park. For a free map, call Cross Country Cycle at (616) 396–7491.

Farmer's Market. In Grand Haven, off Harbor Drive, is a terrific farmer's market every Monday in July and August and Wednesdays and Saturday mornings, June to October.

Fishing. Sport fishing (chinook and coho salmon; lake, brook, and steelhead trout) is a major draw in Grand Haven. Head to Chinook Pier, 2 blocks north of Washington, and you'll find anything and everything that has to do with fishing, right down to the party snacks.

For charters, try Chinook Pier Sport Fishing (616–842–2229) or Marina Jack's Charter Service (616–842–1343).

Golf. Grand Haven Golf Club, 17000 Lincoln, Grand Haven; (616) 842–4040. Play eighteen holes amid the dunes and the pines. Holland Country Club, 51 Country Club Road, Holland; (616) 392–1844.

Parks. Grand Haven State Park (1 mile west of Grand Haven, off U.S. Highway 31) is one of the largest beaches in southwest Michigan. Another popular beach is P. J. Hoffmaster State Park (10 miles northwest of Grand Haven, off U.S. Highway 31), which houses the Gillette Nature Center and provides hiking, biking, and cross-country trails. Kirk Park (between Lake Michigan and Lake Shore Avenue) and Kitchel Dune Reserve in Ferrysburg are frequently mentioned recreational areas. Kitchel's fifty-two acres is the perfect spot for tranquility, but watch out for poison ivy.

Skiing. Mulligan's Hollow Ski Bowl, 519 Washington, Grand Haven; (616) 846–5590. Has 6 runs; its longest run is 700 feet. Rentals, cross-country skiing, and a cafeteria are available.

Baker Furniture Museum, 147 Columbia Avenue, Holland. An impressive collection of period furniture and accessories that dates from the early sixteenth century to the present. Open May to October. Admission: $1.50. Phone (616) 392–8761.

Gillette Nature Center, 1 mile west of U.S. Highway 31, in P. J. Hoffmaster State Park. One of the world's largest accumulations of sand dunes. Lots of hands-on exhibits. Nature trails and observation deck. Park entrance fee: $2.00 per car. Phone (616) 798–3573.

Netherlands Museum, 8 East 12th Street, Holland. More Dutch stuff, including the Netherlands pavilion of the 1939 World's Fair. Phone (616)' 392–9084.

Poll Museum of Transportation, U.S. Highway 31. Collection of about thirty classic and antique cars (1906 Mercedes, 1921 Pierce Arrow roadster), fire trucks, and model trains. Open May 1 to Labor Day. Phone (616) 399–1955.

Special Events

February. Polar Ice Cap Golf Tournament. This unique winter tournament is for brave and hardy golf fanatics who want to test their skills on the challenging course of Spring Lake.

May. Tulip Festival, three parades, 1,500 klompen dancers, and tens of thousands of blossoms. Make sure you have reservations in advance. Holland.

July. Coast Guard Festival. Boats, entertainment, foods. Grand Haven.

December. Classic Homes Holiday Tour. Grand Haven's Victorian homes dressed in their holiday best. Call (616) 842–3200 for information.

Late-November–December. Hans Brinker and the Silver Skates. The skaters of Holland honor their Dutch ancestry with this annual Christmas production. (616) 396–4221.

Other Recommended Restaurants and Lodgings

Grand Haven

Grand Haven Area Bed and Breakfast is a consortium of six B&Bs, assuring a high level of quality: Alberties Waterfront (616–846–4016), Boyden House (616–846–3538), Eastman House (616–837–6474), Riverview (616–677–3921), The Stagecoach Stop (616–677–3940), Washington Street Inn (616–842–1075).

Bil-Mar Inn Supper Club, 1223 Harbor Avenue; (616) 842–5920. Dining on the shores of Lake Michigan. Prime rib and fresh whitefish are specialties of the house.

Holiday Inn of Grand Haven–Spring Lake, 940 West Savidge Street, Spring Lake (State Highway 104 at U.S. 31); (616) 846–1000. Overlooking Grand River. Most rooms with balconies. Two heated pools, sauna, marina. Rates: $60–$90 per night.

Kirby Grill, Washington at Harbor Drive; (616) 846–3299. Another good pasta place, especially for fettucine Alfredo. On Sundays, there's a New Orleans jazz brunch, where the tunes are as lively as the cuisine (rattlesnake sausage).

Holland

Holland Bed & Breakfast Referral Service. There are a number of small B&Bs, and this service can fill you in on their availability and rates. Call (616) 396–3664.

Beechwood Inn, 380 Douglas; (616) 396–2355. The place to go for fresh lake perch. Very popular; closed Sunday.

Dave's Garage, 478 East 16th Street; (616) 392–3017. Steaks, prime rib, and crab legs are the big draws at this popular, car-themed restaurant. Reservations recommended.

The Hatch, 1870 Ottawa Beach Road; (616) 399–9120. Delicious steaks and seafood but equally renowned for Sunday brunch (10:30

A.M.–2:00 P.M.), with reservations strongly recommended.

Pereddie's, 447 Washington Square (between 18th and 19th streets); (616) 394–3061. Classic old Italian restaurant—casual, cheap (for lunch, at least), and comfortable.

Point West Inn and Conference Center, 2150 South Shore Drive, Lake Macatawa; (616) 335–5894. Luxurious suites, many with balconies and patios. Heated pool. Dock and private beach. Tennis and rental bicycles. Rates: $95–$130 per night.

For More Information

Holland Convention and Visitors Bureau, 150 West Eighth Street, Holland, MI 49423. (800) 822–2770 or (616) 396–4221.

Grand Haven/Spring Lake Area Visitors Bureau, 1 South Harbor, Grand Haven, MI 49417. (616) 842–4499.

Detroit

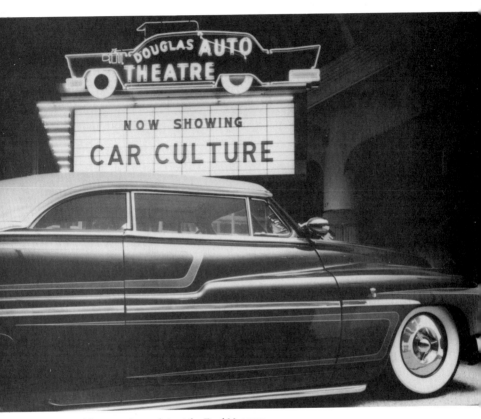

Automotive history and nostalgia at the Ford Museum

Meet Me in Motown

—————————— 3 NIGHTS ——————————

Historic sights • Museums • Zoo • Shopping •
Ethnic dining • Living history museum

No one would every accuse Detroit of being a tourist mecca, and the fact that it's six hours from Chicago makes it an even more questionable choice for a quick trip.

The Henry Ford Museum & Greenfield Village is such a major draw, however, that any Midwest travel book would really be incomplete without it. The complex ranks with Williamsburg, Virginia, as one of the country's best attractions.

The indoor-outdoor complex (technically, it's in Dearborn, but only a purist would quibble) was built by Henry Ford as a tribute to American achievement and can-do spirit. So why endure a six-hour car ride when there are so many wonderful museums right here in Chicago? Because there is nothing locally that makes history seem so vibrant.

There are other eclectic sites, from Greektown to Motown. Also, you can make a quick trip over the border into Windsor. (Detroit is one of the few cities in the United States where you can look due south into Canada.)

Day 1

Morning

Take I–94 all the way to Detroit. If your schedule permits, there are several worthy stops along the way.

In Kalamazoo, 1 mile south of I–94, the **Aviation History Museum** (3101 East Milham Road; 616–382–6555) is a standout. Its twenty-two planes include such World War II fighters as the "Hellcat," the "Wildcat," and the "Bearcat." You can even catch an up-close look at mechanics working on the aircraft. Weather permitting, one of the planes flies daily at 2 P.M., May–September. Open daily except holidays. Get off I–94 at exit 79 and go south on Portage Road, then east on Milham. Admission: adults, $5.00; children, $2.00; under 6, free.

En route to the museum, architecture buffs will enjoy the drive through the **West South Street District** (between Oakland Drive and South Park Street), where there are grand "painted ladies" of the Victorian era.

Lunch: **Great Lakes Shipping Company,** 4525 West KL Avenue; (616) 375–6000. Soups, sandwiches, and salads in a nautical warehouse environment. Also, heartier fare such as prime rib and aged steaks.

Get back on I–94 and travel about another 100 miles to Ann Arbor, home of the University of Michigan and, to many people, the intellectual and cultural center of the state. As proof, you need to look no farther than the half dozen or so bookstores, all centered on or near State Street. The most famous is undoubtedly **Borders,** 303 South State Street (313–668–7652). Many consider this to be the best bookstore in the United States, with a back list that is the envy of much larger operations. It also has a fine collection of maps and poster art.

Snack/Dinner: Even if your timing doesn't land you in Ann Arbor right at meal time, don't miss **Zingerman's Delicatessen,** 422 Detroit

(313–663–3354). Even New Yorkers put this on their itinerary. Along with its matzo ball soup and noodle kugel, Zingerman's Reuben sandwich is so good that it has been known to arouse cravings among former students well after they've hit middle-age.

Back on I–94 and on to Dearborn, about 40 miles away.

Lodging: **The Hyatt Regency-Dearborn** is an excellent choice, not only because of its location (about a five-minute drive to Greenfield Village), but because the pool, Jacuzzi, and sauna provide a great way to unwind after a day of sightseeing. There are a number of weekend packages, which start at about $90 per night. Some options include Henry Ford Museum/Greenfield Village tickets and an adjoining room for children for an additional $25, a small investment to ensure mom and dad a little private time.

Another parenting tip: While most families must stick to a budget, consider upgrading to the Regency Club level. Amenities include a fabulous breakfast, with freshly baked breads, made-to-order omelets, fresh fruit, and just about anything else you can think of. This meal can easily save $40 of food expenses per day—and because it is so substantial, it can keep you satisfied until dinner, which is when complimentary drink and hors d'oeuvres are served.

Day 2

Morning

Breakfast: Hyatt Regency Hotel-Dearborn.

Now, for the main reason for the trip: **Henry Ford Museum & Greenfield Village.** For some children static collections of objects may elicit yawns. But even the most blasé kid will most likely be impressed with the Wright Brothers' Cycle Shop (moved here from Dayton, Ohio) or Thomas Edison's Menlo Park, N.J., laboratory, where more than 400 inventions originated.

You can easily spend your entire weekend here (second-day entry is free with a paid admission). The physical layout as well as the flawless execution of the exhibits make this a unique—and painless—educational experience.

At the museum, eighteenth-century steam engines are displayed alongside sleek convertibles. You'll see the Victorian rocking chair occupied by Abraham Lincoln when he was assassinated at Ford's Theatre, but you'll also get a lighthearted look at how the automobile influenced American life, from Burma-Shave signs to McDonald's. The juxtaposition of rural society and industrial nation allows young visitors to see the connection between past and present in a way that no history book could ever duplicate.

Don't think you need a youngster in tow to justify a visit, however.

Special exhibits such as the Henry Miller Furniture Collection or the automotive design career of General Motors' Bill Mitchell (who created the Corvette Stingray and the Buick Riviera) are strictly of interest to adults.

A few pointers: Because of the size of the complex (Greenfield Village boasts eighty-one acres of space, Henry Ford Museum offers twelve), it's difficult to see everything. If time is limited, focus on the special highlighted exhibits on the map. Also, use the steam train to get around; it allows you to get on and off throughout the village.

If you have young children, opt for Greenfield Village early in the day and save the Henry Ford Museum for the afternoon. Also worth noting for families is the activity room, where kids can pedal a stationary high-wheel bicycle, talk on an antique phone, or operate an old-time printing press.

Lunch: While the cafeteria is very ordinary, it's better to eat lunch on the premises than to go elsewhere. There's really nothing better nearby to make it worth leaving the complex.

The complex is located ½ mile south of U.S. Highway 12 1 mile west of Southfield Road on Oakwood Boulevard. Open daily 9 A.M. to 5 P.M. except Christmas Day. The interiors of Greenfield Village buildings are not open from January 2 to March 16. Combination tickets are the best value at a discounted rate of $18.00 for adults and $9.00 for children under 12 (children under 5 are admitted free). Admission to the museum or the village also may be purchased separately at $10.50 for adults, $5.25 for children. Call (313) 271–1976 for twenty-four-hour information.

Dinner: After a day of walking, you'll want to stay in—easy to do here—since the restaurants are much better than typical hotel fare. They range from sushi to classic French. But probably the most popular is **Giulio and Sons,** which offers some great Italian selections and a build-your-own dessert bar that will have chocoholics thinking they died and went to heaven.

Lodging. Hyatt Regency-Dearborn Hotel.

Day 3

Morning

After your breakfast at the hotel you can visit the auto magnate's estate on the University of Michigan–Dearborn campus (follow the signs to Evergreen Road). The estate, called **Fair Lane,** is where the Fords entertained some of the world's most influential people. Today Fair Lane is prized for its gardens, grottos, and hiking paths (nearly one hundred species of birds have been observed there). Gardeners should note that from April through October, guided walks are conducted to **Jensen's Meadow,** where you'll find what is arguably some of the best examples of landscape architecture. Admission: adults, $6.00; children, $5.00. Check seasonal events. Phone (313) 593–5590.

If you've had about enough of Henry Ford to last a lifetime and are looking for something funkier, then head to the **Motown Historical Museum,** 2648 West Grand Boulevard, about a twenty-minute drive. (Take Highway 10, known as Lodge Freeway, west to Grand Boulevard.) Rare photographs, clothing, and memorabilia of such legends as Diana Ross, the Temptations, Marvin Gaye, and Smokey Robinson cram this old brick home where the original Motown sound was born in 1959. Admission: $3.00 for adults, $2.00 for children. Phone (313) 875–2264.

Lunch: **Tunnel Bar-B-Q,** located just on the other side of the Detroit-Windsor Tunnel. (Follow Highway 12 through the tunnel.) Chicagoans are about as chauvinistic about ribs as they are pizza, but these are just plain hard to beat. Some attribute the juicy smoky flavor to the cooking (slabs are threaded on metal rods), others to the sauce. Whatever the reason, this is a place that truly lives up to the hype. It also does a brisk carry-out business. No bar. Moderate. 58 Park East, Windsor (519–258–2804).

Afternoon

Next stop is **Boblo Island.** This 272-acre island, located on the Detroit River midway between Detroit and Windsor, features more than seventy-five rides and could easily fill a full day. A highlight includes a 300-foot-tall skytower, which provides a bird's-eye view of Canada, Michigan, and Ohio. The island can be reached by ferry from either Detroit or Windsor (actually, the departure point is Amherstburg, near Windsor). The advantage to leaving from the Canadian side is that the ride is much shorter (forty-five minutes vs. ninety minutes from Detroit). Admission is $10–$15, depending on age and where you embark. Price includes round-trip boat transportation and all rides. The park is open daily from late May to Labor Day; weekends only until September 30. Call (313) 848–8800 (Detroit) or (519) 252–4444 (Windsor) for schedule.

If it's off-season for Boblo Island, you can still get some brisk exercise. Get on I–75 and head north to **The Detroit Zoological Park,** 8450 West Ten Mile Road (1 block west of Woodward Avenue) in suburban Royal Oak.

The Detroit Zoo is regarded as one of the largest and most outstanding zoos in the country. The expansive, cageless exhibits are grouped by continents, making it especially easy for first-time visitors. High points are the reptile building, bird-house, and penguinarium. Open daily, 10 A.M.–5 P.M. Admission: adults, $5.00; children, $2.50. Phone (313) 398–0900.

Dinner: **New Hellas Cafe,** 583 Monroe Street, Greektown; (313) 961–5544. The saganaki is especially good, as are the moussaka and Greek salad. Skip dessert and head around the corner to **Susan Hoffman's Fine Pastries** (1219 St. Antoine Street; 313–965–1692).

Also in Greektown is **Trappers Alley,** 508 Monroe Street, a turn-of-the-century complex that houses forty-five shops and eating spots offering souvenir items and food reminiscent of a carnival midway. Kids will love it. Parents may only find the fudge worth buying. At one small shop on the first floor there is a woman with a Dinah Washington voice who belts out a tune while she is stirring the fudge. Only in Detroit.

Lodging: Hyatt Regency-Dearborn Hotel.

Day 4

Morning

Breakfast: **Homemaker's Pantry,** 4648 Woodward Avenue. Grits, eggs, hashbrowns, and biscuits will start your day off right in this soul food–style restaurant. (313) 833–8430.

The **Detroit Institute of Arts,** 5200 Woodward Avenue, houses fine collections of seventeenth-century Dutch and Flemish paintings, nineteenth-century impressionist paintings, and African art. But if you have time to see only one thing, see the one exhibit that is most typically Detroit: Diego Rivera's murals, which portray auto workers in an almost slavelike way. (The art was commissioned by Henry Ford, who was horrified by the results.) Open Tuesday–Sunday, 9:30 A.M.–5:30 P.M. Free admission. Phone (313) 833–7900.

Lunch: Grab a quick lunch at the DIA before stopping at the **Detroit Historical Museum,** just a few blocks away at 5401 Woodward Avenue. This museum does more than simply chronicle the city's history; it also features a quirky exhibit on one hundred years of job-related outfits, including hometown-boy Tom Selleck's baseball cap and Hawaiian shirt and John Salley's Piston uniform. Free admission. Phone (313) 833–1805.

Afternoon

Start the trip home, traveling west on I–94.

There's More

Cranbrook Educational Community, off Lone Pine and Cranbrook roads, just west of Woodward Avenue, Bloomfield Hills. You can easily spend an entire day at Cranbrook, which occupies 315 acres and includes an art museum, science center, gardens, manor house, and a design school of international renown. Just strolling the grounds is an education, with buildings by architects such as Eliel Saarinen (who set up the school's design department) and sculpture by Carl Milles (his beautiful Orpheus Fountain is in front of the museum). If your time is limited, decide which of the public buildings you want to visit. At the Institute of Science, kids will especially enjoy the hands-on exhibits (how often do you get to touch a boa constrictor?) and the observatory (open only on Saturday evenings). Each building has its own hours. A map and general brochure are available by calling (313) 645–3180.

Ann Arbor Hands-On Museum, 219 East Huron Avenue, Ann Arbor; (313) 995–5437. The museum has 160-plus exhibits to intrigue and challenge even the youngest tourist. The do-it-yourself bubble exhibit is an especially big hit. The fact that the museum is located in an old firehouse only adds to the fun. Open Tuesday–Friday, 1:30–5:30 P.M.; Saturday, 10 A.M.–5 P.M.; Sunday, 1–5 P.M. Admission: adults, $3.00; children (ages 3–18), $2.00.

Eastern Farmers' Market, 2934 Russell, Detroit; (313) 833–1560. In operation since the turn of the century, this is one of the largest farmers' markets in the country. Fresh produce, meats, cheeses, spices, and flowers are just some of the items for sale Monday through Saturday.

Domino Farms, Archives and Galleries, 30 Frank Lloyd Wright Drive, Ann Arbor; (313) 995–4258. Tom Monaghan, founder of Domino's Pizza, has made his corporate headquarters a tribute to Frank Lloyd Wright. The center exhibits Monaghan's Wright collection, which includes furniture, glass windows, and other art designed by the architect. Farm includes petting zoo. Open Monday–Friday, 10 A.M.–6 P.M.; Saturday, 10 A.M.–5 P.M.; Sunday, noon–5 P.M. Call for off-season hours. Admission: adults, $4.00; children 12 and over, $3.00.

The complex also houses **Monaghan's Classic Car Museum,** with about fifty cars on display, including an $8.1 million 1931 Bugatti Royale, one of only six in the world. Open Monday–Thursday, 10 A.M.–6 P.M.; Friday and Saturday, 11 A.M.–9 P.M.; Sunday, noon–5 P.M.

Fisher Mansion, 383 Lenox Avenue; (313) 331–6740. The Lawrence P. Fisher mansion is an ornate home of stone, marble, and exotic woods. Guided tours on Friday, Saturday, and Sunday at 12:30 P.M., 2:00 P.M., 3:30 P.M. and 6:00 P.M. Admission: adults, $5.00; students, $4.00.

Historic Fort Wayne, 6325 West Jefferson; (313) 297–9360. This fort pays tribute to Detroit's military history during the eighteenth and nineteenth centuries. It also highlights the National Tuskegee Airmen Museum.

Kalamazoo Nature Center, 7000 North Westnedge Avenue, Kalamazoo; (616) 381–1574. Eleven trails wind through 600 acres of woodlands, herb garden, and arboretum. A two-story glass-domed conservatory displays historical and unusual plants. DeLano Homestead presents demonstrations of pioneer crafts. Hours: Daily, 9 A.M.–6 P.M. Admission: adults, $1.50; children, $1.00.

Gilmore Classic Car Museum, 6865 Hickory Road, Kalamazoo; (616) 671–5089. More than a hundred antique cars are on display. A replica of the Kitty Hawk also garners a lot of attention. Open daily 1–5 P.M. during summer. Check hours the rest of the year. Admission: $4.00.

Museum of African-American History, 301 Frederick Douglass; (313) 833–9800. Exhibits document the achievements and contributions of African Americans.

Renaissance Center, Jefferson at Brush on the Detroit River; (313) 568–5600. "A city within a city" is how the locals describe this retail/office/entertainment complex. It can be a confusing maze, but it has been credited with helping revive riverfront development.

Professional sports. Detroit is a great sports town. If baseball is your game, catch the Detroit Tigers at Tiger Stadium (Michigan Avenue at Trumbull; 313–963–9944). For basketball, the Pistons play at Auburn Hills Complex (3777 Lapeer Road; 313–377–0100) in nearby Pontiac. Football fans also head to Pontiac to see the Lions at the Silverdome (on Highway 59, just west of I–75; 313–335–4151). The Red Wings skate at Joe Louis Arena (Jefferson Avenue at the Riverfront; 313–567–6000).

Ladbroke Race Course, 28001 Schoolcraft Road; Livonia; (313) 525–7300. Thoroughbred racing Wednesday–Sunday, late March to early November.

Skiing. Detroit probably isn't the first city that springs to mind when you think of slopes, but there are five downhill ski areas all within a short drive of the city. They are: Alpine Valley Ski Resort, with 25 runs and 10 chairlifts (6775 East Highland Road, Milford; 313–887–4183); Mt. Brighton Ski Area, with 22 runs and 7 chairlifts (4141 Bauer Road, Mt. Brighton; 313–229–9581); Mt. Holly Inc., with 17 runs and 7 chairlifts (13536 South Dixie Highway, 313–634–8269); Pine Knob Ski Resort, with 20 runs and 5 chairlifts (8 miles north of Pontiac on I–75, exit 189, Clarkston; 313–625–0800; and Riverview Ski Area, with 10 runs and 2 chairlifts (15015 Sibley Road, Riverview; 18 miles south of Detroit on I–75 to exit 34B; 313–479–2080). Longest run: one-third mile; vertical drop, 320 feet.

Special Events

June. Detroit Grand Prix. Of course the Motor City would host a car race through the streets of downtown.

Late June–July 4. International Freedom Festival. Held in Detroit and Windsor, this festival celebrates the camaraderie of the two nations with ethnic foods, fireworks, and entertainment. Various sites in both cities.

June–September. Riverfront Festivals take place at Hart Plaza (at the foot of Woodward Avenue and the Riverfront). Every weekend of the summer, a different nationality is celebrated. Insiders say that the African-American, German, and Polish festivals are the liveliest. Call the Ethnic Festival Hotline, (313) 224–1184.

Late August–Labor Day weekend. Montreux Detroit Jazz Festival features five days of jazz, which attracts national names as well as up-and-comers. Riverfront.

Thanksgiving Day. Santa Claus Parade. The parade travels along Woodward Avenue to the Detroit Institute of Arts.

Other Recommended Restaurants and Lodgings

Dearborn

Best Western Greenfield Inn, 3000 Enterprise Drive; (313) 271–1600. Very comfortable motor inn; some rooms have their own whirlpools. Free transportation to Greenfield Village. Rates range from $65 to $95 per night.

Dearborn Inn and Marriott, 20301 Oakwood Boulevard: (313) 271–2700. Another luxurious property. Large rooms; heated pool; wading pool. All health club privileges. Check weekend packages; kids stay free. Every extra you could want. Rates: $130–$145.

Ritz-Carlton Dearborn, 300 Town Center Drive; (313) 441–2000. Although this is a new construction, the Ritz creates the ambience of an elegant inn with antique furnishings, Oriental rugs, English porcelain, and other appointments. Whirlpool, sauna, tennis, and golf privileges. Rates: $79–$190.

Detroit

American Pizza Cafe, 2239 Woodward Avenue; (313) 964–3122. Funky pizza, with toppings that range from Chinese to chili. Right near the Fox Theatre, it's an excellent late-night choice.

Britt's Cafe, Congress at Shelby; (313) 963–4866. A finely tuned cafeteria that is fast, delicious, and an excellent value. Signature dishes are the Caesar salad and homemade soups. Lots of choices for vegetarians, too.

Fishbones Rhythm Kitchen Cafe, 400 Monroe; (313) 965–4600. Cajun cuisine in the heart of Greektown? Believe it. Sassy, spicy dishes, moderate prices, and a fun atmosphere make this a very popular spot.

Hotel Pontchartrain, 2 Washington Boulevard at Jefferson Avenue; (313) 965–0200. Right in the middle of everything. Luxurious rooms, all newly remodeled. Full health club, outdoor heated pool. Complimentary limo service within the city. Rates range from $125 to $170 per night.

Joe Muer's Seafood, 2000 Gratiot; (313) 567–1088. Located across the street from the Eastern Market. A Detroit institution for sixty years with legions of loyal customers. The Dover sole, Norwegian salmon, and Canadian walleye are consistently top-notch (flown in daily), but you'll pay top dollar, as well.

Omni Hotel, 333 East Jefferson; (313) 222–7700. Detroit's newest hotel is located in the Millender Center (an office complex) and is connected to the Renaissance Center by skyway. The rooms have every amenity imaginable. Facilities include a full fitness center and an Olympic-sized pool. Rates range from $100 to $165 per night.

Rattle Snake Club, in the former Stroh's Brewery, Stroh River Place; (313) 567–4400. The service can be brusque, but the food is very good and very creative—such as the white chocolate ravioli. Be prepared for a long wait, which is made more tolerable with jazz on the patio. Expensive.

Westin Hotel, in the Renaissance Center; (313) 568–8300. The world's tallest hotel with everything done on an equally big scale. Every room has a great view overlooking the Detroit River, Belle Isle, or Hart Plaza. Health club, indoor pool, sauna. Rates range from $100 to $195 per night.

Kalamazoo

The Bartlett-Upjohn House, 229 Stuart Avenue; (616) 342–0230. If you want to stop en route to Detroit, you could do no better than this 1886 gabled manse, located in a historic neighborhood. Lots of Victoriana in the parlors, music room, and dining room. The lovely garden enhances your stay. Rates: $50 to $60 per night.

For More Information

Dearborn Chamber of Commerce, 15544 Michigan Avenue, Dearborn, MI 48126. (313) 584–6100.

Metropolitan Detroit Convention and Visitors Bureau, 100 Renaissance Center, Suite 1950, Detroit, MI 48226. (313) 259–4333.

Index

100 Center Complex, 137
A-1 Beanery, 41
Abe Martin Lodge, 156
Ad Lib, 194
Adam's Rib, 150
Adler Planetarium, 46
Admiralty, 77
Alexander's Steak House, 22
Allen Bradley Four-Faced Clock, 54
Allison Wonderland, 68
American Club, 110
American Old-Fashioned Ice Cream Parlor, 33
American Players Theatre, 77
Amish Acres, 136
Anchor Antiques, 181
Ann Arbor Hands-On Museum, 205
Annie's, 68
Annunciation Greek Orthodox Church, 60
Antiques, 26
Apple Cider Century, 172
Arboreal Inn, 195
Arkins Book Store, 179
Art Barn, 171
Art Institute of Chicago, 46
Artspace, 111
Auction House, 187
Aviation History Museum, 200

Babcock Hall, 80
Bailly Homestead, 128
Baker Furniture Museum, 196
Baker's Oven and Tea Room, 33
Bangor Antique Mall, 180
Bangor Train Factory, 180
Baraboo, 87

Barker Mansion, 127
Basket Emporium, 194
Bauer's, 25
Bay Antiques, 178
Beachway, 185
Beernsen's, 116
Belvedere Mansion & Gardens, 35
Benjamin Harrison Home, 148
Bennett-Curtis House, 19
Berghoff, 44
Bergstrom Mahler Museum, 106
Berrien Springs Courthouse, 173
Bibler's, 134
Big Chief Go-Kart World, 90
Birch Creek Music Center, 119
Bistro 110, 45
Blackwold Run, 112
Blue Heron Tours, 103
Blueberry Store, 179
Boardwalk, 194
Boblo Island, 203
Boerner Botanical Gardens, 60
Bombay Bicycle Club, 55
Bonneyville Mill Park, 143
Borders, 200
Bread Bike Shop, 142
Breadloaf Book Shop, 68
Brewery Works, 109
Bristol Opera House, 143
Brown County
  Convention & Visitors Bureau, 154
  Craft Gallery, 155
  Inn, 155
  Playhouse, 157
  State Park, 156, 164
Bruno's, 135
Buckingham Fountain, 42

Budget Bicycle Center, 78
Buggy Wheel Restaurant, 141
Butch's Anchor Inn, 104

Café Brauer, 43
Cain Gallery, 184
Candy Tour, 26
Canterbury Theatre, 127
Capital Brewery, Gift Haus & Beer Garden, 81
Captain Nemo's, 179
Captain Nichols, 181
Carlyn Gallery, 194
Carol's Antiques, 126
Carriage House, 134
Carriage Ride, 42
Casino Belle, 33–34
Castle Rock , 10
Cave of the Mounds, 75
Cedar Creek Settlement, 109
Cedarburg, 109
Center Street, 136
Chalet of the Golden Fleece, 99
Charles Allis Art Museum, 60
Checkerberry Inn, 141
Checquers, 185
Chelsea Antiques, 119
Chesterfield Inn, 98
Chesterton, 126
Chestnut Mountain Resort, 36
Chiarascuro, 44
Chicago
  Children's Museum, 41
  From the Lake Cruise, 43
  Historical Society, 43
Chief Oshkosh Museum, 120
Children's Museum, 146
Circle Theater, 149

Circus World Museum, 88
City Hall, 55
City Market, 148
Clearbrook GolfCourse,186
Clearing, 119
Clementine's Saloon, 179
Cleo Rogers Memorial
    Library, 163
Clock Tower Coffee Shop,
    75
Clowes Hall, 149
Clown Hall of Fame, 69
Coffee Trader, 58
Columbus Antique Mall,
    163
Columbus Inn, 162
Columbus Visitors Center,
    162
Commons, 163
Conner Prairie, 149, 161
Cook's Energy Informa-
    tion Center, 173
Coral Gables, 186
Country House, 194
Country Mates, 171
Covered Bridge Park, 110
Craft Barn Furniture Shop,
    142
Crafter's Marketplace, 142
Cranbrook Educational
    Community, 204
Crane's Orchards and Pie
    Pantry Restaurant, 187
Crete Antique Mart, 16
Crow Bar, 186
Cucina, 111
Curious Kids Museum,
    177

Damon's, 147
Dana-Thomas House, 24
Das Bauhaus, 184
Das Dutchman Essen-
    haus, 143
David Davis Mansion
    State Historic Site, 21
Davis Mercantile, 142
Dee Lite, 194

DeGrandchamps Blue-
    berry Plantation, 181
DeKlomp Wooden Shoe
    and Delftware Factory,
    193
Design Center, 111
Desoto House Hotel and
    Restaurant, 32
Detroit
    Historical Museum, 204
    Institute of Arts, 204
    Zoological Park, 203
Devil's Lake State Park, 92
Dionne's, 18
Discovery World, 59
Doing the Ducks, 90
Domino Farms, Archives
    and Galleries, 205
Door County
    Maritime Museum, 120
    Museum, 120
Dowling House, 35
Drier's Butcher Shop, 172
Dunes State Park, 128
Dutch Village, 191

EAA Air Adventure Mu-
    seum, 104
Eagle Ridge Inn & Resort,
    33, 36
Eastern Farmers' Market,
    205
Eby's Pines, 143
Edgewater Hotel, 77
Egyptian Theater, 11
Eiteljorg Museum of
    American Indian and
    Western Art, 150
Ek Tradet, 119
Elder's Mill, 70
Ella's Kosher Deli & Ice
    Cream Parlor, 86
Ellwood House Museum,
    12
Elvehjem Museum of Art,
    80
Embassy Suites, 42
Emma's Antiques, 12

Fair Lane, 202
Fancy Fare, 68
Farmer's Home Hotel, 34
Farmer's Market, 81
Fernwood, 173
Field Museum of Natural
    History, 46
Field's Restaurant, 104
Fifth Street Deli, 128
Filoni Vestimenti, 171
First Christian Church, 163
First Presbyterian Church,
    22
Fish Creek, 116
Fish Creek Kite Company,
    117
Fisher Mansion, 205
Floreale/Lindsay's, 24
Four Seasons Hotel, 45
Fulton Brewery Market,
    32

Galena Cellars, 30
Galena/Jo Daviess County
    Historical Society &
    Museum, 30
Galena/Jo Daviess County
    Visitor Information
    Center, 30
Gallery Upstairs, 194
Gallery Vienna, 44
Garden on the Green, 148
Gary's Antiques, 32
Gebhard Woods State
    Park, 4
Gem House, 110
General Store Museum, 31
Geneva Inn, 66
Geneva Lake Cruise Line,
    67
Geneva Lakes Kennel
    Club, 68
George Watts & Son, 55
Gillette Nature Center,
    196
Gilmore Classic Car
    Museum, 206
Geology Museum, 82

Gold Star Sardine Bar, 45
Golda's, 170
Gordon, 44
Governor Dodge/Best
    Western Motor Inn, 97
Governor Noble's Eating
    Place, 161
Governor's Mansion, 26
Granary Restaurant, 105
Grand Opera House, 107
Grand River Dry Goods,194
Grandpa's Barn Antiques,
    110
Grandview Restaurant, 66
Grant Park, 31
Grant's Place, 30
Great Lakes Shipping
    Company, 200
Greater Milwaukee
    Convention & Visitors
    Bureau, 55
Greenery, 55
Greenhouse, 112
Grotto of Our Lady of
    Lourdes, 135

Hall of Fame Museum, 148
Hammer, 44
Hampton Inn, 25
Harbor House Inn, 194
Harbor Trolley, 194
Harborfront Place, 194
Hard Rock Café, 42
Heartland, 16
Helms 4 Seasons Hotel, 117
Henry Ford Museum &
    Greenfield Village, 201
Henry Vilas Park Zoo, 78
Henson Robinson Zoo, 26
Hesston Steam Museum,129
Hilton, 25
Historic Fort Wayne, 205
Hob Nob, 154
Hoffman's Patterns of
    the Past, 6
Holiday Inn, 147
Holiday Inn East Confer-
    ence Center, 25

Holly Market, 178
Homemaker's Pantry, 204
Homestead Restaurant, 35
Honeysuckle Place, 155
Hope Summer Repertory
    Theater, 192
Horicon Marsh, 103
Horse & Plow, 112
Hot Air Balloons, 82
House on the Rock, 75
Hyatt Regency-Dearborn,
    201

Idler, 179
Immigrant, 110
Indiana Dunes National
    Lakeshore, 128
Indiana Repertory The-
    ater, 149
Indianapolis
    Ballet Theater, 149
    Museum of Art, 147
    Opera, 149
    Star, 151
    Zoo, 148
Interlaken Resort, 69
International Crane Foun-
    dation, 91
Ishnala Supper Club, 91

James Whitcomb Riley
    Home, 148
Jensen's Fishery, 178
Jensen's Meadow, 202
John Michael Kohler Arts
    Center, 112
Joyce Petter Gallery, 185

Kal-Haven Trail, 180
Kalamazoo Nature Center,
    205
Kankakee County Histori-
    cal Society Museum, 18
Kankakee River, 18
Karl Ratzsch's Old World
    Restaurant, 58

Kathy's Antiques, 126
Katie's Ice Cream Parlor,
    127
Keewatin, 186
Keyes West, 77
Kilwin's, 68
Kingsbury Fish and
    Wildlife Area, 129
Kingston Inn, 31
Kirsch's, 69
Knight's Action Park, 27
Kohler Company, 111
Kohler-Andrae State Park,
    113
Kopp's, 59
Krasl Art Center, 178
Kristina's, 87

Ladbroke Race Course, 206
Lake Bluff Park, 177
Lake County Courthouse,
    129
Lake Geneva Municipal
    Beach, 67
Lake Michigan Maritime
    Museum, 179
Lake Monroe, 164
Lakeside Gallery, 171
Land's End, 98
Landmark Cruise, 42
LaPort County Museum,
    129
Lasalle County Historical
    Museum, 6
Laser Light Show, 127
Le Grand Trunk, 171
Left Bank, 162
Lemon Creek Fruit Farms,
    Vineyards, and Win-
    ery, 173
Lighthouse Place, 127
Lincoln
    Depot, 22
    Elementary School, 163
    Home Visitors Center, 22
    Memorial Garden &
    Nature Center, 26
    Park Zoo, 43

Lincoln's New Salem State Historic Site, 25
Lincoln's Tomb, 24
Little Nashville Opry, 157
Loaf & Mug, 184
Log Cabin Lodge, 112
Looms, 98
Lost Canyon Tours, 91
Lou Mitchell's, 42
Lowden State Park, 10

Madame Walker Urban Life Center, 150
Mader's, 56
Madison
  Art Center, 80
  Children's Museum, 82
  Civic Center, 80
Maldaner's, 23
Mallard Duck Hatchery, 36
Manitowoc Maritime Museum, 116
Manufacturer's Marketplace, 104, 162, 193
Marketplace Antiques, 16
Marquette University, 56
Matthiessen, 6
Max's, 181
Mayfair Regent Hotel, 46
Menno-Hof Visitors Center, 141
Michiana Antiques Mall, 173
Michigan, The, 179
Mid-Continent Railroad Museum, 88
Midwest Museum of American Art, 140
Miller Bakery Cafe, 128
Miller Brewing Company, 57
Miller's Country House, 171
Millie's Restaurant and Shopping Village, 69
Milwaukee
  Art Museum, 58
  Center, 56
  Historical Center, 59

Public Museum, 58
Zoo, 59
Mineral Point Antiques Center, 98
Mining Museum, 97
Mitchell Park Conservatory, 57
Monaghan's Classic Car Museum, 205
Mongerson Wunderlich, 44
Monk's Bar & Grill, 89
Monte Carlo Resort Model, 87
Moser's Dried Flower Barn, 195
Motown Historical Museum, 202
Mount Baldy, 128
Mountain Made Music, 155
Mount Baldhead, 185
Murray's Irish House, 117
Museum of African-American History, 206
Museum of Norman Rockwell Art, 92
Museum of Science and Industry, 46
Musical Fountain, 195

Nashville, 154
National New York Central Railroad Museum, 140
Neenah, 107
Netherlands Museum, 196
New Glarus
  Hotel, 98
  Bakery & Tea Room, 99
New Hellas Cafe, 203
Newport State Park, 118
Noah's Ark, 90
North Beach, 178
North Beach Inn, 181
North Christian Church, 163
North Shore Aquasports, 178

North Shore Deli, 180
Notre Dame Golf Course, 137

O Gallery, 68
Objects, 44
Olbrich Gardens, 78
Old Bag Factory, 142
Old Harbor Village, 179
Old Heidelberg, 127
Old Holland Inn, 192
Old Lighthouse Museum, 129
Old Market House State Historic Site, 31
Old Post Office Shops, 184
Old Saint Mary's Church, 55
Old State Capitol, 23
Old Stockade Refuge, 31
Old Wade House and Wisconsin Carriage Museum, 112
Old World Wisconsin, 61
Olson Planetarium, 60
Original Pancake House, 147
Oshkosh Public Museum, 105
Oval Beach, 185
Ovens of Brittany, 79
Oz Museum, 126

Pabst Mansion, 57
Paine Art Center and Arboretum, 105
Palmer's Antiques, 180
Panozzo's Cafe, 170
Parthenon Gyros Restaurant, 80
Patchwork Quilt Country Inn, 142
Patrick and Beatrice Haggerty Museum of Art, 57
Paul Bunyan's Lumberjack Meals, 89

Pendarvis, 97
Peninsula Art School, 119
Peninsula Players, 118
Peninsula State Park, 117
Performing Arts Center, 56
Peter's Bay, 164
Pine Garth Inn, 170
Pinehill Bed & Breakfast, 11
Pioneer Inn, 104
Pirates' Cove Adventure Golf, 90
Poll Museum of Transportation, 196
Popeye's Gallery, 67
Portage Charter Fishing Fleet Inc., 129
Potato Creek State Park, 137
Potowatomi, 118
Pump Room, 45
Pumpernickel's, 185

Queen of Saugatuck, 186
Queens Inn, 191
Quivey's Grove, 79

Rabbit Run Antiques, 171
Ragamuffin Dolls, 32
Rainbotique, 126
Rainbow's End Antiques, 171
Ramada, 25
Ramada Renaissance, 22
Randall's Sports Emporium, 113
Rathskeller, 78, 186
Ray's Cherry Hut, 116
Red Barn Playhouse, 186
Red Geranium, 68
Red Rooster, 97
Red's Antiques, 32
Reddick Mansion, 6
Reflections, 155
Renaissance Center, 206
Richmond, 70
Rick's Cafe American, 147

Ripley's Believe It or Not, 91
River North, 44
River wildlife, 111
Rock 'n' Roll McDonald's, 41
Rock Island State Park, 118
Rollo Jamison Museum, 97
Royal Veil Antiques, 171
Rue's Meat Market, 99
Russ & Barb, 126
Ruthmere Museum, 140

Sacred Heart Church, 135
Sanderling Nature Center, 113
Sandpiper, 192
Sandwich Antiques Market, 6
Saugatuck
  Drug, 184
  Antique and Auction Center, 187
Dune Rides, 186
Dunes State Park, 186
Sauk County Historical Museum, 91
Saz's, 57
Schoolhouse Shop, 126
Schooner Valley Stable, 157
Sea Wolf, 178
Sears Tower Skydeck Observatory, 43
Seasons Lodge, 155
Shake Rag Valley, 98
Sheboygan County Museum, 112
Sheboygan Indian Mound Park, 113
Shedd Aquarium, 42
Shenandoah Riding Center, 35
Sherman's Dairy Bar, 179
Shipshewana Flea Market and Auction, 141
Shops at Woodlake, 111
Silver Annie's Ltd. 96

Silver Crane Gallery, 171
Silver Ridge Golf Course, 12
Sinnissippi Forest, 12
Sister Bay Bowl, 117
Skiing, 206
Skylight Opera Theatre, 55
Snite Museum of Art, 135
South Bend Marriott, 134
South Haven Antique Mall, 181
South Pier, 180
Speedway, 148
Spielman's Wood Works, 117
Sports Core, 112
Spring Green Restaurant, 76
Springfield Convention & Visitors Center, 25
St. Elmo's, 149
St. Joan of Arc Chapel, 56
Starfire, 68
Starved Rock State Park, 4
State Capitol of Wisconsin, 80
State Historical Museum, 79
State of Illinois Center, 44
State Street, 80
State of Illinois Artisan Center, 44
Statue of Chief John Big Tree, 104
Steele, T.C., home of, 156
Stone Mill Winery, 109
Store Next Store, 32
Story Inn, 156
Storybook Gardens, 91
Studebaker Archives Center, 135
Studebaker Museum, 135
Sturgeon Bay Maritime Museum, 120
Surrey Antiques & Collectibles, 16
Susan Hoffman's Fine Pastries, 203

Swiss Historic Village, 99
Swiss Miss Lace Factory,
    99

Tabor Hill Winery and
    Vineyard, 172
Talisman, 25
Tannebaum, 119
Terra Museum of Ameri-
    can Art, 46
Thomas L. Brisch Book-
    seller, 32
Three Oaks Bicycle Mu-
    seum and Information
    Center, 172
Three Pelicans, 180
Thumb Fun Park, 120
Til Midnight, 193
Timbers Supper Club, 96
Time Museum, 29
Tin-Pan Alley Antiques, 32
Touch of Country, 142
Toy Shop, 193
Trappers Alley, 204
Tree-Mendus fruit, 173
Tri-Cities Historical Mu-
    seum, 195
Tunnel Bar-B-Q, 203
Turners Bar & Restaurant,
    54

Ulysses S. Grant Home,
    30
Union Station, 147
Unity Chapel, 77
University Arboretum, 78
Upper Crust, 90
U.S. Forest Products Labo-
    ratory, 82

Usinger's Famous
    Sausage, 56

Vachel Lindsay Home, 26
Van Buren State Park, 181
Veldheer Tulip Gardens,
    192
Victor's, 110
Viking Restaurant, 119
Village Cafe, 118
Vinegar Hill Historic Lead
    Mine Museum, 35

Wacky Pirate Cruise, 41
Waelderhaus, 113
Walking Tour of the
    Loop, 43
Walworth II, 67
Warren Dunes, 170
Washington Avenue
    Antiques, 110
Washington Park Botani-
    cal Gardens, 26
Washington Park Zoo, 129
Washington Street
    Mercantile & Coffee
    House, 11
Wateway Visitors' Center, 6
West Shore Golf Club, 188
West South Street District,
    200
Whad Ya' Know Radio
    Show, 82
White Gull Inn, 118–19
White Pines
    Deer Park, 12
    Forest State Park, 10
    Inn, 11
    Ranch, 12

Whitefish Dunes, 118
Whitnall Park, 60
Wichwook Inn, 185
Wilbur's Ice Cream and
    Sandwich Shop, 177
Williams Bay Municipal
    Breaches, 67
Windmill Island Municipal
    Park, 193
Winnebago Indian Mu-
    seum, 91
Wisconsin
    Cheese Mart, 56
    Opry, 91
    Room, 111
    Shakespeare Festival, 97
Wolline Stables, 69
Woodlake Market, 111
Wright, Frank Lloyd, Hill-
    side Home School at
    Taliesin, 76

Yellow Jersey, 78
Yelton Manor, 178
Yerkes Observatory, 68
Yesterday's Treasures, 126
Yoder's Popcorn Shoppe,
    142
Yvette Wintergarden, 44

Zaharako's Confectionery,
    163
Zim's, 99
Zingerman's Delicatessen,
    200
Zionsville, 150
Zurkrone, 54